More praise for

Inventing Human Rights

"Remarkable. . . . She covers so much ground in so few pages and with such clarity, *Inventing Human Rights* is a tour de force."
—Gordon S. Wood, *New York Times Book Review*

"To connect human rights to social history in this way is an original and interesting approach to the subject. . . . [Hunt] offers a lively and informative history."
—Joshua Muravchick, *Wall Street Journal*

"Lynn Hunt has shown, in this book and throughout her career, there is much to be learned by drawing connections between the political events that shaped modern politics and the literary developments that shaped modern sensibilities."
—*London Review of Books*

"Lynn Hunt's elegant *Inventing Human Rights* offers lucid and original answers. . . . Hunt skillfully situates their discourse of rights within a series of broader cultural changes that transformed how (Western) human beings related to one another. . . . Hunt's mastery of the 18th-century European landscape allows the book to double as a fresh interpretation of Enlightenment culture."
—Maya Jasanoff, *Washington Post*

"As Americans begin to hold their leaders accountable for the mistakes made in the war against terror, this book ought to serve as a guide for thinking about one of the most serious mistakes of all, the belief that America can win that war by revoking the Declaration that brought the nation into being."
—Alan Wolfe, *Commonweal*

"The enterprise of writing the history of human rights has become a widespread activity only in the past decade. Lynn Hunt's *Inventing Human Rights* is its most prominent result. . . . Highly readable."   —Samuel Moyn, *The Nation*

"Hunt . . . has written a book that is now the inevitable starting point in thinking about the history of human rights. Essential."
—S. N. Katz, *Choice*

"Lynn Hunt has achieved nearly everything she set out to do with *Inventing Human Rights.* . . . . Clearly, Hunt has a passion for the subject, as it comes through in her writing and the angle from which she attacks the issue . . . colorful, in-depth narrative."   —Cristoph Mark, *The Daily Yomiuri* (Japan)

"[*Inventing Human Rights*] offers a cogent summary of a subject that is important to every thinking man and woman. Recommended."   —Bob Williams, *The Compulsive Reader*

"Hunt's history places an insightful emphasis on the idea of human rights as a project to be continuously extended, a project whose promise is not yet fulfilled."
—Alexander Bevilacqua, *Harvard Book Review*

"Cultural history of a high order; recommended for academic and large public collections."   —David Keymer, *Library Journal*

ALSO BY LYNN HUNT

Politics, Culture and Class in the French Revolution

The New Cultural History

The Family Romance of the French Revolution

Beyond the Culture Turn: New Directions in the Study of Society and Culture

The Making of the West: Peoples and Cultures

Inventing

HUMAN RIGHTS

A History

Lynn Hunt

 W. W. NORTON & COMPANY | NEW YORK LONDON

For information about permission to reproduce selections from
this book, write to Permissions, W. W. Norton & Company, Inc.,
500 Fifth Avenue, New York, NY 10110

Manufacturing by LSC Harrisonburg
Book design by Judith Stagnitto Abbate / Abbate Design
Production manager: Andrew Marasia

Library of Congress Cataloging-in-Publication Data

Hunt, Lynn Avery.
    Inventing human rights / Lynn Hunt.
        p. cm.
Includes bibliographical references and index.
    ISBN-13: 978-393-06095-9 (hardcover)
    ISBN-10: 0-393-06095-0 (hardcover)
    1. Human rights—History.   2. Human rights in literature.
    3. Torture—History.   I. Title.
JC585.H89 2007
323.09—dc22   2006027599

ISBN 978-0-393-33199-8 pbk.

W. W. Norton & Company, Inc.
500 Fifth Avenue, New York, N.Y. 10110
www.wwnorton.com

W. W. Norton & Company Ltd.
15 Carlisle Street, London W1D 3BS

15 14

To Lee and Jane
Sisters, Friends, Inspirers

Contents

Acknowledgments

While writing this book I benefited from countless suggestions offered by friends, colleagues, and participants in various seminars and lectures. No expression of gratitude on my part could possibly repay the debts that I have been fortunate enough to incur, and I only hope that some will recognize their input in certain passages or footnotes. Giving the Patten Lectures at Indiana University, the Merle Curti Lectures at the University of Wisconsin, Madison, and the James W. Richard Lectures at the University of Virginia provided invaluable opportunities to try out my preliminary notions. Excellent insights came as well from audiences at Camino College; Carleton College; Centro de Investigación y Docencia Económicas, Mexico City; Fordham University, Institute of Historical Research, University of London, Lewis & Clark College; Pomona College; Stanford University; Texas A&M University; the University of Paris; the University of Ulster, Coleraine; the University of Washington, Seattle; and my home institution, UCLA. Funding for most of my research came from the Eugen Weber Chair in Modern European History at UCLA, and the research was greatly facilitated by the truly exceptional riches of the UCLA libraries.

Most people think that teaching follows behind research in the list of priorities for university professors, but the idea for this book came originally from a document collection that I edited and translated for the purpose of teaching undergraduates: *The French Revolution and Human Rights: A Brief Documentary History* (Boston and New York: Bedford/St. Martin's Press, 1996).

A fellowship from the National Endowment for the Humanities helped me complete that project. Before writing this book, I published a brief sketch, "The Paradoxical Origins of Human Rights," in Jeffrey N. Wasserstrom, Lynn Hunt, and Marilyn B. Young, eds., *Human Rights and Revolutions* (Lanham, MD: Rowman & Littlefield, 2000), pp. 3–17. Some of the arguments in chapter 2 were first developed in a different way in "Le Corps au XVIIIe siècle: les origines des droits de l'homme," *Diogène*, 203 (July–September 2003): 49–67.

From idea to final execution, the road, at least in my case, is long and sometimes arduous, but made passable by help from those near and dear. Joyce Appleby and Suzanne Desan read early drafts of my first three chapters and made marvelous suggestions for improvement. My editor at W. W. Norton, Amy Cherry, provided the kind of close attention to writing and argument that most authors only dream of. Without Margaret Jacob, I would not have written this book. She kept me going with her own excitement about research and writing, her braveness about venturing into new and controversial domains, and not least, her ability to put it all aside in favor of preparing an exquisite dinner. She knows how much I owe to her. My father died while I was writing this book, but I can still hear his words of encouragement and support. I dedicate this book to my sisters Lee and Jane in recognition, however inadequate, of all we have shared over many years. They taught me my first lessons about rights, resolution of conflict, and love.

Inventing

HUMAN
RIGHTS

INTRODUCTION

*"We hold these truths to
be self-evident"*

GREAT THINGS sometimes come from rewriting under pressure. In his first draft of the Declaration of Independence, prepared in mid-June 1776, Thomas Jefferson wrote, "We hold these truths to be sacred & undeniable; that all men are created equal & independant [sic], that from that equal creation they derive rights inherent & inalienable, among which are the preservation of life, & liberty, & the pursuit of happiness." Largely thanks to his own revisions, Jefferson's sentence soon shook off its hiccups to speak in clearer, more ringing tones: "We hold these truths to be self-evident, that all men are created equal, that they are endowed by their Creator with certain unalienable Rights, that among these are Life, Liberty and the pursuit of Happiness." With this one sentence Jefferson turned a typical eighteenth-century document about political grievances into a lasting proclamation of human rights.[1]

Thirteen years later, Jefferson was in Paris when the French began to think about drawing up a statement of their rights. In January 1789—several months before the fall of the Bastille—Jefferson's friend, marquis de Lafayette, veteran of the War of American Independence, drafted a French declaration, most likely with Jefferson's help. When the Bastille fell on July 14, and the French Revolution began in earnest, the demand for an official declaration gathered momentum. Despite Lafayette's best efforts, no one hand shaped the document as had Jefferson for the American Congress. On August 20, the new National Assembly opened discussion of twenty-four articles drafted by an unwieldy committee of forty deputies. After six days of tumultuous debate and endless amendments, the French deputies had only approved seventeen articles. Exhausted by the continuing contention and needing to turn to other pressing matters, the deputies voted on August 27, 1789, to suspend discussion of the draft and provisionally adopt the already approved articles as their Declaration of the Rights of Man and Citizen.

The document so frantically cobbled together was stunning in its sweep and simplicity. Never once mentioning king, nobility, or church, it declared the "natural, inalienable and sacred rights of man" to be the foundation of any and all government. It assigned sovereignty to the nation, not the king, and pronounced everyone equal before the law, thus opening positions to talent and merit and implicitly eliminating all privilege based on birth. More striking than any particular guarantee, however, was the universality of the claims made. References to "men," "man," "every man," "all men," "all citizens," "each citizen," "society," and "every society" dwarfed the single reference to the French people.

As a result, the publication of the declaration immediately galvanized worldwide opinion on the subject of rights, both for and against. In a sermon given in London on November 4, 1789, Richard Price, friend of Benjamin Franklin and frequent critic of the English government, waxed lyrical on the new rights of man. "I have lived to see the rights of men better understood than ever, and nations panting for liberty, which seemed to have lost the idea of it." Outraged by Price's naive enthusiasm for the "metaphysical abstractions" of the French, the well-known essayist and member of Parliament Edmund Burke dashed off a furious response. His pamphlet, *Reflections on the Revolution in France* (1790), gained instant recognition as the founding text of conservatism. "We are not the converts of Rousseau," Burke thundered. "We know that *we* have made no discoveries, and we think that no discoveries are to be made, in morality. . . . We have not been drawn and trussed, in order that we may be filled, like stuffed birds in a museum, with chaff and rags and paltry blurred shreds of paper about the rights of man." Price and Burke had agreed about the American Revolution; they both supported it. But the French Revolution upped the ante enormously, and battle lines soon formed: was it the dawn of a new era of freedom based on reason or the beginning of a relentless descent into anarchy and violence?[2]

For nearly two centuries, despite the controversy provoked by the French Revolution, the Declaration of the Rights of Man and Citizen incarnated the promise of universal human rights. In 1948, when the United Nations adopted the Universal Declaration of Human Rights, Article 1 read, "All human beings are born free and equal in dignity and rights." In 1789, Article I of the Declaration of the Rights of Man and Citizen had already proclaimed, "Men are born and remain free and equal in rights." Although the modifications in language were meaningful, the echo between the two documents is unmistakable.

The origins of documents do not necessarily tell us something significant about their consequences. Does it really matter that Jefferson's rough draft went through eighty-six alterations made by himself, the Committee of Five, or Congress? Jefferson and Adams clearly thought so, since they were still arguing about who contributed what in the 1820s, in the last decade of their long and eventful lives. Yet the Declaration of Independence had no constitutional standing. It simply declared intentions, and fifteen years passed before the states finally ratified a very different Bill of Rights in 1791. The French Declaration of the Rights of Man and Citizen claimed to safeguard individual freedoms, but it did not prevent the emergence of a French government that repressed rights (known as the Terror), and future French constitutions—there were many of them—formulated different declarations or went without declarations altogether.

More troubling still, those who so confidently declared rights to be universal in the late eighteenth century turned out to have something much less all-inclusive in mind. We are not surprised that they considered children, the insane, the imprisoned, or foreigners to be incapable or unworthy of full participation in the political process, for so do we. But they also excluded those without property, slaves, free blacks, in some cases religious minorities, and always and everywhere, women. In recent years, these limitations on "all men" have drawn much commentary, and some scholars have even questioned whether the declarations had any real emancipatory meaning. The founders, framers, and declarers have been judged elitist, racist, and misogynist for their inability to consider everyone truly equal in rights.

We should not forget the restrictions placed on rights by eighteenth-century men, but to stop there, patting ourselves on the back for our own comparative "advancement," is to miss the point. How did these men, living in societies built on slavery, subordination, and seemingly natural subservience, ever come to imagine men not at all like them and, in some cases, women too, as equals? How did equality of rights become a "self-evident" truth in such unlikely places? It is astounding that men such as Jefferson, a slaveowner, and Lafayette, an aristocrat, could speak as they did of the self-evident, inalienable rights of all men. If we could understand how this came to pass, we would understand better what human rights mean to us today.

The Paradox of Self-Evidence

Despite their differences in language, the two eighteenth-century declarations both rested on a claim of self-evidence. Jefferson made this explicit when he wrote, "We hold these truths to be self-evident." The French Declaration stated categorically that "ignorance, neglect or contempt of the rights of man are the sole causes of public misfortunes and governmental corruption." Not much had changed in this regard by 1948. True, the United Nations Declaration took a more legalistic tone: "WHEREAS recognition of the inherent dignity and of the equal and inalienable rights of all members of the human family is the foundation of freedom, justice and peace in the world." Yet this too constituted a claim of self-evidence, for "whereas" literally means "it being the fact that." In other words, "whereas" is simply a legalistic way of asserting a given, something self-evident.

This claim of self-evidence, crucial to human rights even now, gives rise to a paradox: if equality of rights is so self-evident, then why did this assertion have to made and why was it only made in specific times and places? How can human rights be universal if they are not universally recognized? Shall we rest content with the explanation given by the 1948 framers that "we agree about the rights but on condition no one asks us why"? Can they be "self-evident" when scholars have argued for more than two hundred years about what Jefferson meant by his phrase? Debate will continue forever because Jefferson never felt the need to explain himself. No one from the Committee of Five or Congress wanted to revise his claim, even though they extensively modified other sections of his preliminary version. They apparently agreed with him. Moreover, if Jefferson had explained himself, the self-evidence of the claim would have evaporated. An assertion that requires argument is not self-evident.[3]

I believe that the claim of self-evidence is crucial to the history of human rights, and this book is devoted to explaining how it came to be so convincing in the eighteenth century. Happily, it also provides a point of focus in what tends to be a very diffuse history. Human rights have become so ubiquitous in the present time that they seem to require an equally capacious history. Greek ideas about the individual person, Roman notions of law and right, Christian doctrines of the soul . . . the risk is that the history of human rights becomes the history of Western civilization or now, sometimes, even the history of the entire world. Do not ancient Babylon, Hinduism, Buddhism, and Islam all make their contributions, too? How then do we account for the sudden crystallization of human rights claims at the end of the eighteenth century?

Human rights require three interlocking qualities: rights must be *natural* (inherent in human beings); *equal* (the same for everyone); and *universal* (applicable everywhere). For rights to be *human* rights, all humans everywhere in the world must possess them equally and only because of their status as human beings.

It turned out to be easier to accept the natural quality of rights than their equality or universality. In many ways, we are grappling still with the implications of the demand for equality and universality of rights. At what age does someone have the right to full political participation? Do immigrants—non-citizens—share in rights, and which ones?

Yet even naturalness, equality, and universality are not quite enough. Human rights only become meaningful when they gain political content. They are not the rights of humans in a state of nature; they are the rights of humans in society. They are not just human rights as opposed to divine rights, or human rights as opposed to animal rights; they are the rights of humans vis-à-vis each other. They are therefore rights guaranteed in the secular political world (even if they are called "sacred"), and they are rights that require active participation from those who hold them.

The equality, universality, and naturalness of rights gained direct political expression for the first time in the American Declaration of Independence of 1776 and the French Declaration of the Rights of Man and Citizen of 1789. While the English Bill of Rights of 1689 referred to the "ancient rights and liberties" established by English law and deriving from English history, it did not declare the equality, universality, or naturalness of rights. In contrast, the Declaration of Independence insisted that "all men are created equal," and that all of them possess "unalienable rights." Similarly, the Declaration of the Rights of Man and Citizen proclaimed that "Men are born and remain free and equal in rights." Not French men, not white men, not Catholics, but "men," which then as now means not just males but also persons, that is, members of the human race. In other words, sometime between 1689 and 1776 rights that had been viewed most often as the rights of a particular people—freeborn

English men, for example—were transformed into human rights, universal natural rights, what the French called *les droits de l'homme* or "the rights of man."[4]

Human Rights and "The Rights of Man"

A brief foray into the history of terms will help pin down the moment of emergence of human rights. Eighteenth-century people did not often use the expression "human rights," and when they did, they usually meant something different by it than what we mean. Before 1789, Jefferson, for example, spoke most often of "natural rights." He began to use the term "rights of man" only after 1789. When he employed "human rights," he meant something more passive and less political than natural rights or the rights of man. In 1806, for example, he used the term in referring to the evils of the slave trade:

> I congratulate you, fellow citizens, on the approach of the period at which you may interpose your authority constitutionally, to withdraw the citizens of the United States from all further participation in those violations of human rights which have been so long continued on the unoffending inhabitants of Africa, and which the morality, the reputation, and the best interests of our country, have long been eager to proscribe.

In maintaining that Africans enjoyed human rights, Jefferson drew no implications for African-American slaves at home. Human rights, by Jefferson's definition, did not enable Africans— much less African-Americans—to act on their own behalf.[5]

During the eighteenth century, in English and in French, "human rights," "rights of mankind," and "rights of humanity" all proved to be too general to be of direct political use. They referred to what distinguished humans from the divine on one end of the scale and from animals on the other, rather than to politically relevant rights such as freedom of speech or the right to participate in politics. Thus, in one of the earliest uses (1734) of "rights of humanity" in French, the acerbic literary critic Nicolas Lenglet-Dufresnoy, himself a Catholic priest, satirized "those inimitable monks of the sixth century who so entirely renounced all 'the rights of humanity' that they grazed like animals and ran around completely naked." Similarly, in 1756 Voltaire could proclaim tongue-in-cheek that Persia was the monarchy in which one most enjoyed the "rights of humanity" because Persians had the greatest "resources against boredom." The term "human right" appeared in French for the first time in 1763 and could mean something like "natural right," but it did not catch on despite its use by Voltaire in his widely influential *Treatise on Tolerance*.[6]

While English speakers continued to prefer "natural rights" or just plain "rights" throughout the eighteenth century, the French invented a new expression in the 1760s—"rights of man" (*droits de l'homme*). "Natural right(s)" or "natural law" (*droit naturel* has both meanings in French) had longer histories going back hundreds of years, but perhaps as a consequence, "natural right(s)" had too many possible meanings. It sometimes meant simply making sense within the traditional order. Thus, for example, Bishop Bossuet, a spokesman for Louis XIV's absolute monarchy, used "natural right" only when describing Jesus Christ's entry to heaven ("he entered heaven by his own natural right").[7]

"Rights of man" gained currency in French after its appearance in Jean-Jacques Rousseau's *Social Contract* of 1762, even though Rousseau gave the term no definition and even though—or perhaps because—Rousseau used it alongside "rights of humanity," "rights of the citizen," and "rights of sovereignty." Whatever the reason, by June 1763, "rights of man" had become a common term according to an underground newsletter:

> the actors of the *Comédie française* today played, for the first time, *Manco* [a play about the Incas in Peru], of which we previously spoke. It is one of the most badly constructed tragedies. There is a role in it for a savage which could be very beautiful; he recites in verse everything that we have read scattered about on kings, liberty, the rights of man, in *The Inequality of Conditions*, in *Emile*, in *The Social Contract*.

Although the play does not in fact use the precise phrase "the rights of man," but rather the related one, "rights of our being," the term had clearly entered intellectual usage, and it was in fact directly associated with the works of Rousseau. Other Enlightenment writers, such as baron d'Holbach, Raynal, and Mercier, then picked it up in the 1770s and 1780s.[8]

Before 1789, "rights of man" had little crossover into English. But the American Revolution prompted the French Enlightenment champion marquis de Condorcet to make a first pass at defining "the rights of man," which for him included security of person, security of property, impartial and fair justice, and the right to contribute to the formulation of the laws. In his 1786 essay "On the Influence of the American Revolution on Europe," Condorcet explicitly linked the rights of man to the American Revolution: "The spectacle of a great people, where the rights of man are respected, is useful to all others, despite the difference in climate, customs, and constitutions." The American Declaration of Independence, he proclaimed, was nothing less than "a simple and sublime exposition of these rights that are at once so sacred and so long forgotten." In January 1789, Emmanuel-Joseph Sieyès used the expression in his incendiary anti-noble pamphlet, *What Is the Third Estate?* Lafayette's January 1789 draft of a declaration of rights made explicit reference to "the rights of man," as did Condorcet's own draft of early 1789. From the spring of 1789—that is, even before the fall of the Bastille on July 14—talk of the need for a declaration of the "rights of man" permeated French political circles.[9]

When the language of human rights emerged in the second half of the eighteenth century, there was at first little explicit definition of those rights. Rousseau offered no explanation when he used the term "rights of man." The English jurist William Blackstone defined them as "the natural liberty of mankind," that is, the "absolute rights of man, considered as a free agent, endowed with discernment to know good from evil." Most of those using the phrase in the 1770s and 1780s in France, such as the controversial Enlightenment figures d'Holbach and Mirabeau, referred to the rights of man as if they were obvious and needed no justification or definition; they were in other words self-evident. D'Holbach argued, for instance, that if men feared death less, "the rights of man would be more boldly defended." Mirabeau denounced his persecutors, who had "neither character nor soul, because they have no idea at all of the rights of men." No one offered a precise list of those rights before 1776 (the date of George Mason's Virginia Declaration of Rights).[10]

The ambiguity of human rights was captured by the French

Calvinist pastor Jean-Paul Rabaut Saint-Etienne, who wrote to the French king in 1787 to complain about the limitations of a proposed Edict of Toleration for Protestants like himself. Emboldened by the rising sentiment in favor of the rights of man, Rabaut insisted, "we know today what natural rights are, and they certainly give to men much more than the edict accords to Protestants. . . . The time has come when it is no longer acceptable for a law to overtly overrule the rights of humanity that are very well known all over the world." They may have been "well known," yet Rabaut himself granted that a Catholic king could not officially sanction the Calvinist right of public worship. In short, everything depended—as it still does—on the interpretation given to what was "no longer acceptable."[11]

How Rights Became Self-Evident

Human rights are difficult to pin down because their definition, indeed their very existence, depends on emotions as much as on reason. The claim of self-evidence relies ultimately on an emotional appeal; it is convincing if it strikes a chord within each person. Moreover, we are most certain that a human right is at issue when we feel horrified by its violation. Rabaut Saint-Etienne knew that he could appeal to the implicit knowledge of what was "no longer acceptable." In 1755, the influential French Enlightenment writer Denis Diderot had written of *droit naturel* that "the use of this term is so familiar that there is almost no one who would not be convinced inside himself that the thing is obviously known to him. This interior feeling is common both to the philosopher and to the man who has not reflected at all." Like others of the time, Diderot gave only a vague indication of the meaning of natural rights; "as a man," he concluded, "I have no other natural rights that are truly inalienable than those of humanity." But he had put his finger on the most important quality of human rights; they required a certain widely shared "interior feeling."[12]

Even the austere Swiss natural law philosopher Jean-Jacques Burlamaqui insisted that liberty could only be proved by each man's inner feelings: "Such proofs of feeling are above all objection and produce the most deep-seated *conviction*." Human rights are not just a doctrine formulated in documents; they rest on a disposition toward other people, a set of convictions about what people are like and how they know right and wrong in the secular world. Philosophical ideas, legal traditions, and revolutionary politics had to have this kind of inner emotional reference point for human rights to be truly "self-evident." And, as Diderot insisted, these feelings had to be felt by many people, not just the philosophers who wrote about them.[13]

Underpinning these notions of liberty and rights was a set of assumptions about individual autonomy. To have human rights, people had to be perceived as separate individuals who were capable of exercising independent moral judgment; as Blackstone put it, the rights of man went along with the individual "considered as a free agent, endowed with discernment to know good from evil." But for these autonomous individuals to become members of a political community based on those independent moral judgments, they had to be able to empathize with others. Everyone would have rights only if everyone could be seen as in some fundamental way alike. Equality was not just an abstract concept or a political slogan. It had to be internalized in some fashion.

While we take the ideas of autonomy and equality, along

with human rights, for granted, they only gained influence in the eighteenth century. The contemporary moral philosopher J. B. Schneewind has traced what he calls "the invention of autonomy." "The new outlook that emerged by the end of the eighteenth century," he asserts, "centered on the belief that all normal individuals are equally able to live together in a morality of self-governance." Behind those "normal individuals" lies a long history of struggle. In the eighteenth century (and indeed, right up to the present), all "people" were not imagined as equally capable of moral autonomy. Two related but distinct qualities were involved: the ability to reason and the independence to decide for oneself. Both had to be present if an individual was to be morally autonomous. Children and the insane lacked the necessary capacity to reason, but they might someday gain or regain that capacity. Like children, slaves, servants, the propertyless, and women lacked the required independence of status to be fully autonomous. Children, servants, the propertyless, and perhaps even slaves might one day become autonomous, by growing up, by leaving service, by buying property, or by buying their freedom. Women alone seemed not to have any of these options; they were defined as inherently dependent on either their fathers or husbands. If the proponents of universal, equal, and natural human rights automatically excluded some categories of people from exercising those rights, it was primarily because they viewed them as less than fully capable of moral autonomy.[14]

Yet the newfound power of empathy could work against even the longest held prejudices. In 1791, the French revolutionary government granted equal rights to Jews; in 1792, even men without property were enfranchised; and in 1794, the French government officially abolished slavery. Neither autonomy nor empathy were fixed; they were skills that could be learned, and the "acceptable" limitations on rights could be—and were—challenged. Rights cannot be defined once and for all because their emotional basis continues to shift, in part in reaction to declarations of rights. Rights remain open to question because our sense of who has rights and what those rights are constantly changes. The human rights revolution is by definition ongoing.

Autonomy and empathy are cultural practices, not just ideas, and they are therefore quite literally embodied, that is, they have physical as well as emotional dimensions. Individual autonomy hinges on an increasing sense of the separation and sacredness of human bodies: your body is yours and my body is mine, and we should both respect the boundaries between each other's bodies. Empathy depends on the recognition that others feel and think as we do, that our inner feelings are alike in some fundamental fashion. To be autonomous, a person has to be legitimately separate and protected in his or her separation; but to have rights go along with that bodily separation a person's selfhood must be appreciated in some more emotional fashion. Human rights depend both on self-possession and on the recognition that all others are equally self-possessed. It is the incomplete development of the latter that gives rise to all the inequalities of rights that have preoccupied us throughout all history.

Autonomy and empathy did not materialize out of thin air in the eighteenth century; they had deep roots. Over the long term of several centuries, individuals had begun to pull themselves away from the webs of community and had become increasingly independent agents both legally and psychologically. Greater respect for bodily integrity and clearer lines of demarcation between individual bodies had been produced by the ever-rising threshold of shame about bodily functions and the growing sense of bodily decorum. Over time, people began to sleep alone or only with a spouse in bed. They used utensils to eat and began to consider repulsive such previously acceptable behavior as throwing food on the floor or wiping bodily excretions on clothing. The constant evolution of notions of interiority and depth of psyche from the Christian soul to the Protestant conscience to eighteenth-century notions of sensibility filled the self with a new content. All these processes took place over a long time period.

But there was a spurt in the development of these practices in the second half of the eighteenth century. The absolute authority of fathers over their children was questioned. Audiences started watching theatrical performances or listening to music in silence. Portraiture and genre painting challenged the dominance of the great mythological and historical canvases of academic painting. Novels and newspapers proliferated, making the stories of ordinary lives accessible to a wide audience. Torture as part of the judicial process and the most extreme forms of corporal punishment both came to be seen as unacceptable. All of these changes contributed to a sense of the separation and self-possession of individual bodies, along with the possibility of empathy with others.

The notions of bodily integrity and empathetic selfhood, traced in the next chapters, have histories not unlike those of human rights, to which they are so intimately related. That is, the changes in views seem to happen all at once in the mid-eighteenth century. Consider, for example, torture. Between 1700 and 1750, most uses of the word "torture" in French referred to the difficulties a writer had in finding a felicitous expression. Thus, Marivaux in 1724 referred to "torturing one's mind in order to draw out reflections." Torture, that is, legally authorized torture to get confessions of guilt or names of accomplices, became a major issue after Montesquieu attacked the practice in his *Spirit of Laws* (1748). In one of his most influential passages, Montesquieu insists that "So many clever people and so many men of genius have written against this practice [judicial torture] that I dare not speak after them." Then he goes on rather enigmatically to add, "I was going to say that it might be suitable for despotic government, where everything inspiring fear enters more into the springs of government; I was going to say that slaves among the Greeks and Romans. . . . But I hear the voice of nature crying out against me." Here too self-evidence—"the voice of nature crying out"—provides the grounding for the argument. After Montesquieu, Voltaire and many others, especially the Italian Beccaria, would join the campaign. By the 1780s, the abolition of torture and barbarous forms of corporal punishment had become essential articles in the new human rights doctrine.[15]

Changes in reactions to other people's bodies and selves provided critical support for the new secular grounding of political authority. Although Jefferson wrote that "their Creator" had endowed men with their rights, the role of the Creator ended there. Government no longer depended on God, much less on a church's interpretation of God's will. "Governments are instituted among Men," said Jefferson, "to secure these Rights," and they derive their power "from the Consent of the Governed." Similarly, the French Declaration of 1789 maintained that "The purpose of all political association is the preservation of the natural and imprescriptible rights of man" and "The principle of all sovereignty rests essentially in the nation." Political authority, in this view, derived from the innermost nature of individuals and their ability to create community through consent. Political scientists and historians have examined this conception of political authority from various angles, but they have paid little attention to the view of bodies and selves that made it possible.[16]

My argument will make much of the influence of new kinds of experiences, from viewing pictures in public exhibitions to reading the hugely popular epistolary novels about love and marriage. Such experiences helped spread the practices of autonomy and empathy. The political scientist Benedict Anderson has argued that newspapers and novels created the "imagined community" that nationalism requires in order to flourish. What might be termed "imagined empathy" serves as the foundation of human rights rather than of nationalism. It is imagined, not in the sense of made up, but in the sense that empathy requires a leap of faith, of imagining that someone else is like you. Accounts of torture produced this imagined empathy through new views of pain. Novels generated it by inducing new sensations about the inner self. Each in their way reinforced the notion of a community based on autonomous, empathetic individuals who could relate beyond their immediate families, religious affiliations, or even nations to greater universal values.[17]

There is no easy or obvious way to prove or even measure the effect of new cultural experiences on eighteenth-century people, much less on their conceptions of rights. Scientific studies of present-day responses to reading or watching television have proved difficult enough, and they have the advantage of living subjects who can be exposed to ever-changing research strategies. Still, neuroscientists and cognitive psychologists have been making some progress in linking the biology of the brain to psychological and eventually even to social and cultural outcomes. They have shown, for example, that the ability to construct narratives is based in the biology of the brain and is crucial to the development of any notion of self. Certain kinds of brain lesions affect narrative comprehension, and diseases such as autism show that the capacity for empathy—for the recognition that others have minds like your own—has a biological basis. For the most part, however, these studies only address one side of the equation: the biological. Although most psychiatrists and even some neuroscientists would agree that the brain itself is influenced by social and cultural forces, this interaction has been harder to study. Indeed, the self itself has proved very difficult to examine. We know that we have an experience of having a self, but neuroscientists have not succeeded in pinning down the site of that experience, much less explaining how it works.[18]

If neuroscience, psychiatry, and psychology are still uncertain about the nature of the self, then it is perhaps not surprising that historians have stayed away from the subject altogether. Most historians probably believe that the self is to some extent shaped by social and cultural factors, that is, that selfhood meant something different in the tenth century from what it means to us today. Yet little is known about the history of personhood as a set of experiences. Scholars have written at great length about the emergence of individualism and autonomy as doctrines, but much less about how the self itself might change over time. I agree with other historians that the meaning of the self changes over time, and I believe that the experience—not just the idea—of it changes for some people in decisive ways in the eighteenth century.

My argument depends on the notion that reading accounts of torture or epistolary novels had physical effects that translated into brain changes and came back out as new concepts about the organization of social and political life. New kinds of reading (and viewing and listening) created new individual experiences (empathy), which in turn made possible new social and political concepts (human rights). In these pages I try to untangle how that process worked. Because my own discipline of history has for so long disdained any form of psychological argument—we historians often speak of psychological reductionism but never of sociological or cultural reductionism—it has largely overlooked the possibility of an argument that depends on an account of what goes on inside the self.

I am trying to refocus attention on what goes on within individual minds. It might seem like an obvious place to look for an explanation of transformative social and political changes, but individual minds—other than those of great thinkers and writers—have been surprisingly overlooked in recent work in the humanities and social sciences. Attention has been focused on the social and cultural contexts, not on the way individual minds understand and reshape that context. I believe that social and political change—in this case, human rights—comes about because many individuals had similar experiences, not because they all inhabited the same social context but because through their interactions with each other and with their reading and viewing, they actually created a new social context. In short, I am insisting that any account of historical change must in the end account for the alteration of individual minds. For human rights to become self-evident, ordinary people had to have new understandings that came from new kinds of feelings.

1

"TORRENTS OF EMOTION"

Reading Novels and Imagining Equality

A YEAR BEFORE ROUSSEAU PUBLISHED the *Social Contract*, he gained international attention with a best-selling novel, *Julie, or the New Héloïse* (1761). Although modern readers find the epistolary or letter form of the novel sometimes excruciatingly slow to develop, eighteenth-century readers reacted viscerally. The subtitle excited their expectations, for the medieval story of the doomed love of Héloïse and Abelard was well known. The twelfth-century philosopher and Catholic cleric Peter Abelard seduced his pupil Héloïse and paid a high price at the hands of her uncle: castration. Separated forever, the two lovers then exchanged intimate letters that captivated readers down through the centuries. Rousseau's contemporary takeoff seemed at first to point in a very different direction. The new Héloïse, Julie, falls in love with her tutor, too, but she gives up the penniless Saint-Preux to satisfy the demand of her authoritarian father that she marry Wolmar, an older Russian soldier who once saved her father's life. She not only surmounts her passion for Saint-Preux but also appears to have learned to love him simply as a friend, when she dies after saving her young son from drowning. Did Rousseau mean to celebrate her submission to parental and spousal authority or did he intend to portray her sacrifice of her own desires as tragic?

The plot, even with its ambiguities, can hardly account for the explosion of emotions experienced by Rousseau's readers. What moved them was their intense identification with the characters, especially Julie. Since Rousseau already enjoyed international celebrity, news of the imminent publication of his novel spread like wildfire, in part because he read sections of it aloud to various friends. Although Voltaire derided it as "this miserable trash," Jean Le Rond d'Alembert, Diderot's co-editor of the *Encyclopédie*, wrote to Rousseau to say that he had "devoured" the book. He warned Rousseau to expect censure in "a country where one speaks so much of sentiment and passion and knows them so little." The *Journal des Savants* admitted that the novel had defects and even some long-winded passages, but it concluded that only the cold-hearted could resist these "torrents of emotion that so ravage the soul, that so imperiously, so tyrannically extract such bitter tears."[1]

Courtiers, clergy, military officers, and all manner of ordinary people wrote to Rousseau to describe their feelings of a "devouring fire," their "emotions upon emotions, upheavals upon upheavals." One recounted that he had not cried over Julie's death, but rather was "shrieking, howling like an animal." (Figure 1) As one twentieth-century commentator on these letters to Rousseau remarked, eighteenth-century readers of the novel did not read it with pleasure but rather with "passion, delirium,

FIGURE 1. *Julie's Deathbed*
This scene provoked more distress than any other in *Julie, or the New Héloïse*. The engraving by Nicolas Delaunay, based on a drawing by the well-known artist Jean-Michel Moreau, appeared in a 1782 edition of Rousseau's collected works.

spasms and sobs." The English translation appeared within two months of the French original; ten editions in English followed between 1761 and 1800. One hundred fifteen editions of the French version were published in the same period to meet the voracious appetite of an international French-reading public.[2]

Reading *Julie* opened up its readers to a new form of empathy. Although Rousseau gave currency to the term "rights of man," human rights are hardly the main subject of his novel, which revolves around passion, love, and virtue. Nevertheless, *Julie* encouraged a highly charged identification with the characters and in so doing enabled readers to empathize across class, sex, and national lines. Eighteenth-century readers, like people before them, empathized with those close to them and with those most obviously like them—their immediate families, their relatives, the people of their parish, in general their customary social equals. But eighteenth-century people had to learn to empathize across more broadly defined boundaries. Alexis de Tocqueville recounts a story told by Voltaire's secretary about Madame Duchâtelet, who did not hesitate to undress in front of her servants, "not considering it a proven fact that valets were men." Human rights could only make sense when valets were viewed as men too.[3]

Novels and Empathy

Novels like *Julie* drew their readers into identifying with ordinary characters, who were by definition unknown to the reader personally. Readers empathized with the characters, especially the heroine or hero, thanks to the workings of the narrative form itself. Through the fictional exchange of letters, in other words, epistolary novels taught their readers nothing less than a new psychology and in the process laid the foundations for a new social and political order. Novels made the middle-class Julie and even servants like Pamela, the heroine of Samuel Richardson's novel by that name, the equal and even the better of rich men such as Mr. B, Pamela's employer and would-be seducer. Novels made the point that all people are fundamentally similar because of their inner feelings, and many novels showcased in particular the desire for autonomy. In this way, reading novels created a sense of equality and empathy through passionate involvement in the narrative. Can it be coincidental that the three greatest novels of psychological identification of the eighteenth century—Richardson's *Pamela* (1740) and *Clarissa* (1747–48) and Rousseau's *Julie* (1761)—were all published in the period that immediately preceded the appearance of the concept of "the rights of man"?

Needless to say, empathy was not invented in the eighteenth century. The capacity for empathy is universal because it is rooted in the biology of the brain; it depends on a biologically based ability to understand the subjectivity of other people and to be able to imagine that their inner experiences are like one's own. Children who suffer from autism, for example, have great difficulty decoding facial expressions as indicators of feelings and in general have trouble attributing subjective states to others. Autism, in short, is characterized by the inability to empathize with others.[4]

Normally, everyone learns empathy from an early age. Although biology provides an essential predisposition, each culture shapes the expression of empathy in its own particular fashion. Empathy only develops through social interaction; therefore, the forms of that interaction configure empathy in important ways. In the eighteenth century, readers of novels learned to extend their purview of empathy. In reading, they empathized across traditional social boundaries between nobles and commoners, masters and servants, men and women, perhaps even adults and children. As a consequence, they came to see others—people they did not know personally—as like them, as having the same kinds of inner emotions. Without this learning process, "equality" could have no deep meaning and in particular no political consequence. The equality of souls in heaven is not the same thing as equal rights here on earth. Before the eighteenth century, Christians readily accepted the former without granting the latter.

The ability to identify across social lines might have been acquired in any number of ways, and I do not pretend that novel reading was the only one. Still, novel reading seems especially pertinent, in part because the heyday of one particular kind of novel—the epistolary novel—coincides chronologically with the birth of human rights. The epistolary novel surged as a genre between the 1760s and 1780s and then rather mysteriously died out in the 1790s. Novels of all sorts had been published before, but they took off as a genre in the eighteenth century, especially after 1740, the date of publication of Richardson's *Pamela*. In France, 8 new novels were published in 1701, 52 in 1750, and 112 in 1789. In Britain, the number of new novels increased sixfold between the first decade of the eighteenth century and the 1760s: about 30 new novels appeared every year in the 1770s, 40 per year in the 1780s, and 70 per year in the 1790s. In addition, more people could read, and novels now featured ordinary people as central characters facing the everyday problems of love, marriage, and getting ahead in the world. Literacy had increased to the point where even servants, male and female, read novels in the big cities, though novel reading was not then, nor is it now, common among the lower classes. French peasants, who made up as much as 80 percent of the population, did not usually read novels, when they could read at all.[5]

Despite the limitations in readership, the ordinary heroes and heroines of the eighteenth-century novel, from Robinson Crusoe and Tom Jones to Clarissa Harlowe and Julie d'Etanges, became household names, even on occasion to those who could not read. Aristocratic characters such as Don Quixote and the Princess of Cleves, so prominent in seventeenth-century novels, now gave way to servants, sailors, and middle-class girls (as the daughter of a minor Swiss nobleman, even Julie seems rather middle class). The remarkable rise of the novel to prominence in the eighteenth century did not go unnoticed, and scholars have linked it over the years to capitalism, the aspiring middle class, the growth of the public sphere, the appearance of the nuclear family, a shift in gender relations, and even the emergence of nationalism. Whatever the reasons for the rise of the novel, I am concerned with its psychological effects and how they connect to the emergence of human rights.[6]

To get at the novel's encouragement of psychological identification, I focus on three especially influential epistolary novels: Rousseau's *Julie* and two novels by his English predecessor and avowed model, Samuel Richardson, *Pamela* (1740) and *Clarissa* (1747–48). My argument could have encompassed the eighteenth-century novel in general and would then have considered the many women who wrote novels, and male characters, such as Tom Jones or Tristram Shandy, who certainly attracted their share of attention. I have chosen to concentrate on *Julie*, *Pamela*, and *Clarissa*, three novels written by men and centered on female heroines, because of their indisputable cultural impact. They did not produce the changes in empathy traced here all on their own, but a closer examination of their reception does show the new learning of empathy in operation. To understand what was new about the "novel"—a label only embraced by writers in the second half of the eighteenth century—it helps to see how specific ones worked on their readers.

In the epistolary novel, there is no one authorial point of view outside and above the action (as later in the nineteenth-century realist novel); the authorial point of view is the characters' perspectives as expressed in their letters. The "editors" of the letters, as Richardson and Rousseau styled themselves, created a vivid sense of reality precisely because their authorship was obscured within the letters' exchange. This made possible a heightened sense of identification, as if the character were real, not fictional. Many contemporaries commented on this experience, some with joy and amazement, others with concern, even disgust.

The publication of Richardson and Rousseau's novels produced instantaneous reactions—and not just in the country of their original appearance. An anonymous French man, now known to be a cleric, published a 42-page letter in 1742 detailing the "avid" reception given the French translation of *Pamela*: "You cannot go into a house without finding a Pamela." Although the author claims that the novel suffers from many shortcomings, he confesses, "I devoured it." ("Devouring" would turn out to be the most common metaphor for reading these novels.) He describes Pamela's resistance to the advances of Mr. B, her employer, as if they were real people rather than fictional characters. He finds himself caught up in the plot. He trembles when Pamela is in danger, feels outrage when aristocratic characters such as Mr. B act in an unworthy fashion. His choice of words and style of speaking repeatedly reinforce the sense of emotional absorption created by the reading.[7]

The novel made up of letters could produce such striking psychological effects because its narrative form facilitated the development of a "character," that is, a person with an inner self. In one of the early letters of *Pamela*, for example, our heroine describes to her mother how her employer has tried to seduce her:

> . . . he kissed me two or three times, with frightful Eagerness.—At last I burst from him, and was getting out of the summer-house; but he held me back, and shut the door. I would have given my Life for a Farthing. And he said, I'll do you no Harm, *Pamela*; don't be afraid of me. I said, I won't stay. You won't, Hussy! Said he: Do you know whom you speak to? I lost all Fear, and all Respect, and said, Yes, I do, sir, too well!—Well may I forget that I am your Servant, when you forget what belongs to a Master. I SOBB'D and cry'd most sadly. What a foolish Hussy you are! said he: Have I done you any Harm?—Yes, Sir, said I, the greatest Harm in the World: You have taught me to forget myself, and what belongs to me; and have lessen'd the Distance that Fortune has made between us, by demeaning yourself, to be so free to a poor Servant.

We read the letter along with the mother. No narrator, indeed no quotation marks, stand between us and Pamela herself. We cannot help but identify with Pamela and experience with her the potential erasure of social distance as well as the threat to her self-possession.[8] (Figure 2)

FIGURE 2. *Mr. B Reads One of Pamela's Letters to Her Parents*
In one of the opening scenes of the novel, Mr. B bursts in upon Pamela and
demands to see the letter she is writing. Writing is her means of autonomy.
Artists and publishers could not resist adding visual renditions of the key
scenes. This engraving by the Dutch artist Jan Punt appeared in an early
French translation published in Amsterdam.

Although the scene has many theatrical qualities, and is staged for Pamela's mother in the writing, it also differs from theater because Pamela can write at greater length about her inner emotions. Much later on, she will write pages about her thoughts of suicide when her plans for escape run awry. A play, in contrast, could not linger in this way on the unfolding of an inner self, which on the stage usually has to be inferred from action or speech. A novel of many hundreds of pages could bring out a character over time and do so, moreover, from the perspective of inside the self. The reader does not just follow Pamela's actions; the reader participates in the blossoming of her personality as she writes. The reader simultaneously becomes Pamela even while imagining him-/herself as a friend of hers and as an outside observer.

As soon as Richardson's authorship of *Pamela* became known in 1741 (he published it anonymously), he began receiving letters, mostly from enthusiasts. His friend Aaron Hill proclaimed it "the soul of religion, good breeding, discretion, good nature, wit, fancy, fine thought, and morality." Richardson had sent a copy to Aaron Hill's daughters in early December 1740, and Hill dashed off an immediate response: "I have done nothing but read it to others, and hear others again read it to me, ever since it came into my hands; and I find I am likely to do nothing else, for the Lord knows how long yet to come . . . it takes possession, all night, of the fancy. It has witchcraft in every page of it; but it is the witchcraft of passion and meaning." The book cast a kind of spell on its readers. The narrative—the exchange of letters—unexpectedly swept them out of themselves into a new set of experiences.[9]

Hill and his daughters were not alone. The *Pamela* craze soon engulfed England. In one village, it was said, the inhabitants rang the church bells upon hearing the rumor that Mr. B had finally married Pamela. A second printing appeared in January 1741 (the original was only published on November 6, 1740), a third in March, a fourth in May, and a fifth in September. By then, others had already penned parodies, lengthy critiques, poems, and knockoffs of the original. They were to be followed over the years by many theatrical adaptations and paintings and prints of the major scenes. In 1744, the French translation made its way onto the papal Index of Forbidden Books, where it would soon be joined by Rousseau's *Julie*, along with many other works of the Enlightenment. Not everyone found in such novels "the soul of religion" or "morality" that Hill had claimed to see.[10]

When Richardson began to publish *Clarissa* in December 1747, expectations ran high. By the time the last volumes (there were seven in all, ranging from 300 to over 400 pages each!) appeared in December 1748, Richardson had already received letters begging him to offer a happy ending. Clarissa runs off with the rake Lovelace to escape the loathsome suitor proposed by her own family. She then has to fend off Lovelace, who eventually rapes Clarissa after drugging her. Despite Lovelace's repentant offer of marriage, and her own feelings for him, Clarissa dies, her heart broken by the rake's assault on her virtue and her sense of self. Lady Dorothy Bradshaigh recounted to Richardson her response on reading the death scene: "My Spirits are strangely seized, my Sleep is disturbed, waking in the Night I burst into a Passion of crying, so I did at Breakfast this Morning, and just now again." The poet Thomas Edwards wrote in January 1749, "I never felt so much distress in my life as I have done for that dear girl," referred to earlier as "the divine Clarissa."[11]

Clarissa appealed more to highbrow readers than to the general public, yet it nonetheless went through five editions in the next thirteen years and was soon translated into French (1751), German (1752), and Dutch (1755). A study of French personal libraries set up between 1740 and 1760 showed that *Pamela* and *Clarissa* ranked among the three English novels (Henry Fielding's *Tom Jones* was the other) most likely to be found in them. *Clarissa*'s length no doubt put off some readers; even before the thirty manuscript volumes went into print, Richardson worried and tried to cut it. A Parisian literary newsletter offered a mixed judgment on reading the French translation: "In reading this book I experienced something not at all ordinary, the most intense pleasure and the most tedious boredom." Yet two years later another contributor to the newsletter announced that Richardson's genius for presenting so many individualized characters made *Clarissa* "perhaps the most surprising work that ever came from a man's hands."[12]

Although Rousseau believed his own novel to be superior to Richardson's, he nonetheless ranked *Clarissa* the best of the rest: "No one has ever yet written, in any language, a novel equal to *Clarissa*, not even one approaching it." Comparisons between *Clarissa* and *Julie* continued right through the century. Jeanne-Marie Roland, wife of a minister and informal coordinator of the Girondin political faction during the French Revolution, confessed to a friend in 1789 that she reread Rousseau's novel every year, yet she still considered Richardson's work the acme of perfection. "There is not a people in the world who offer a novel capable of sustaining a comparison with *Clarissa*; it is the chef-d'oeuvre of the genre, the model and the despair of every imitator."[13]

Men and women alike identified with the female heroines of these novels. From letters to Rousseau, we know that men, even military officers, reacted intensely to *Julie*. One Louis François, a retired military officer, wrote to Rousseau: "You have driven me crazy about her. Imagine then the tears that her death must have wrung from me. . . . Never have I wept such delicious tears. That reading created such a powerful effect on me that I believe I would have gladly died during that supreme moment." Some readers explicitly acknowledged their identification with the female heroine. C. J. Panckoucke, who would become a well-known publisher, told Rousseau, "I have felt pass through my heart the purity of Julie's emotions." The psychological identification that leads to empathy clearly took place across gender lines. Male readers of Rousseau did not just identify with Saint-Preux, the lover Julie is forced to renounce, and empathized even less with Wolmar, her bland husband, or baron d'Etange, her tyrannical father. Like female readers, men identified with Julie herself. Her struggle to overcome her passions and live a virtuous life became their struggle.[14]

By its very form, then, the epistolary novel was able to demonstrate that selfhood depended on qualities of "interiority" (having an inner core), for the characters express their inner feelings in their letters. In addition, the epistolary novel showed that all selves had this interiority (many of the characters write), and consequently that all selves were in some sense equal because all were alike in their possession of interiority. The exchange of letters turns the servant girl Pamela, for example, into a model of proud autonomy and individuality rather than a stereotype of the downtrodden. Like Pamela, Clarissa and Julie come to stand for individuality itself. Readers become more aware of their own and every other individual's capacity for interiority.[15]

Needless to say, everyone did not experience the same feelings when reading these novels. The English novelist and wit

Horace Walpole derided the "tedious lamentations" of Richardson, "which are pictures of high life as conceived by a bookseller, and romances as they would be spiritualized by a Methodist teacher." Yet many quickly sensed that Richardson and Rousseau had struck a vital cultural nerve. Just one month after the publication of the final volumes of *Clarissa*, Sarah Fielding, the sister of Richardson's great rival and a successful novelist herself, anonymously published a 56-page pamphlet defending the novel. Although her brother Henry had published one of the first sendups of *Pamela* (*An Apology for the Life of Mrs. Shamela Andrews, In which, the many notorious Falsehoods and Misrepresentations of a Book called "Pamela," are exposed and refuted*, 1741), Sarah had become good friends with Richardson, who printed one of her novels. One of her fictional characters, Mr. Clark, insists that Richardson has so succeeded in drawing him into the web of illusion "that for my own part I am as intimately acquainted with all the *Harlows* [sic], as if I had known them from my Infancy." Another character, Miss Gibson, insists on the virtues of Richardson's literary technique: "Most truly, Sir, do you remark, that a Story told in this Manner can move but slowly, that the Characters can be seen only by such as attend strictly to the Whole; yet this Advantage the Author gains by writing in the present Tense, as he himself calls it, and in the first Person, that his Strokes penetrate immediately to the Heart, and we feel all the Distresses he paints; we not only weep for, but with *Clarissa*, and accompany her, step by step, through all her Distresses."[16]

The noted Swiss physiologist and literary scholar Albrecht von Haller published an anonymous appreciation of *Clarissa* in the *Gentleman's Magazine* in 1749. Von Haller struggled mightily to grasp the nettle of Richardson's originality. Although he appreciated the many virtues of earlier French novels, von Haller insisted that they provided "generally no more than representations of the illustrious actions of illustrious persons," whereas in Richardson's novel, the reader sees a character "in the same station of life with ourselves." The Swiss author paid close attention to the epistolary format. Although readers might have trouble believing that all the characters liked to spend their time writing down their every innermost feeling and thought, the epistolary novel could offer minutely accurate portrayals of individual characters and thereby evoke what Haller termed compassion: "The pathetic has never been exhibited with equal power, and it is manifest, in a thousand instances that the most obdurate and insensible tempers have been softened into compassion, and melted into tears, by the death, the sufferings, and the sorrows of Clarissa." He concluded that "We have not read any performance, in any language, that so much as approaches to a competition."[17]

Degradation or Uplift?

Contemporaries knew from their own experience that reading these novels had effects on bodies and not just minds, but they disagreed about the consequences. Catholic and Protestant clergy denounced the potential for obscenity, seduction, and moral degradation. As early as 1734, Nicolas Lenglet-Dufresnoy, a Sorbonne-trained cleric himself, found it necessary to defend novels against his colleagues, albeit under a pseudonym. He teasingly rebutted all the objections that led authorities to prohibit novels "as so many pricks that serve to inspire in us sentiments that are too lively and too marked." Insisting that novels were appropriate in any period, he conceded that "at all times credulity, love and women have reigned; thus in all times novels have been followed and savoured." It would be better to concentrate on making them good, he suggested, rather than trying to suppress them altogether.[18]

The attacks did not end when novel production took off at midcentury. In 1755, another Catholic cleric, abbé Armand-Pierre Jacquin, wrote a 400-page work to show that reading novels undermined morality, religion, and all the principles of social order. "Open these works," he insisted, "and you will see in almost all of them, the rights of divine and human justice violated, parents' authority over their children scorned, the sacred bonds of marriage and friendship broken." The danger lay precisely in their attractive powers; by constantly harping on the seductions of love, they encouraged readers to act on their worst impulses, to refuse the advice of their parents and church, to ignore the moral strictures of the community. The only reassurance that Jacquin could offer was the lack of staying power of novels. The reader might devour one the first time around but never read it again. "Was I wrong to prophesy that the novel of *Pamela* would soon be forgotten? . . . It will be the same in three years for *Tom Jones* and *Clarissa*."[19]

Similar complaints flowed from the pens of English Protestants. Reverend Vicesimus Knox summed up decades of lingering anxieties in 1779 when he proclaimed novels degenerate, guilty pleasures that diverted young minds from more serious and edifying reading. The upsurge in British novels only served to broadcast French libertine habits and accounted for the corruption of the present age. Richardson's novels, Knox admitted, had been written with "the purest intentions." But inevitably the author had recounted scenes and excited sentiments that were incompatible with virtue. Clerics were not alone in their contempt for the novel. A rhyme in the *Lady's Magazine* for 1771 summed up a view widely shared:

> With Pamela, by name,
> No better acquainted;
> For as novels I hate,
> My mind is not tainted.

Many moralists feared that novels sowed discontent in the minds especially of servants and young girls.[20]

The Swiss physician Samuel-Auguste Tissot linked novel reading to masturbation, which he thought led to physical, mental, and moral degeneration. Tissot believed that bodies naturally tended to deteriorate and that masturbation hastened the process in both men and women. "All that I can say is that idleness; inactivity; staying in bed too long; a bed that is too soft; a rich, spicy, salty, and wine-filled diet; suspect friends; and licentious books are the causes most apt to lead to these excesses." By "licentious," Tissot did not mean frankly pornographic; in the eighteenth century, "licentious" meant anything tending to the erotic but it was distinguished from the much more objectionable "obscene." Novels about love—and the majority of eighteenth-century novels told stories about love—easily slipped into the category of the licentious. In England, girls in boarding schools seemed especially at risk because of their ability to get hold of such "immoral and repugnant" books and read them in bed.[21]

Clerics and doctors thus agreed in viewing novel reading in terms of loss—of time, vital fluids, religion, and morality. They assumed that the reader would imitate the action in the novel, to her great regret. A female reader of *Clarissa*, for example, might disregard the wishes of her family and like Clarissa agree to escape with a Lovelace-like rake who would lead her, willy-nilly, to her ruin. In 1792, an anonymous English critic could still insist that "The increase of novels will help to account for the increase of prostitution and for the numerous adulteries and elopements that we hear of in the different parts of the kingdom." In this view, novels overstimulated the body, encouraged a morally suspect self-absorption, and provoked actions destructive of familial, moral, and religious authority.[22]

Richardson and Rousseau claimed the role of editor rather than author so that they could sidestep the disrepute associated with novels. When Richardson published *Pamela*, he never referred to it as a novel. The full title of the first edition is a study in protesting too much: *Pamela: Or, Virtue Rewarded. In a Series of Familiar Letters from a Beautiful Young Damsel, to her Parents: Now first Published In order to cultivate the Principles of Virtue and Religion in the Minds of the Youth of Both Sexes. A Narrative which has its Foundation in Truth and Nature: and at the same time that it agreeably entertains, by a Variety of curious and affecting Incidents, is intirely [sic] divested of all those Images, which, in too many Pieces calculated for Amusement only, tend to inflame the Minds they should instruct.* Richardson's preface "by the editor" justifies the publication of "the following Letters" in moral terms; they will instruct and improve the minds of the young, inculcate religion and morality, paint vice "in its proper colours," etc.[23]

Although Rousseau referred to himself as editor too, he did clearly consider the work a novel. In the first sentence of the preface to *Julie*, Rousseau linked novels to his well-known criticism of the theater: "Great cities must have theaters; and corrupt peoples, Novels." As if this were not enough warning, Rousseau also provided a preface consisting of a "Conversation about Novels between the Editor and a Man of Letters." In it, the character "R" [Rousseau] lays out all the usual charges against the novel for playing upon the imagination to create desires they cannot virtuously fulfill:

> We hear it complained that Novels trouble people's minds: I can well believe it. By endlessly setting before their readers' eyes the pretended charms of an estate that is not their own, they seduce them, lead them to view their own with contempt, and trade it in their imagination for the one they are induced to love. Trying to be what we are not, we come to believe ourselves different from what we are, and that is the way to go mad.

And yet Rousseau then proceeded to offer a novel to his readers. He even threw down the gauntlet with defiance. If anyone wants to criticize me for having written it, says Rousseau, let him say so to everyone on earth except to me. For my part, I could never have any esteem for such a man. The book might scandalize almost everyone, Rousseau gladly admits, but it will at least not afford a merely tepid pleasure. Rousseau fully expected his readers to have violent reactions.[24]

Despite Richardson and Rousseau's own worries about their reputations, some critics had already begun to develop a much more positive view of the workings of the novel. Already in defending Richardson, Sarah Fielding and von Haller had drawn attention to the empathy or compassion stimulated by reading *Clarissa*. In this new view, novels worked on readers to make them more sympathetic toward others, rather than just self-absorbed, and therefore more moral, not less. One of the most articulate defenders of the novel was Diderot, author of the article on natural right for the *Encyclopédie* and himself a novelist. When Richardson died in 1761, Diderot wrote a eulogy comparing Richardson to the greatest authors among the ancients, Moses, Homer, Euripides, and Sophocles. Diderot dwelled, however, on the immersion of the reader in the world of the novel: "One takes, despite all precautions, a role in his works, you are thrown into conversation, you approve, you blame, you admire, you become irritated, you feel indignant. How many times did I not surprise myself, as it happens to children who have been taken to the theater for the first time, crying: 'Don't believe it, he is deceiving you. . . . If you go there, you will be lost.'" Richardson's narrative creates the impression that you are present, Diderot recognizes, and moreover, this is your world, not a far distant country, not an exotic locale, not a fairy tale. "His characters are taken from ordinary society . . . the passions he depicts are those I feel in myself."[25]

Diderot does not use the terms "identification" or "empathy," but he does provide a compelling description of them. You recognize yourself in the characters, he acknowledges, you imaginatively leap into the midst of the action, you feel the same feelings that the characters are feeling. In short, you learn to empathize with someone who is not yourself and can never be directly accessible to you (unlike, say, members of your family) and yet who is in some imaginative way also yourself, that being a crucial element in identification. This process explains why Panckoucke wrote to Rousseau, "I have felt pass through my heart the purity of Julie's emotions."

Empathy depends on identification. Diderot sees that Richardson's narrative technique draws him ineluctably into this experience. It is a kind of hothouse of emotional learning: "In the space of a few hours I went through a great number of situations which the longest life can hardly offer across its entire duration. . . . I felt that I had acquired experience." So much does Diderot identify that he feels bereft at the novel's end: "I felt the same sensation that men feel who have been closely entwined and lived together for a long time and who are now on the point of separating. At the end, it suddenly seemed to me that I was left alone."[26]

Diderot has simultaneously lost himself in the action and regained himself in the reading. He has more of a sense of the separateness of his self than before—he now feels lonely—but he also has more of a sense that others have selves too. In other words, he has what he himself called that "interior feeling" that is necessary to human rights. Diderot grasps, morever, that the effect of the novel is unconscious: "One feels oneself drawn to the good with an impetuosity one does not recognize. When faced with injustice you experience a disgust you do not know how to explain to yourself." The novel has worked its effect through the process of involvement in the narrative, not through explicit moralizing.[27]

Reading fiction got its most serious philosophical treatment in Henry Home, Lord Kames's *Elements of Criticism* (1762). The Scottish jurist and philosopher did not discuss novels per se in the work, but he did argue that fiction in general creates a kind of "ideal presence" or "waking dream," in which the reader imagines himself transported to the depicted scene. Kames described this "ideal presence" as a trancelike state. The reader is "thrown into a kind of reverie," and "losing the consciousness of self, and of reading, his present occupation, he conceives every incident as passing in his presence, precisely as if he were an eyewitness." Most important for Kames, this transformation fosters morality. "Ideal presence" opens up the reader to feelings that strengthen the bonds of society. Individuals are drawn out of their private interests and motivated to perform "acts of generosity and benevolence." "Ideal presence" was another term for Aaron Hill's "witchcraft of passion and meaning."[28]

Thomas Jefferson apparently shared this view. When Robert Skipwith, who married the half sister of Jefferson's wife, wrote to Jefferson in 1771 asking for a list of recommended books, Jefferson suggested many of the classics, ancient and modern, in politics, religion, law, science, philosophy, and history. Kames's *Elements of Criticism* was on the list, but Jefferson began his catalogue with poetry, plays, and novels, including those of Laurence Sterne, Henry Fielding, Jean-François Marmontel, Oliver Goldsmith, Richardson, and Rousseau. In the letter that went with the reading list Jefferson waxed eloquent on "the entertainments of fiction." Like Kames, he insisted that fiction could imprint both the principles and practice of virtue. Citing Shakespeare, Marmontel, and Sterne by name, Jefferson explained that in reading such works, we experience the "strong desire in ourselves of doing charitable and grateful acts" and conversely are disgusted by evil deeds or immoral conduct. Fiction, he insisted, produces the desire for moral emulation even more effectively than reading history.[29]

Ultimately at stake in this conflict of views about the novel was nothing less than the valorization of ordinary secular life as the foundation for morality. In the eyes of the critics of novel reading, sympathy with a novelistic heroine encouraged the worst in the individual (illicit desires and excessive self-regard) and demonstrated the irrevocable degeneration of the secular world. For the adherents of the new view of empathetic moralization, in contrast, such identification showed that the arousal of passion could help transform the inner nature of the individual and produce a more moral society. They believed that the inner nature of humans provided a grounding for social and political authority.[30]

The magical spell cast by the novel thus turned out to be far-reaching in its effects. Although the adherents of the novel did not say so explicitly, they understood that writers such as Richardson and Rousseau were effectively drawing their readers into daily life as a kind of substitute religious experience. Readers learned to appreciate the emotional intensity of the ordinary and the capacity of people like themselves to create on their own a moral world. Human rights grew out of the seedbed sowed by these feelings. Human rights could only flourish when people learned to think of others as their equals, as like them in some fundamental fashion. They learned this equality, at least in part, by experiencing identification with ordinary characters who seemed dramatically present and familiar, even if ultimately fictional.[31]

The Strange Fate of Women

In the three novels singled out here, the focus of psychological identification is a young female character created by a male author. Needless to say, identification with male characters also took place. Jefferson, for instance, avidly followed the fortunes of Sterne's *Tristram Shandy* (1759–67) and Sterne's alter ego, Yorick, in *A Sentimental Journey* (1768). Women writers, too, had their enthusiasts among both female and male readers. The French penal reformer and abolitionist Jacques-Pierre Brissot quoted Rousseau's *Julie* constantly, but his favorite English novel was Fanny Burney's *Cecilia* (1782). As the example of Burney confirms, however, female characters enjoyed pride of place; all three of her novels bore the names of their featured heroines.[32]

Female heroines were so compelling because their quest for autonomy could never fully succeed. Women had few legal rights separate from their fathers or husbands. Readers found the heroine's search for independence especially poignant because they immediately understood the constraints such a woman inevitably faced. In a happy ending, Pamela marries Mr. B and accepts the implied limits on her freedom. In contrast, Clarissa dies, rather than marry Lovelace after he rapes her. While Julie seems to accept being forced by her father to renounce the man she loves, she too dies in the final scene.

Some modern critics have seen masochism or martyrdom in these stories, but contemporaries could see other qualities. Male and female readers alike identified with these characters because the women displayed so much will, so much personality. Readers did not just want to save the heroines; they wanted to be like them, even like Clarissa and Julie, despite their tragic deaths. Almost all of the action in the three novels turns on expressions of female will, usually a will that has to chafe against parental or societal restrictions. Pamela must resist Mr. B in order to maintain her sense of virtue and her sense of self, and her resistance eventually wins him over. Clarissa stands firm against her family and then Lovelace for much the same reasons, and by the end Lovelace wants desperately to marry Clarissa, an offer she refuses. Julie must give up Saint-Preux and learn to love her life with Wolmar; the struggle is entirely hers. In each novel, everything comes back to the heroine's desire for independence. The actions of the male characters only serve to highlight this female will. Readers empathizing with the heroines learned that all people—even women—aspired to greater

autonomy, and they imaginatively experienced the psychological effort that struggle entailed.

Eighteenth-century novels reflected a deeper cultural preoc-
cupation with autonomy. Enlightenment philosophers firmly
believed that they had effected a breakthrough in this area in the
eighteenth century. When they talked of freedom, they meant
individual autonomy, whether it was the freedom to express
opinions or practice one's chosen religion or the independence
taught to boys if one followed Rousseau's precepts in his educational guide, *Emile* (1762). The Enlightenment narrative of the
conquest of autonomy reached its culmination in Immanuel
Kant's 1784 essay, "What is Enlightenment?" He famously
defined it as "mankind's exit from its self-incurred immaturity."
Immaturity, he went on, "is the inability to make use of one's
own understanding without the guidance of another." Enlightenment, for Kant, meant intellectual autonomy, the ability to
think for oneself.[33]

The Enlightenment's emphasis on individual autonomy
grew out of the seventeenth-century revolution in political
thinking started by Hugo Grotius and John Locke. They had
argued that the autonomous male entering into a social compact
with other such individuals was the only possible foundation of
legitimate political authority. If authority justified by divine
right, Scripture, and history was to be replaced by a contract
between autonomous men, then boys had to be taught to think
for themselves. Educational theory, shaped most influentially by
Locke and Rousseau, therefore shifted from an emphasis on obedience enforced through punishment to the careful cultivation
of reason as the chief instrument of independence. Locke
explained the significance of the new practices in *Some
Thoughts Concerning Education* (1693): "We must look upon

our Children, when grown up, to be like ourselves. . . . We would be thought Rational Creatures, and have our Freedom; we love not to be uneasie under constant rebukes and Browbeatings." As Locke recognized, political and intellectual autonomy depended on educating children (in his case, both boys and girls) in new dispositions; autonomy required a new relationship to the world, not just new ideas.[34]

Thinking and deciding for oneself therefore required psychological and political changes as much as philosophical ones. In *Emile*, Rousseau called on mothers to build psychological walls between their children and all external social and political pressures. "Set up early on," he urged, "an enclosure around your child's soul." The English preacher and political pamphleteer Richard Price insisted in 1776, when writing in support of the American colonists, that one of the four general aspects of liberty was physical liberty, "that principle of *Spontaneity*, or *Self-determination*, which constitutes us *Agents*." For him, liberty was synonymous with self-direction or self-government, the political metaphor in this case suggesting a psychological one, but the two were closely related.[35]

Enlightenment-inspired reformers wanted to go beyond shielding the body or enclosing the soul as Rousseau urged. They demanded a widening of the compass of individual decision making. French revolutionary laws on the family demonstrate the depth of concern felt about traditional limitations on independence. In March 1790, the new National Assembly abolished primogeniture, which gave special inheritance rights to the first-born male child, and the infamous *lettres de cachet*, which allowed families to incarcerate children without hearings. In August of the same year, the deputies established family councils to hear disputes between parents and children up to age twenty rather than permitting fathers exclusive control over their children. In April 1791, the Assembly decreed that all children, both male and female, must inherit equally. Then, in August and September 1792, the deputies lowered the age of majority from twenty-five to twenty-one, declared that adults could no longer be subject to paternal authority, and instituted divorce for the first time in French history, making it available on the same legal grounds for both men and women. In short, the revolutionaries did everything they could to push out the boundaries of personal autonomy.[36]

In Great Britain and its North American colonies, the desire for greater autonomy can be traced more easily in autobiographies and novels than in the law, at least before the American Revolution. In fact, in 1753, the Marriage Act (26 Geo II, c. 33) made marriages in England of those under twenty-one illegal unless the father or guardian consented. Despite this reaffirmation of paternal authority, the old-style patriarchal domination of husbands over wives and fathers over children declined in the eighteenth century. From Daniel Defoe's *Robinson Crusoe* (1719) to Benjamin Franklin's *Autobiography* (written between 1771 and 1788), English and American writers celebrated independence as a cardinal virtue. Defoe's novel of the shipwrecked sailor provided a primer on how a man could learn to fend for himself. It is hardly surprising, then, that Rousseau made Defoe's novel required reading for young Emile or that *Robinson Crusoe* was first printed in the American colonies in 1774, right in the midst of the burgeoning independence crisis. *Robinson Crusoe* was one of the American colonial best sellers of 1775, rivaled only by *Lord Chesterfield's Letters to His Son* and John Gregory's *A Father's Legacy to His Daughters*, popularizations of Locke's views on education for boys and girls.[37]

Trends in the lives of real people moved in the same direction, if more haltingly. Young people increasingly expected to make their own choices in marriage, though families still exerted great pressure on them, as could be seen in any number of novels whose plots revolve around this point (e.g., *Clarissa*). Child-rearing practices also reveal subtle changes in attitude. The English abandoned the swaddling of infants before the French (Rousseau can take considerable credit for dissuading the French) but kept beating boys in school longer. By the 1750s, English aristocratic families had stopped using leading strings to guide their children's walking, weaned children sooner, and because the children were no longer swaddled, also toilet-trained them earlier, all signs of increasing emphasis on independence.[38]

The record was sometimes more muddled, however. Divorce in England, unlike other Protestant countries, was virtually impossible in the eighteenth century; between 1700 and 1857, when the Matrimonial Causes Act set up a special court for hearing divorce cases, only 325 divorces were granted by private act of Parliament for England, Wales, and Ireland. Though the number of divorces did grow, from 14 in the first half of the eighteenth century to 117 in the second half, divorce was limited to all intents and purposes to a few aristocratic men, since the grounds required made divorce almost impossible to obtain for women. The numbers translate to only 2.34 divorces granted per year in the second half of the eighteenth century. After the French revolutionaries instituted divorce, in contrast, some 20,000 divorces were granted in France between 1792 and 1803, or 1,800 a year. The British North American colonies generally followed English practice in forbidding divorce while allowing some form of legal separation; but after independence, divorce petitions began to be accepted by the new courts in most states.

Establishing a trend then repeated in Revolutionary France, women filed most of the petitions for divorce in the first years of independence of the new United States.[39]

In notes written in 1771 and 1772 about a legal case for divorce, Thomas Jefferson clearly linked divorce to natural rights. Divorce would restore "to women their natural right of equality." It was, he insisted, in the nature of contracts by mutual consent that they must be dissolvable if one party broke the bargain—the same argument the French revolutionaries would use in 1792. Moreover, the possibility of legal divorce would ensure "liberty of affection," also a natural right. "The pursuit of happiness," made famous by the Declaration of Independence, would have included the right to divorce since the "end of marriage is Propagation & Happiness." The right to pursue happiness therefore required divorce. It is hardly an accident that Jefferson would make similar arguments for an American divorce from Great Britain four years later.[40]

As eighteenth-century people pushed for the expansion of self-determination, they ran up against a dilemma: what would provide the source of community in this new order that highlighted the rights of the individual? It was one thing to explain how morality could be derived from human reason rather than Divine Scripture or how autonomy should be preferred to blind obedience. But it was quite another to reconcile this self-directed individual with the greater good. The Scottish philosophers of midcentury put the question of secular community at the center of their work, and they offered a philosophical answer that resonated with the practice of empathy taught by the novel. The philosophers, like eighteenth-century people more generally, called their answer "sympathy." I have used the term "empathy" because though it entered English only in the twentieth century, it better captures the active will to identify with others. Sympathy now often signifies pity, which can imply condescension, a feeling incompatible with a true feeling of equality.[41]

"Sympathy" had a very broad meaning in the eighteenth century. For Francis Hutcheson, sympathy was a kind of sense, a moral faculty. More noble than sight or hearing, senses shared with animals, but less noble than conscience, sympathy or fellow feeling made social life possible. By the power of human nature, prior to any reasoning, sympathy acted like a kind of social gravitational force to bring people outside of themselves. Sympathy ensured that happiness could not be defined by self-satisfaction alone. "By a sort of contagion or infection," Hutcheson concluded, "all our pleasures, even those of the lowest kind, are strangely increased by their being shared with others."[42]

Adam Smith, author of the *Wealth of Nations* (1776) and a student of Hutcheson, devoted one of his earlier works to the question of sympathy. In the opening chapter of his *Theory of Moral Sentiments* (1759), he uses the example of torture to get at its operation. What makes us sympathize with the suffering of someone on the rack? Even if the sufferer is a brother, we can never directly experience what he feels. We can only identify with his suffering by virtue of our imagination, which lets us place ourselves in his situation and endure the same torments; "we enter as it were into his body and become in some measure him." This process of imaginative identification—sympathy— permits the observer to feel what the torture victim feels. The observer is able to become a truly moral being, however, only when he takes the next step and understands that he too is the subject of such imaginative identification. When he can see himself as the object of others' feelings, he is able to develop within himself an "impartial spectator," which serves as his moral compass. Autonomy and sympathy therefore go together for Smith. Only an autonomous person can develop an "impartial spectator" within himself; yet he can only do so, Smith explains, if he first identifies with others.[43]

Sympathy or sensibility—the latter term was much more common in French—had a broad cultural resonance on both sides of the Atlantic in the last half of the eighteenth century. Thomas Jefferson read Hutcheson and Smith, though he specifically cited the novelist Laurence Sterne as offering "the best course of morality." Given the ubiquity of reference to sympathy and sensibility in the Atlantic world, it hardly seems accidental that the first novel written by an American, published in 1789, carried as its title *The Power of Sympathy*. Sympathy and sensibility so permeated literature, painting, and even medicine that some physicians began to worry about an excess of them, which they feared might lead to melancholia, hypochondria, or "the vapors." Physicians thought that ladies of leisure (women readers) were especially susceptible.[44]

Sympathy and sensibility worked in favor of many disenfranchised groups, but not women. Capitalizing on the success of the novel in calling forth new forms of psychological identification, early abolitionists encouraged freed slaves to write their own novelistic autobiographies, sometimes partially fictionalized, to gain adherents to the budding movement. The evils of slavery came to life when described firsthand by men such as Olaudah Equiano, whose book *The Interesting Narrative of the Life of Olaudah Equiano, Or Gustavus Vassa, The African. Written by Himself*, was first published in London in 1789. Yet most of the abolitionists failed to make a connection to women's rights. After 1789, many French revolutionaries would take public and vociferous stands in favor of rights for Protestants, Jews,

free blacks, and even slaves, and at the same time actively
oppose granting rights to women. In the new United States,
though slavery came up immediately for heated debate, women's
rights elicited even less public commentary than in France.
Women did not get equal political rights anywhere before the
twentieth century.[45]

Eighteenth-century people, like almost everyone in human
history before them, viewed women as dependents defined by
their family status and thus by definition not fully capable of
political autonomy. They could stand for self-determination as a
private, moral virtue without establishing a link to political
rights. They had rights, but not political ones. This view became
explicit when the French revolutionaries drew up a new constitution in 1789. Abbé Emmanuel-Joseph Sieyès, a leading inter-
preter of constitutional theory, explained the emerging
distinction between natural and civil rights on the one hand and
political rights on the other. All the inhabitants of a country,
including women, enjoyed the rights of a passive citizen: the
right to the protection of their person, property, and liberty. But
all are not active citizens, he maintained, with the right to
directly participate in public affairs. "Women, at least in the
present state, children, foreigners, those who contribute nothing
to maintaining the public establishment" were defined as the
passive citizens. Sieyès's qualifier "at least in the present state"
left a slight opening for future changes in the rights of women.
Others would try to exploit that opening, but without success in
the short term.[46]

The few who did advocate women's rights in the eighteenth
century expressed ambivalence about novels. Traditional opponents of novels believed that women were especially susceptible
to the enchantment of reading about love, and even defenders of

novels, such as Jefferson, worried about their effects on young girls. In 1818, a much older Jefferson than the one who had enthused about his favorite novelists in 1771 warned about "the inordinate passion" for novels among girls. "The result is a bloated imagination" and "sickly judgment." It is not surprising then that ardent defenders of women's rights took these suspicions to heart. Like Jefferson, Mary Wollstonecraft, the mother of modern feminism, explicitly contrasted novel reading—"the only kind of reading calculated to interest an innocent frivolous mind"—to reading history and to active rational understanding more generally. Yet Wollstonecraft herself wrote two novels centered on female heroines, reviewed many novels in print, and constantly referred to them in her correspondence. Despite her objections to Rousseau's prescriptions for female education in *Emile*, she avidly read *Julie*, and she used remembered phrases from *Clarissa* and Sterne's novels to convey her own emotions in her letters.[47]

Learning to empathize opened the path to human rights, but it did not ensure that everyone would be able to take that path right away. No one understood this better or agonized over it more than the author of the Declaration of Independence. In a letter of 1802 to the English clergyman, scientist, and reformer Joseph Priestley, Jefferson held up the American example for the whole world: "It is impossible not to be sensible that we are acting for all mankind; that circumstances denied to others but indulged to us have imposed on us the duty of proving what is the degree of freedom and self-government in which a society may venture to leave its individual members." Jefferson pushed for the highest imaginable "degree of freedom," which for him meant opening political participation to as many white men as possible and perhaps eventually even to Native American men, if they could be turned into farmers. Although he recognized the humanity of African-Americans and even the rights of slaves as human beings, he did not envision a polity in which they or women of any color took an active part. But that was the highest imaginable degree of freedom for the vast majority of Americans and Europeans, even twenty-four years later on the day of Jefferson's death.[48]

2

"BONE OF
THEIR BONE"

Abolishing Torture

IN 1762, THE SAME YEAR that Rousseau introduced the term "rights of man," a court in the southern French city of Toulouse convicted a sixty-four-year-old French Protestant named Jean Calas of murdering his son to prevent him from converting to Catholicism. The judges sentenced Jean to death by breaking on the wheel. Before execution, Calas first had to endure judically supervised torture known as the "preliminary question," which was designed to get those already convicted to name their accomplices. With his wrists tied tightly to a bar behind him, Calas was stretched by a system of cranks and pulleys that steadily drew his arms up while an iron weight kept his feet in place. (Figure 3) When Calas refused to provide names after two applications, he was tied to a bench and pitchers of water were forced down his throat while his mouth was held open by two

FIGURE 3. *Judicial Torture*
Representations of judicially sanctioned torture are almost impossible to find. This sixteenth-century full-page woodcut (21.6 cm x 14.4 cm) purports to show a method employed in Toulouse which resembles that endured by Jean Calas two centuries later. It is a version of the most commonly used judicial torture in Europe, called the *strappado*, derived from the Italian word for a sharp pull or tear.

small sticks. (Figure 4) Pressed again to name names, he reportedly responded, "Where there is no crime, there cannot be any accomplices."

Death did not follow promptly nor was it meant to do so. Breaking on the wheel, reserved to men convicted of homicide or highway robbery, took place in two stages. First, the executioner tied the condemned man to an X-shaped cross and systematically crushed the bones in his forearms, legs, thighs, and arms by striking each one with two sharp blows. Using a winch fastened to the halter around the condemned man's neck, an assistant under the scaffold then dislocated the vertebrae of the neck with violent tugs on the halter. Meanwhile, the executioner struck the midsection with three hard blows of the iron rod. Then the executioner took down the broken body and fastened it, limbs bent excruciatingly backward, to a carriage wheel on top of a ten-foot pole. There the condemned man remained long after death, concluding "a most dreadful spectacle." In a secret instruction, the court granted Calas the grace of being strangled to death after two hours of torment, before his body was attached to the wheel. Calas died still protesting his innocence.[1]

The Calas "affair" galvanized attention when the case was taken up by Voltaire a few months after the execution. Voltaire raised money for the family, wrote letters in the name of various Calas family members purporting to give their firsthand views of events, and then published a pamphlet and a book based on the case. The most famous of these was his *Treatise on Tolerance on the Occasion of the Death of Jean Calas*, in which he first used the expression "human right"; the gist of his argument was that intolerance could not be a human right (he did not make the positive argument that freedom of religion was a human right). Voltaire did not initially protest against either

FIGURE 4. *Water Torture*
This sixteenth-century woodcut (21.6 cm x 14.4 cm) shows a French method of water torture. It is not exactly the same as the one Calas endured but is close enough to convey the general idea.

torture or breaking on the wheel. What enraged him was the religious bigotry that he concluded had motivated the police and the judges: "It is impossible to see, how, following this principle [human right] one man could say to another, 'believe what I believe and what you cannot believe or you will die.' That's how they talk in Portugal, Spain, and Goa [countries infamous for their inquisitions]."[2]

As public Calvinist worship had been banned in France since 1685, it was apparently not too much of a stretch for the authorities to believe that Calas had killed his son to prevent his conversion to Catholicism. After dinner one night, the family had found Marc-Antoine hanging from a doorway to a rear storeroom, an apparent suicide. In order to avoid scandal, they claimed to have discovered him on the floor, presumably a victim of murder. Suicide was punishable under the law in France; a person who committed suicide could not be buried in consecrated ground, and if found guilty at a hearing, the body could be exhumed, dragged through town, then hung by the feet and thrown in the garbage dump.

The police seized upon the inconsistencies in the family's testimony and promptly arrested the father, mother, and brother along with their servant and a visitor and charged them all with murder. A local court sentenced the father, mother, and brother to torture in order to elicit confessions of guilt (called the "preparatory question"), but on appeal the Parlement of Toulouse overruled the local court, refused to apply torture before conviction, and found only the father guilty, hoping that he would name the others when tortured just before his execution. Voltaire's unrelenting publicity about the affair paid off for the rest of the family, which had not yet been cleared. The Royal Council first set aside the verdicts on technical grounds in 1763 and 1764 and then in 1765 voted for acquittal of everyone involved and the return of the family's confiscated goods.

During the storm over the Calas Affair, Voltaire's focus of attention began to shift, and increasingly the criminal justice system itself, and especially its use of torture and cruelty, came under fire. In his initial writings about Calas in 1762–63, Voltaire never once used the general term "torture" (employing instead the legal euphemism "the question"). He denounced judicial torture for the first time in 1766 and thereafter linked Calas and torture together frequently. Natural compassion makes everyone detest the cruelty of judicial torture, insisted Voltaire, though he himself had not said so earlier. "Torture has been abolished in other countries, and with success; the question therefore is decided." So much did Voltaire's views shift that in 1769 he felt compelled to add an article on "Torture" to his *Philosophical Dictionary*, first published in 1764 and already on the papal Index of Forbidden Books. In the article, Voltaire uses his habitual alternation of ridicule and fulmination to condemn French practices as uncivilized; foreigners judge France by its plays, novels, verses, and beautiful actresses without knowing that there is no nation crueler than the French. A civilized nation, Voltaire concludes, can no longer follow "atrocious old customs." What had long seemed acceptable to him and many others now came into doubt.[3]

As with human rights more generally, new attitudes about both torture and humane punishment first crystallized in the 1760s, not only in France but elsewhere in Europe and in the American colonies. Voltaire's friend, Frederick the Great of Prussia, had already abolished judicial torture in his lands in 1754.

Others followed in the next decades: Sweden in 1772, and Austria and Bohemia in 1776. In 1780, the French monarchy eliminated the use of torture to extract confessions of guilt before sentencing, and in 1788, it provisionally abolished the use of torture just prior to execution to produce the names of accomplices. In 1783, the British government discontinued the public procession to Tyburn, where executions had become a major popular entertainment, and introduced the regular use of "the drop," a raised stage dropped by the executioner in order to ensure quicker and more humane hangings. In 1789, the French revolutionary government renounced all forms of judicial torture, and in 1792 it introduced the guillotine, which was meant to make the execution of the death penalty uniform and as painless as possible. By the end of the eighteenth century, public opinion seemed to demand an end to judicial torture and to the many indignities visited on the bodies of the condemned. As the American physician Benjamin Rush insisted in 1787, we should not forget that even criminals "possess souls and bodies composed of the same materials as those of our friends and relations. They are bone of their bone."[4]

Torture and Cruelty

Judicially supervised torture to extract confessions had been introduced or reintroduced in most European countries in the thirteenth century as a consequence of the revival of Roman law and the example of the Catholic Inquisition. In the sixteenth, seventeenth, and eighteenth centuries, many of Europe's finest legal minds devoted themselves to codifying and regularizing the use of judicial torture in order to prevent abuses of it by overly zealous or sadistic judges. Great Britain had supposedly replaced judicial torture with juries in the thirteenth century, yet torture still took place there in the sixteenth and seventeenth centuries in cases of sedition and witchcraft. Against witches, for example, the more severe Scottish magistrates used pricking, sleep deprivation, and torture by "boots" (crushing legs), burning with hot irons, and other methods. Torture to obtain the names of accomplices was allowed under Massachusetts colonial law, but apparently never ordered.[5]

Brutal forms of punishment upon conviction were ubiquitous in Europe and the Americas. Although the British Bill of Rights of 1689 expressly prohibited cruel punishment, judges still sentenced criminals to the whipping post, ducking stool, stocks, pillory, branding, and execution by drawing and quartering (dismemberment by horses) or, for women, drawing and quartering and burning at the stake. What constituted "cruel" punishment clearly depended on cultural expectations. Only in 1790 did Parliament forbid burning women at the stake. Previously, however, it had dramatically increased the number of capital offenses, which by some estimates tripled in the eighteenth century, and in 1752 it had acted to make punishments for murder yet more horrible in order to increase their deterrence. It ordered that all murderers' bodies be given to surgeons for dissection—at this time viewed as ignominious—and it gave judges the discretionary authority to order that any male murderer's body be hung in chains after execution. Despite growing discomfort with this gibbeting of the corpses of murderers, the practice was not finally abolished until 1834.[6]

Punishment in the colonies not surprisingly followed the patterns established in the imperial center. Thus, one third of all sentences in the Massachusetts Superior Court even in the last

half of the eighteenth century called for public humiliations ranging from wearing signs to cutting off an ear, branding, and whipping. A contemporary in Boston described how "women were
taken from a huge cage, in which they were dragged on wheels
from prison, and tied to the post with bare backs, on which
thirty or forty lashes were bestowed amid the scream of the cul-
prits and the uproar of the mob." The British Bill of Rights did
not protect slaves because they were not viewed as persons with
legal rights. Virginia and North Carolina expressly permitted the
castration of slaves for heinous offenses, and in Maryland, in
cases of petty treason or arson by a slave, the right hand was cut
off and the slave then hanged, the head cut off, the body quar-
tered, and the dismembered parts displayed in public. As late as
the 1740s, slaves in New York could be burnt to death in agoniz-
ingly slow fashion, broken on the wheel, or hung in chains until
death by starvation.[7]

Most sentences mandated by the French courts in the last half
of the eighteenth century still included some form of public corporal punishment such as branding, whipping, or wearing the iron
collar (which was attached to a pole or to the pillory—Figure 5). In
the same year that Calas was executed, the Parlement of Paris rendered appellate penal judgments against 235 men and women first
tried by the Châtelet court (a lower court) of Paris: 82 were sentenced to banishment and branding, usually combined with whipping; 9 to the same combination along with the iron collar; 19 to
branding and imprisonment; 20 to confinement in the General
Hospital after branding and/or the iron collar; 12 to hanging; 3 to
breaking on the wheel; and 1 to burning at the stake. If all the
other courts of Paris were included in the count, the number of
public humiliations and mutilations would climb to 500 or 600,
with some 18 executions—in just one year in one jurisdiction.[8]

Escroc
et fabricateur
d'une Loterie
et de Libelles
Diffamatoires

Le veritable Portrait tiré d'aprés nature sur la Place du Palais Royal, d'Emmanuel Jean de la Coste, comdamné par Jugement souverain de M.ʳ le Licutenant G.ˡ de Police, du 28. Aouſt 1760. au Carcan pendant 3. jours a la marqu et aux Galeres a perpétuité).

FIGURE 5. *The Iron Collar*
The point of this punishment was public humiliation. This print by an unknown artist shows a man convicted of fraud and libel in 1760. According to the caption, he was first attached to the iron collar for three days, thcn brandcd and scnt to the galleys for life.

The death penalty could be imposed in five different ways in France: decapitation for nobles; hanging for common criminals; drawing and quartering for offenses against the sovereign known as *lèse-majesté*; burning at the stake for heresy, magic, arson, poisoning, bestiality, and sodomy; and breaking on the wheel for murder or highway robbery. Judges ordered drawing and quartering and burning at the stake infrequently in the eighteenth century, but breaking on the wheel was quite common; in the southern French jurisdiction of the Parlement of Aix-en-Provence, for example, nearly half the fifty-three death sentences imposed between 1760 and 1762 called for breaking on the wheel.[9]

Yet from the 1760s onward, campaigns of various sorts led to the abolition of state-sanctioned torture and a growing moderation of punishment (even for slaves). The reformers credited their accomplishments to the spread of Enlightenment humanitarianism. In 1786, the English reformer Samuel Romilly looked back and confidently asserted that "in proportion as men have reflected and reasoned upon this important subject, the absurd and barbarous notions of justice, which prevailed for ages, have been exploded, and human and rational principles have been adopted in their stead." Much of the immediate impetus for reasoning on the subject came from the short, punchy *Essay on Crimes and Punishments*, published in 1764 by a twenty-five-year-old Italian aristocrat, Cesare Beccaria. Promoted by the circles around Diderot, quickly translated into French and English, and eagerly read by Voltaire in the midst of the Calas Affair, Beccaria's little book trained the spotlight on every nation's criminal justice system. The Italian upstart rejected not only torture and cruel punishment but also—in a move remarkable for the time—the death penalty itself. Against the absolute power of rulers, religious orthodoxy, and the privileges of the titled, Beccaria held forth a democratic standard of justice: "the greatest happiness of the greatest number." Virtually every reformer thereafter, from Philadelphia to Moscow, cited him.[10]

Beccaria helped valorize the new language of sentiment. For him, the death penalty could only be "pernicious to society, from the example of barbarity it affords," and when objecting to "torments and useless cruelty" in punishment, he derided them as "the instrument of furious fanaticism." Moreover, in justifying his intervention, he expressed his hope that if "I shall contribute to save from the agonies of death one unfortunate victim of tyranny, or of ignorance, equally fatal; his blessing and tears of transport, will be a sufficient consolation to me for the contempt of all mankind." After reading Beccaria, the English jurist William Blackstone made the connection that would become characteristic ever after of the Enlightenment view: the criminal law, affirmed Blackstone, should always be "conformable to the dictates of truth and justice, the feelings of humanity, and the indelible rights of mankind."[11]

Yet, as the example of Voltaire shows, the educated elite, and even many of the leading reformers, did not immediately grasp the connection between the emerging rights language and torture and cruel punishment. Voltaire railed against the miscarriage of justice in the Calas case, but he did not originally object to the fact that the old man had been tortured or broken on the wheel. If natural compassion makes everyone detest the cruelty of judicial torture, as Voltaire said later, then why was this not obvious before the 1760s, even to him? Evidently some kind of blinder had operated to inhibit the operation of empathy before then.[12]

Once Enlightenment writers and legal reformers began to

question torture and cruel punishment, an almost complete turnabout in attitudes took place over a couple of decades. The discovery of fellow feeling was part of this change, but only part. What was needed in addition to empathy—indeed, in this case a necessary precondition for empathy with the judicially condemned—was a new concern for the human body. Once sacred only within a religiously defined order, in which individual bodies could be mutilated or tortured for the greater good, the body became sacred on its own in a secular order that rested on the autonomy and inviolability of individuals. There are two parts to this development. Bodies gained a more positive value as they became more separate, more self-possessed, and more individualized over the course of the eighteenth century, while violations of them increasingly aroused negative reactions.

The Self-Contained Person

Although it might seem that bodies are always inherently separate from each other, at least after birth, boundaries between bodies became more sharply defined after the fourteenth century. Individuals became more self-contained as they increasingly felt the need to keep their bodily excretions to themselves. The threshold of shame lowered, while pressure for self-control rose. Defecation and urination in public became increasingly repellent. People began to use handkerchiefs rather than blowing their noses into their hands. Spitting, eating out of a common bowl, and sleeping in a bed with a stranger became disgusting or at least unpleasant. Violent outbursts of emotion and aggressive behavior became socially unacceptable. These changes in attitudes toward the body were the surface indications of an underlying transformation. They all signaled the advent of the self-enclosed individual, whose boundaries had to be respected in social interaction. Self-possession and autonomy required increasing self-discipline.[13]

Eighteenth-century changes in musical and theatrical performances, domestic architecture, and portraiture built upon these longer-term alterations in attitudes. Morever, these new experiences proved to be crucial to the emergence of sensibility itself. In the decades after 1750, operagoers began to listen in silence to the music rather than walking about to visit and converse with their friends, allowing them to feel strong individual emotions in response to the music. One woman recounted her reaction to Gluck's opera *Alceste*, which premiered in Paris in 1776: "I listened to this new work with profound attention. . . . From the first measures I was seized by such a strong feeling of awe, and felt within me so intensely that religious impulse . . . that without even knowing it I fell to my knees in my box and stayed in this position, suppliant and with my hands clasped, until the end of the piece." This woman's reaction is especially striking because she (the letter is signed Pauline de R***) draws an explicit parallel to religious experience. The ground of all authority was shifting from a transcendental religious framework to an inner human one; but this shift could only make sense to people if it was experienced in a personal, even intimate, fashion.[14]

Theater patrons displayed more of a penchant for rowdiness during performances than music lovers, but even in the theater new practices heralded a different future in which plays would be performed in something akin to religious silence. Through much of the eighteenth century, Parisian spectators coordinated coughing, spitting, sneezing, and farting to disrupt performances they disliked, and public displays of drunkenness and fighting often interrupted the performers' lines. To put spectators at a greater distance and thus make disruption more difficult, sitting on the stage was eliminated in France in 1759. In 1782, efforts to establish order in the pit or *parterre* culminated in the installation of benches at the Comédie Française; before then, spectators in the pit roamed freely and sometimes acted more like a mob than an audience. Although the benches were hotly contested in the press of the time and seen by some as a dangerous attack on the freedom and frankness of the pit, the direction of developments had become clear: collective outbursts were to give way to individual and quieter inner experiences.[15]

Home architecture reinforced this sense of individual separateness. The "chamber" (*chambre*) in French houses increasingly became more specialized in the second half of the eighteenth century. The once general purpose room became the "bedroom," and in better-off families children would have bedrooms separate from their parents. Two thirds of Parisian houses had bedrooms by the second half of the eighteenth century, whereas only one in seven had dedicated dining rooms. The elite of Parisian society began to insist on a variety of rooms for private use ranging from *boudoirs* (which comes from the French *bouder* for "pouting"—a room for pouting in private) to toilet and bathing cabinets. Still, the move toward individual privacy should not be exaggerated, at least in France. English travelers complained incessantly about the French practice of sleeping three or four strangers to a room in an inn (albeit in separate beds), the use of commodes in common view, urinating in the fireplace, and throwing the contents of chamberpots out of windows into the street. Their complaints testify, however, to an ongoing process in both countries. In England, one notable new example was the circuit-walk garden developed on country estates between the 1740s and 1760s; the closed loop with its carefully chosen vistas and monuments was designed to intensify private contemplation and remembrance.[16]

Bodies had always been central to European painting, but before the seventeenth century, these had most often been the bodies of the Holy Family and Catholic saints or rulers and their courtiers. In the seventeenth and especially the eighteenth century, more ordinary people began to order paintings of themselves and their families. After 1750, regular public exhibitions—themselves a new feature of social life—showed increasing numbers of portraits of ordinary people in London and Paris, even though history painting still ranked officially as the premier genre.

In the British North American colonies, portraiture dominated the visual arts, in part because European ecclesiastical and political traditions weighed less heavily. Portraits only gained importance in the eighteenth-century colonies: four times as many portraits were painted in the colonies between 1750 and 1776 as were painted between 1700 and 1750, and many of these depicted ordinary townspeople and landowners. (Figure 6) When history painting gained new prominence in France under the Revolution and the Napoleonic Empire, portraits still made up some 40 percent of the paintings shown in the Salons. The prices commanded by portrait painters rose in the last decades of the eighteenth century, and prints brought portraits to a wide audience beyond the original sitters and their families. The most famous English painter of the age, Sir Joshua Reynolds, made his reputation as a portraitist and, according to Horace Walpole, "ransomed portrait-painting from insipidity."[17]

FIGURE 6. *Portrait of Captain John Pigott by Joseph Blackburn*
Like many artists active in the American colonies, Joseph Blackburn was born
and most likely trained in England before going to Bermuda in 1752 and the
following year to Newport, Rhode Island. After painting scores of portraits in
Newport, Boston, and Portsmouth, New Hampshire, he returned to England in
1764. This oil painting from the late 1750s or early 1760s (127 cm x 101.6 cm)
forms a companion piece with the portrait of Pigott's wife. Blackburn was
known for his close attention to lace and other clothing details.

One contemporary viewer expressed his disdain upon seeing the number of portraits in the French exhibition of 1769:

The multitude of portraits, Sir, which strikes me everywhere, forces me in spite of myself to speak of this subject now and to treat of this arid and monotonous matter which I had reserved for the end. In vain has the public long since complained of the multitude of obscure bourgeois which it must incessantly pass by in review. . . . The facility of the genre, its utility and the vanity of all these petty personnages encourages our emerging artists. . . . Thanks to the unhappy taste of the century, the Salon is becoming nothing more than a gallery of portraits.

The century's "unhappy taste" emanated from England, according to the French, and it signaled for many the impending victory of commerce over true art. In his article "Portrait" for Diderot's multivolume *Encyclopédie*, chevalier Louis de Jaucourt concluded that "the genre of painting that is most followed and most sought after in England is that of the portrait." Later in the century, the writer Louis-Sébastien Mercier tried to sound a reassuring note: "the English excell in portraits, and nothing surpasses the portraits of *Regnols* [sic], of which the principal examples are full-length, life-size, and on a par with history paintings." (Figure 7) In his usual astute fashion, Mercier had seized on the critical element—in England, portraits were comparable to the leading genre in the French Academy of Fine Arts, history paintings. The ordinary person could now be heroic merely by virtue of his individuality. The ordinary body now had distinction.[18]

J. Reynolds pinx.   *J. M. Ardell fecit*

Lady Charlotte Fitz-William.

FIGURE 7. *Portrait of Lady Charlotte Fitz-William, mezzotint by James MacArdell of painting by Sir Joshua Reynolds, 1754*
Reynolds gained fame by painting portraits of leading figures in British society. He often painted only the faces and hands of his sitters, farming out the drapery and costumes to specialists or assistants. Charlotte was only eight at the time of this portrait, but her hairdressing and pearl earrings and brooch give her an older look. Prints such as this one spread Reynolds's fame even further. James MacArdell did mezzotints of many Reynolds portraits. The caption reads: "J. Reynolds pinxt. J. McArdell fecit. Lady Charlotte Fitz-William. Publish'd by J. Reynolds according to Act of Parliament 1754."

True, portraits could convey something quite different from individuality. As commercial wealth grew by leaps and bounds in Great Britain, France, and their colonies, commissioning portraits as a mark of status and gentility reflected a more general rise of consumerism. Likeness did not always take pride of place in these commissions. Ordinary people did not wish to look ordinary in their portraits, and some portrait painters gained reputations for their ability to render laces, silks, and satins more than faces. Yet, though portraits sometimes focused on representations of types or on allegories of virtues or wealth, in the second half of the eighteenth century such portraits declined in significance as artists and their clients began to prefer more natural-looking renderings of psychological and physiognomical individuality. Moreover, the very proliferation of individual likenesses itself encouraged the view that each person was an individual—that is, single, separate, distinctive, and original, and therefore should be depicted as such.[19]

Women played a sometimes surprising role in this development. The rage for novels like *Clarissa*, which focused on ordinary women with rich inner lives, made allegorical paintings of female subjects with masklike faces seem irrelevant or simply decorative. Yet, as painters increasingly sought forthrightness and psychological intimacy in their portraits, the relationship between painter and sitter became more fraught with overt sexual tension, especially when women painted men. In 1775, James Boswell recorded Samuel Johnson's strictures against women portraitists: "He [Johnson] thought portrait-painting an improper employment for a woman. 'Public practice of any art, and staring in men's faces, is very indelicate in a female.'" Several women portrait painters nonetheless became veritable celebrities in the last half of the eighteenth century. Denis

Diderot had his portrait painted by one of them, the German artist Anna Therbusch. In his review of the Salon of 1767, where the painting appeared, Diderot felt he had to defend himself against the suggestion that he had slept with her, "a woman who is not pretty." Yet he also had to admit that his daughter was so struck by the likeness of Therbusch's portrait that she had to keep herself from kissing it a hundred times in her father's absence for fear of ruining it.[20]

Thus, though likeness in portraits might have been judged by some critics to be secondary to aesthetic value, resemblance was obviously highly regarded by many clients and an increasing number of critics. In his self-revelatory *Journal to Eliza*, written in 1767, Laurence Sterne refers repeatedly to "your sweet senti-mental Picture"—the portrait of Eliza, probably by Richard Cosway, that is all he has of his absent love. "Your Picture is Yourself—all Sentiment, Softness, and Truth. . . . Dearest Origi-nal! How like unto thee does it seem—and will seem—till thou makest it vanish, by thy presence." As with the epistolary novel, so too in portrait painting, women played a highly charged role in the process of empathy. Even while most men, in theory, wanted women to maintain the roles of modesty and virtue, in practice women inevitably stood for and thus evoked sentiment, a feeling that always threatened to overflow its boundaries.[21]

So valued was likeness, eventually, that in 1786 the French musician and engraver Gilles-Louis Chrétien invented a machine called the physionotrace, which produced profile por-traits mechanically (see Figure 8). The original life-size profile was then reduced and engraved on copperplate. Among the hun-dreds produced by Chrétien, first in collaboration with Edmé Quenedey, a miniaturist, and then in rivalry with him, was one of Thomas Jefferson taken in April 1789. A French émigré intro-

FIGURE 8. *Physionotrace of Jefferson*
The caption reads, "Quenedy del. ad vivum et sculpt." (Drawn from life and engraved by Quenedey.)

duced the process to the United States, and Jefferson had another done in 1804. Now a historical curiosity long obscured by the appearance of photography, physionotrace is yet another indicator of the interest in representing ordinary people—Jefferson aside—and in capturing the smallest differences between each person. Moreover, as Sterne's comments suggest, the portrait, especially in miniature, often served as a memory trigger and an occasion for recapturing a fond emotion.[22]

The Public Spectacle of Pain

Garden walks, listening to music in silence, using a handkerchief, and viewing portraits all seem to go along with the image of the empathetic reader, and they seem utterly incongruous alongside the torture and execution of Jean Calas. Yet the same judges and legislators who upheld the traditional legal system and even defended its harshness no doubt listened quietly to music, commissioned portraits, and owned houses with bedrooms, though they may not have read novels because of their association with seduction and debauchery. Magistrates endorsed the traditional system of crime and punishment because they believed that those guilty of crime could only be controlled by an external force. In the traditional view, ordinary people could not regulate their own passions. They had to be led, prodded to do good, and deterred from following their baser instincts. This tendency toward evil in mankind resulted from original sin, the Christian doctrine that all people have been innately predisposed to sin ever since Adam and Eve fell from God's grace in the Garden of Eden.

The writings of Pierre-François Muyart de Vouglans give us

rare insight into the traditionalist position because he was one of the very few jurists who rushed to take up Beccaria's gauntlet and defend the old ways in print. In addition to his many works on the criminal law, Muyart also wrote at least two pamphlets defending Christianity and attacking its modern critics, especially Voltaire. In 1767, he published a point-by-point refutation of Beccaria. He objected in the strongest terms to Beccaria's attempt to found his system on "the ineffable sentiments of the heart." "I pride myself on having as much sensibility as anyone else," he insisted, "but no doubt I do not have an organization of fibers [nerve endings] as loose as that of our modern criminalists, for I did not feel that gentle shuddering of which they speak." Muyart instead felt surprise, not to say shock, when he saw that Beccaria built his system on the ruins of all received wisdom.[23]

Muyart derided Beccaria's rationalist approach. "Sitting in his study, [the author] undertakes to trace the laws of all the nations and make us see that until now we have never had an exact or solid thought on this crucial subject." The reason it was so difficult to reform criminal law, according to Muyart, was that it was based on positive law and depended less on reasoning than on experience and practice. What experience taught was the need to control the unruly, not coddle their sensibilities. "Who does not know in fact that because men are shaped by their passions, most often their temper dominates over their sentiments?" Men must be judged as they are, not as they should be, he insisted, and only the awe-inspiring power of an avenging justice could rein in those tempers.[24]

The pageantry of pain at the scaffold was designed to instill terror in observers and in this way served as a deterrence. Those present—and the crowds were frequently immense—were meant to identify with the condemned person's pain and through it to feel the overpowering majesty of the law, the state, and ultimately God. Muyart therefore found it revolting that Beccaria tried to justify his arguments by reference to "the sensitivity to pain of the guilty." That sensitivity made the traditional system work. "Precisely because each man identified with what happened to another and because he had a natural horror of pain, it was necessary to prefer, in the choice of punishments, that which was the cruelest for the body of the guilty."[25]

Under the traditional understanding, the pains of the body did not belong entirely to the individual condemned person. Those pains had the higher religious and political purposes of redemption and reparation of the community. Bodies could be mutilated in the interest of inscribing authority, and broken or burned in the interest of restoring the moral, political, and religious order. In other words, the offender served as a kind of sacrificial victim whose suffering would restore wholeness to the community and order to the state. The sacrificial nature of the rite in France was underlined by the inclusion in many French sentences of a formal act of penitence (the *amende honorable*), in which the condemned criminal carried a burning torch and stopped in front of a church to demand forgiveness on the way to the scaffold.[26]

Because punishment was a sacrificial rite, festivity inevitably accompanied and sometimes overshadowed the fear. Public executions brought thousands of people together to celebrate the community's recovery from crime's injury. Executions in Paris took place in the same square—the Place de Grève—where fireworks celebrated births and marriages in the royal family. As observers frequently recounted, however, such festivity had an unpredictable quality about it. The English educated classes increasingly expressed their disapproval of the "most amazing scenes of drunkenness and debauchery" that accompanied every execution at Tyburn. (Figure 9) Letter writers bemoaned the crowd's ridiculing of the clergy sent in attendance on the prisoners, the fights between surgeons' apprentices and the friends of the executed over the dead bodies, and just generally the expression of a "kind of Mirth, as if the Spectacle they had beheld had afforded Pleasure instead of Pain." Reporting on a hanging in the winter of 1776, the *Morning Post* of London complained that the "remorseless multitude behaved with the most inhuman indecency—shouting, laughing, throwing snowballs at each other, particularly at those few who had a proper compassion for the misfortunes of their fellow creatures."[27]

Even when the crowd was more subdued, something about its sheer size could be disturbing. A British visitor to Paris reported on an execution by breaking on the wheel in 1787: "The noise of the multitude was like the hoarse murmur caused by the waves of the sea breaking along a rocky shore: For a moment it subsided, and in an awful silence the multitude beheld the executioner take up an iron bar, and begin the tragedy, by striking his victim on the fore arm." Most troubling to this and many other observers was the large number of women watching: "It is amazing, how the more delicate part of the creation, whose feelings are so exquisitely tender and refined, should come in crouds to see so bloody a spectacle: Yet without doubt, it is the pity, the kind compassion which they feel, that makes them so anxious about the tortures inflicted on our fellow creatures." Needless to say, it is not "without doubt" that this was the predominant emotion of the women. The crowd no longer felt the emotions the spectacle had been designed to elicit.[28]

Pain, punishment, and the public spectacle of suffering all gradually lost their religious moorings in the second half of the

FIGURE 9. *Procession to Tyburn by William Hogarth, 1747*
The Idle 'Prentice executed at Tyburn is Plate 11 of Hogarth's series *Industry and Idleness*, which compares the fates of two apprentices. This one represents the sorry end of Thomas Idle, the idle apprentice. The gallows can be seen back right of center next to the grandstand for the crowd. A Methodist preacher is haranguing the prisoner, who is probably reading his Bible while being transported by cart along with his coffin. A man sells cakes in the right foreground. His basket is ringed by four candles because he has been there since dawn serving people who came early to get good places. An urchin is picking his pocket. Behind the woman hawking the confession of Thomas Idle is another selling gin from the basket at her waist. In front of her a woman punches a man, while another man standing near her prepares to throw a dog at the preacher. Hogarth captures all the unruliness of the execution crowd. The caption reads: "Design'd & Engrav'd by Wm Hogarth Publish'd according to Act of Parliamt Sep. 30. 1747."

eighteenth century; but the process did not happen all at once, and it was not very well understood at the time. Even Beccaria failed to see all the consequences of the new thinking he did so much to crystallize. He wanted to put the law on a Rousseauian rather than religious footing; laws "ought to be conventions between men in a state of freedom," he maintained. Yet, though he argued for a moderation of punishment—it should be "the least possible in the case given" and "proportioned to the crime"—he still insisted that it should be public. For him, public exposure guaranteed the transparency of the law.[29]

In the emerging individualistic and secular view, pains belonged only to the sufferer in the here-and-now. The attitude toward pain did not change because of medical improvement in the treatment of pain. Medical practitioners certainly tried to alleviate pain at the time, but the real breakthroughs in anesthesia only came in the mid-nineteenth century with the use of ether and chloroform. Instead, the change in attitude came about as a consequence of the reevaluation of the individual body and its pains. Since pain and the body itself now belonged only to the individual, rather than to the community, the individual could no longer be sacrificed to the good of the community or to a higher religious purpose. As the English reformer Henry Dagge insisted, "the good of society is best promoted by a regard for individuals." Rather than expiating sin, punishment should be viewed as repaying a "debt" to society, and clearly no payment could be forthcoming from a mutilated body. Where pain had served as the symbol of reparation under the old regime, now pain seemed an obstacle to any meaningful quittance. In one example of this change of views, many judges in the British North American colonies began to impose fines for property offenses rather than whipping.[30]

In the new view, consequently, cruel punishment exacted in a public setting constituted an assault on society rather than a reaffirmation of it. Pain brutalized the individual—and by identification, the spectators—rather than opening the door to salvation through repentance. The English lawyer William Eden therefore denounced the exposure of corpses: "we leave each other to rot like scare-crows in the hedges; and our gibbets are crowded with human carcasses. May it not be doubted, whether a forced familiarity with such objects can have any other effect, than to blunt the sentiments, and destroy the benevolent prejudices of the people?" By 1787, Benjamin Rush could brush aside even the last doubts. "The reformation of a criminal can never be effected by a public punishment," he flatly asserted. Public punishment destroys any sense of shame, produces no changes in attitude, and instead of working as a deterrence has the opposite effect on the spectators. Although agreeing with Beccaria in opposing the death penalty, Dr. Rush parted company when he argued that punishment should be private, administered behind the walls of a prison, and oriented toward rehabilitation, that is, the restoration of a criminal to society and to his personal liberty, "so dear to all men."[31]

Torture's Last Throes

The conversion of elites to the new views of pain and punishment took place in stages between the early 1760s and the end of the 1780s. Many lawyers published briefs in the 1760s denouncing the injustice of the Calas conviction, for example, but like Voltaire, none of them opposed the use of judicial torture or breaking on the wheel. They too focused on the religious fanaticism which they were convinced had motivated both the common people and the judges in Toulouse. The briefs lingered on the moment of Jean Calas's torture and death, but without challenging their legitimacy as penal instruments.

In fact, the briefs in favor of Calas essentially upheld the assumptions that lay behind torture and cruel punishment. Defenders of Calas assumed that the body in pain would tell the truth; Calas proved his innocence when he maintained it even in pain and suffering. (Figure 10) In language typical of the pro-Calas side, Alexandre-Jérôme Loyseau de Mauléon insisted that "Calas withstood the question [torture] with that heroic resignation that only belongs to innocence." As his bones were being crushed one by one, Calas uttered "these affecting words": "I die innocent; Jesus-Christ, innocence itself, fervently wished to die by an even crueler suffering. God punishes in me the sin of that unfortunate one [Calas's son] who did himself in . . . God is just, and I adore his punishments." Loyseau argued, moreover, that the "majestic perseverance" of old Calas marked the turning point in the sentiments of the populace. Seeing him repeatedly affirm his innocence during his torments, the people of Toulouse began to feel compassion and to repent of their earlier unreasoning suspicion of the Calvinist. Each blow of the iron rod "sounded in the bottom of the souls" of those witnessing the execution, and "torrents of tears were unleashed, too late, from all the eyes present." The "torrents of tears" would always be "too late" as long as the assumptions behind torture and cruel punishment remained unchallenged.[32]

Chief among those assumptions was that torture could prod the body to speak the truth even when the individual mind resisted. A long physiognomic tradition in Europe had held that character could be read from body marks or signs. In the late

FIGURE 10. *Sentimentalizing the Calas Affair*
The most widely circulated print of the Calas Affair was this large-size one
[originally 34 cm x 45 cm] by the German artist and printmaker Daniel
Chodowiecki, which he engraved after his own oil painting of the scene. The
etching established his reputation and kept alive the outrage caused far and
wide by Calas's punishment. Chodowiecki had married into a French Protestant refugee family in Berlin just three years before he produced this print.

sixteenth and seventeenth centuries, various works on "metoposcopy" had been published, promising to teach readers how to read a person's character or fortune from lines, wrinkles, or blemishes on the face. Typical of such titles was that of Richard Saunders's *Physiognomie, and Chiromancie, Metoposcopie, The Symmetrical Proportions and Signal Moles of the Body, Fully and Accurately Explained; with Their Natural-Predictive Significations Both to Men and Women*, published in 1653. Without having to endorse the more extreme variants of this tradition, many Europeans believed that bodies could reveal the inner person in an involuntary fashion. Although remnants of such thinking could be still found in the late eighteenth and early nineteenth centuries, in the form, for example, of phrenology, most scientists and physicians turned against it after 1750. They argued that the exterior appearance of the body had no relationship to the inner soul or character. Thus, the criminal could dissimulate, and the innocent person might well confess to a crime he or she did not commit. As Beccaria insisted when arguing against torture, "the robust will escape, and the feeble be condemned." Pain, in Beccaria's analysis, could not be "the test of truth, as if truth resided in the muscles and fibres of a wretch in torture." Pain was merely a sensation without connection to moral sentiment.[33]

The lawyers' accounts said relatively little about Calas's reaction to torture because "the question" took place in private, away from the eyes of observers. The private administration of torture made it especially repugnant in Beccaria's eyes. It meant that the accused lost his "public protection" even before being found guilty and that any deterrent value of punishment was lost as well. French judges evidently also began to feel some doubts, especially about torture to gain confessions of guilt. After 1750, the French parlements (regional courts of appeal) began to intervene to prevent the use of torture before judgment of the case ("preparatory torture"), as the Parlement of Toulouse did in the Calas case. They also decreed the death penalty less frequently, and more often ordered that the condemned be strangled before being burnt at the stake or placed on the wheel.[34]

But the judges did not give up on torture altogether, and they would not have agreed with Beccaria's contempt for the religious framing of torture. The Italian reformer summarily denounced "another ridiculous motive for torture, namely, *to purge a man from infamy.*" This "absurdity" could only be explained as "the offspring of religion." Since torture rendered the victim infamous in the first place, it could hardly wash away the stain. Muyart de Vouglans defended torture against Beccaria's arguments. The example of one innocent falsely convicted paled in comparison to the "million others" who were guilty but could never have been convicted without the use of torture. Not only was judicial torture therefore useful, it could also be justified by the antiquity and universality of its use. The frequently cited exceptions only proved the rule, Muyart insisted, which should be sought in the history of France itself and the Holy Roman Empire. According to Muyart, Beccaria's system contradicted canon law, civil law, international law, and the "experience of all the centuries."[35]

Beccaria himself did not stress the connection between his views on torture and nascent rights language. But others were prepared to do so on his behalf. His French translator, abbé André Morellet, modified the order of Beccaria's presentation to draw attention to the link to the "rights of man." Morellet took Beccaria's only reference to his aim of supporting the "rights of man" (*i diritti degli uomini*) out of the end of chapter 11 in the original Italian edition of 1764 and moved it into the introduction of the 1766 French translation. Defending the rights of man now appeared to be Beccaria's chief aim, and those rights were affirmed as the essential bulwark against individual suffering. Morellet's rearrangement was adopted in many subsequent translations and even later Italian editions.[36]

Muyart's best efforts notwithstanding, the tide turned against torture in the 1760s. Although attacks on torture had been published before, the trickle of publications now became a stream. Leading the charge were the many translations, reprintings, and re-editions of Beccaria. Some twenty-eight Italian editions, many with false imprints, and nine French ones came out before 1800, even though the book appeared on the papal Index of Forbidden Books in 1766. An English translation was published in London in 1767, and was followed by editions from Glasgow, Dublin, Edinburgh, Charleston, and Philadelphia. German, Dutch, Polish, and Spanish translations followed soon after. The London translator of Beccaria captured the changing mood of the times: "penal laws . . . are still so imperfect, and are attended with so many unnecessary circumstances of cruelty in all nations, that an attempt to reduce them to the standard of reason must be interesting to all of mankind."[37]

So dramatic was Beccaria's growing influence that opponents of the Enlightenment claimed to have seen the hand of conspiracy at work. Was it a coincidence that the Calas Affair should have been followed by the defining tract on penal reform? Penned, moreover, by an otherwise unknown Italian with only a cursory knowledge of the law? In 1779, the always inflammatory journalist Simon-Nicolas-Henri Linguet reported that a witness had laid it all out for him:

Shortly after the Calas Affair, the Encyclopédists, armed
with his torments and profiting from propitious circumstances, though without compromising themselves
directly, as is their wont, wrote Reverend Father Barn-
abite in Milan, their Italian banker and a well-known
mathematician. They told him that it was the moment
to unleash a declamation against the rigor of punishments and intolerance; that Italian philosophy should
furnish the artillery, and they would secretly make use
of it in Paris.

Linguet complained that Beccaria's tract was widely viewed as
an indirect brief in favor of Calas and other recent sufferers of
injustice.[38]

Beccaria's influence helped galvanize the campaign against
torture, but it proceeded only slowly at first. Two articles on torture in Diderot's *Encyclopédie*, both published in 1765, capture
the ambiguity. In the first article, on the jurisprudence of torture, Antoine-Gaspard Boucher d'Argis matter-of-factly refers to
the "violent torments" to which the accused is subjected, but
with no judgment on their merit. In the next article, however,
which considered torture as part of criminal procedure, chevalier
de Jaucourt hammers away at its use, deploying all the available
arguments from "the voice of humanity" to the defects of torture in providing sure evidence of guilt or innocence. During the
second half of the 1760s, five new books appeared advocating
criminal law reform. In the 1780s, in contrast, thirty-nine such
books were published.[39]

During the 1770s and 1780s, the campaign for the abolition
of torture and for the moderation of punishment gained momentum, as learned societies in the Italian states, the Swiss cantons,

and France offered prizes for the best essays on penal reform. The French government found the rising pitch of criticism so worrisome that it ordered the academy of Châlons-sur-Marne to stop printing copies of the essay by its 1780 winner, Jacques-Pierre Brissot de Warville. Brissot's vituperative rhetoric, rather than any new proposals, set off alarms:

> These sacred rights that man holds from nature, which society violates so often with its judicial apparatus, still require the suppression of a portion of our mutilating punishments and the softening of those which we must preserve. It is inconceivable that a gentle [*douce*] nation, living in a temperate climate under a moderate government, could combine an amiable character and peaceful customs with the atrocity of cannibals. For our judicial punishments breathe only blood and death and tend only to inspire rage and despair in the heart of the accused.

The French government did not like to see itself compared to cannibals, but by the 1780s the barbarism of judicial torture and cruel punishment had become a reform mantra. In 1781, Joseph-Michel-Antoine Servan, a longtime advocate of penal reform, applauded Louis XVI's recent abolition of torture to get a confession of guilt, "this infamous torture which for so many centuries usurped the temple of justice itself and made it into a school of suffering, where the executioners professed the refinement of pain." Judicial torture was for him "a kind of sphinx . . . an absurd monster barely worthy of finding an asylum with savage peoples."[40]

Encouraged by other reformers despite his youth and lack of

experience, Brissot then undertook to publish a ten-volume *Philosophical Library of the Legislator, Politician, and Jurist* (1782–85), which had to be printed in Switzerland and smuggled into France. It brought together Brissot's own and other reform writings. Although only a synthesizer, Brissot clearly linked torture to the rights of man: "Is one too young when it is a question of defending the outraged rights of humanity?" The term "humanity" ("the spectacle of suffering humanity," for example) appeared again and again in his pages. In 1788, Brissot founded the Society of the Friends of Blacks, the first French society for the abolition of slavery. The campaign for penal reform thus became ever more closely associated with the general defense of human rights.[41]

Brissot deployed the same rhetorical strategies as the lawyers writing briefs in the various French *causes célèbres* of the 1780s; they not only defended their wrongly accused clients but also increasingly indicted the legal system as a whole. Those writing briefs usually adopted the first-person voice of their clients to develop melodramatic novelistic narratives that drove home their point. This rhetorical strategy culminated in two briefs written by one of Brissot's correspondents, Charles-Marguerite Dupaty, a magistrate from Bordeaux living in Paris, who intervened on behalf of three men condemned to be broken on the wheel for aggravated theft. Dupaty's first brief of 1786, 251 pages long, not only denounced every misstep in the judicial process but also included a detailed account of his meeting with the three men in prison. In it, Dupaty cleverly shifts from his first-person view of the scene to the prisoners' own: "And me, Bradier [one of the condemned] then said, half of my body was swollen for six months. And me, Lardoise [another of the condemned] said, thanks to God I was able to resist [the epidemic illness in the prison]; however, the pressure of my irons (I [i.e., Dupaty] can well believe it, thirty months in irons!) so injured my leg that gangrene set in; they almost had to cut it off." The scene concludes with Dupaty in tears. In this way the lawyer makes the most of his fellow feeling with the prisoners.[42]

Dupaty then switches perspective again, this time addressing the judges directly: "Judges of Chaumont, Magistrates, Criminalists, do you hear it? . . . Here is the cry of reason, truth, justice and the Law." Finally, Dupaty calls directly on the king to intervene. He begs the monarch to listen to the blood of the innocent, from Calas to his own three accused thieves: "deign, from the height of your Throne, deign to take a look at all the bloody pitfalls of your criminal Legislation, where we have perished, where every day innocent people perish!" The brief then concludes with several pages imploring Louis XVI to reform criminal legislation in the line with reason and humanity.[43]

Dupaty's brief so aroused public opinion in favor of the accused and against the legal system that the Parlement of Paris voted to have it publicly burned. The court's spokesman denounced the novelistic style of the brief; Dupaty "sees beside him humanity trembling and reaching out to him, a dishevelled fatherland showing him its wounds, the whole nation taking on his voice and commanding him to speak in its name." But the court proved powerless in holding back the swelling tide of opinion. Jean Caritat, marquis de Condorcet, soon to be the French Revolution's most consistent and far-reaching defender of human rights, published two pamphlets in favor of Dupaty in late 1786. Though not himself a lawyer, Condorcet attacked the court's "scorn for man" and the continuing "manifest violation of natural law" that had been shown in the Calas case and other unfair judgments rendered since then.[44]

By 1788, the French crown itself had signed on to many of the new attitudes. In the decree provisionally abolishing torture before execution to get names of accomplices, Louis XVI's government spoke of "reassuring innocence . . . removing any excess of severity from punishment . . . [and] punishing evildoers with all the moderation that humanity demands." In his 1780 treatise about French criminal law, Muyart recognized that in defending the validity of confessions won through torture, "I do not at all ignore the fact that I must combat a system that has more than ever gained credence in recent times." But he refused to enter into the debate, insisting his opponents were simply polemicists and that he had the force of the past behind his position. So successful was the campaign for penal reform in France that in 1789 correction of abuses in the criminal code ranked as one of the most frequently cited issues in the grievance lists prepared for the forthcoming Estates-General.[45]

The Passions and the Person

In the course of this increasingly one-sided debate, the new meanings assigned to the body had become more fully evident. The broken body of Calas, or even the gangrenous leg of Dupaty's accused thief Lardoise, gained a new dignity. In the back-and-forth on torture and cruel punishment, this dignity first emerged in negative reactions to the judicial assaults on it. But over time it became the subject, as was evident in Dupaty's briefs, of positive feelings of empathy. Only toward the end of the eighteenth century did the assumptions of the new model become explicit. In his short yet illuminating eighteen-page pamphlet of 1787, Dr. Benjamin Rush linked the defects of public punishment to the new notion of the autonomous yet sympathetic individual. As a physician, Rush would admit some use for bodily pain in punishment, though he clearly preferred "labour, watchfulness, solitude, and silence," an acknowledgment of the criminal's individuality and potential usefulness. Public punishment proved most objectionable, in his view, for its tendency to destroy sympathy, "the vice-regent of the divine benevolence in our world." These were the key words: sympathy—or what we now call empathy—provided the grounds for morality, the spark of the divine in human life, "in our world."

"Sensibility is the sentinel of the moral faculty," Rush affirmed. He likened that sensibility to "a sudden sense of right," a kind of learned reflex for the moral good. Public punishment short-circuited sympathy: "as the distress which the criminals suffer, is the effect of a law of the state, which cannot be resisted, the sympathy of the spectator is rendered abortive, and returns empty to the bosom in which it was awakened." Public punishment thus undermined social feelings by making spectators increasingly callous; spectators lost their feelings of "universal love" and the sense that criminals had bodies and souls like their own.[46]

Although Rush certainly counted himself a good Christian, his model of the person differed in almost every respect from the one put forth by Muyart de Vouglans in his defense of torture and traditional corporal punishments. For Muyart, original sin explained the inability of humans to control their passions. True, passions provided the motivating force to life, but their inherent turbulence, even rebelliousness, had to be brought under control by reason, community pressures, the church, and failing that, in the case of crime, the state. In Muyart's view, the sources of crime (vice) were the passions desire and fear, "the desire of acquiring things that one does not have, and the fear of losing those that one has." These passions suffocated the sentiments of honor and justice engraved by natural law on the human heart. Divine Providence gave kings supreme authority over the life of men which they delegated to judges, reserving for themselves the right to pardon. The chief purpose, therefore, of criminal law was the prevention of the triumph of vice over virtue. Containment of humanity's inherent evil was the motto of Muyart's view of justice.[47]

The reformers ultimately reversed the philosophical and political assumptions of this model and advocated in its place the cultivation through education and experience of inherently good human qualities. By the middle of the eighteenth century, some Enlightenment philosophers had embraced a position on the passions not unlike the one proposed recently by the neurologist Antonio Damasio, who insists that emotions are crucial to reasoning and consciousness, not at odds with them. Although Damasio traces his intellectual roots back to the seventeenth-century Dutch philosopher Spinoza, European elites only came to generally accept a more positive evaluation of the emotions—the passions, in their terms—in the eighteenth century. "Spinozism" had a bad reputation as leading to materialism (the soul is only matter, hence there is no soul) and atheism (God is nature, therefore there is no God). By the mid-eighteenth century, some in the educated professions had nonetheless accepted a kind of implicit or soft materialism, which made no theological claims about the soul, but did argue that matter could think and feel. This version of materialism led logically to the egalitarian position that all humans have the same physical and mental organization and therefore that experience and education, rather than birth, explain the differences between them.[48]

Whether they subscribed to an explicitly materialist philosophy or not—and most people did not—many in the educated elites came to hold a very different view of the passions than Muyart's. Emotion and reason were now seen as partners. The passions were "the unique Motor of Sensible Being, and of intelligent Beings," according to the Swiss physiologist Charles Bonnet. The passions were good and could be mobilized by education for improvement of humanity, which was now seen as perfectible rather than inherently evil. By this view, criminals had made mistakes but could be reeducated. Moreover, the passions, based in biology, fed into moral sensibility. Sentiment was the emotional reaction to a physical sensation, and morality was the education of this sentiment to bring out its social component (sensibility). Laurence Sterne, Thomas Jefferson's favorite novelist, put the new credo of the age into the mouth of his central character Yorick in his tellingly titled novel, *A Sentimental Journey*:

> Dear sensibility! . . . eternal fountain of our feelings!—
> 'tis here I trace thee—and this is thy divinity which stirs
> within me . . . that I feel some generous joys and gener-
> ous cares beyond myself—all comes from thee, great—
> great SENSORIUM of the world! which vibrates, if a hair of
> our heads but falls upon the ground, in the remotest
> desert of thy creation.

Sterne found this sensibility even in "the roughest peasant."[49]

It might seem rather a stretch to link blowing one's nose into a handkerchief, listening to music, reading a novel, or ordering a portrait to the abolition of torture and the moderation of cruel punishment. Yet legally sanctioned torture did not end just because the judges gave up on it or because Enlightenment writers eventually opposed it. Torture ended because the traditional framework of pain and personhood fell apart, to be replaced, bit by bit, by a new framework, in which individuals owned their bodies, had rights to their separateness and to bodily inviolability, and recognized in other people the same passions, sentiments, and sympathies as in themselves. "The men, or perhaps the women," to return to the good doctor Rush one last time, "whose persons we detest [convicted criminals], possess souls and bodies composed of the same materials as those of our friends and relations." If we contemplate their miseries "without emotion or sympathy," then "the principle of sympathy" itself "will cease to act altogether; and . . . will soon lose its place in the human breast."[50]

3

"THEY HAVE SET A GREAT EXAMPLE"

Declaring Rights

DECLARATION: The action of stating, telling, setting forth, or announcing openly, explicitly or formally; positive statement or assertion; an assertion, announcement or proclamation in emphatic, solemn, or legal terms. . . . A proclamation or public statement as embodied in a document, instrument, or public act. — *Oxford English Dictionary*, electronic 2nd. ed.

WHY MUST RIGHTS be set forth in a declaration? Why do countries and citizens feel the need for such a formal statement? The campaigns to abolish torture and cruel punishment point to one answer: a formal, public statement confirms the changes in underlying attitudes that have taken place. Yet the declarations of rights in 1776 and 1789 went further still. They did not just signal transformations in general attitudes and expectations.

They helped effect a transfer of sovereignty, from George III and the British Parliament to a new republic in the American case, and from a monarchy claiming supreme authority to a nation and its representatives in the French one. In 1776 and 1789, declaring opened up whole new political vistas. The campaigns against torture and cruel punishment would from then onward be fused with a whole host of other human rights causes, whose relevancy only emerged after the declarations had been made.

The history of the word "declaration" gives a first indication of the shift in sovereignty. The English word "declaration" comes from the French *déclaration*. In French, the word originally referred to a catalogue of lands to be given in exchange for swearing homage to a feudal lord. Over the course of the seventeenth century, it increasingly pertained to the public statements of the king. In other words, the act of declaring was linked to sovereignty. As authority shifted from feudal lords to the French king, so too did the power of making declarations. In England, the converse also held: when subjects wanted a reaffirmation of their rights from their kings, they drew up their own declarations. Thus, the Magna Carta ("Great Charter") of 1215 formalized the rights of English barons in relation to the English king; the Petition of Right of 1628 confirmed the "diverse Rights and Liberties of the Subjects"; and the English Bill of Rights of 1689 validated "the true, ancient and indubitable rights and liberties of the people of this kingdom."[1]

In 1776 and 1789, the words "charter," "petition," and "bill" seemed inadequate to the task of guaranteeing rights (the same would be true in 1948). "Petition" and "bill" both implied a request or appeal to a higher power (a bill was originally "a petition to the sovereign"), and "charter" often meant an old document or deed. "Declaration" had less of a musty, submissive air.

Moreover, unlike "petition," "bill," or even "charter," "declaration" could signify the intent to seize sovereignty. Jefferson therefore began the Declaration of Independence with this explanation of the need to proclaim it: "When in the Course of human events, it becomes necessary for one people to dissolve the political bands which have connected them with another, and to assume among the powers of the earth, the separate and equal station to which the Laws of Nature and of Nature's God entitle them, a decent respect to the opinions of mankind requires that they should *declare* [my emphasis] the causes which impel them to the separation." An expression of "decent respect" could not obscure the main point: the colonies were declaring themselves a separate and equal state and seizing their own sovereignty.*

In contrast, in 1789 the French deputies were not yet ready to explicitly repudiate the sovereignty of their king. Yet they nonetheless accomplished nearly as much by deliberately omitting any mention of him in their Declaration of the Rights of Man and Citizen: "The representatives of the French people, constituted as a National Assembly, and considering that ignorance, neglect or contempt of the rights of man are the sole causes of public misfortunes and governmental corruption, have resolved to set forth in a solemn *declaration* [my emphasis] the natural, inalienable and sacred rights of man." The Assembly had to do more than give speeches or draft laws on specific questions. It had to put in writing for posterity that rights flowed not from a compact between ruler and citizens, less still from a petition to him or a charter granted by him, but rather from the nature of human beings themselves.

These acts of declaring were at once backward- and forward-looking. In each case, the declarers claimed to be confirming

---

*See the Appendix for the full text.

rights that already existed and were unquestionable. But in so doing they effected a revolution in sovereignty and created an entirely new basis for government. The Declaration of Independence asserted that King George III had trampled on the preexisting rights of the colonists and that his actions justified the establishment of a separate government: "whenever any Form of Government becomes destructive of these ends [the securing of rights], it is the Right of the People to alter or to abolish it, and to institute new Government." Similarly, the French deputies declared that these rights had simply been ignored, neglected, or disdained; they did not claim to have invented them. "Henceforward," however, the declaration proposed that these rights constitute the foundation of government, though they had not been in the past. Even while claiming these rights already existed and they were merely defending them, the deputies created something radically new: governments justified by their guarantee of universal rights.

Declaring Rights in America

The Americans did not begin with a clear plan to separate from Great Britain. No one imagined in the 1760s that rights would lead them into such new territory. Reshaping of sensibility helped make the idea of rights more tangible to the educated classes, in the debates over torture and cruel punishment, for example, but the notion of rights also changed in response to political circumstances. Two versions of rights language were available in the eighteenth century: a particularistic version (rights specific to a people or national tradition) and a universalistic one (rights of man in general). The Americans used one or the other or both in combination, depending on the circumstances. During the Stamp Act crisis of the mid-1760s, for example, American pamphleteers emphasized their rights as colonists within the British Empire, whereas the Declaration of Independence of 1776 clearly invoked the universal rights of all men. The Americans then set up their own particularistic tradition in the Constitution of 1787 and the 1791 Bill of Rights. In contrast, the French almost immediately embraced the universalistic version, in part because it undercut the particularistic and historical claims of the monarchy. In the debates over the French Declaration, duc Mathieu de Montmorency exhorted his fellow deputies to "follow the example of the United States: they have set a great example in the new hemisphere; let us give one to the universe."[2]

Before the Americans and French declared the rights of man, the leading proponents of universalism lived on the margins of the great powers. Perhaps that very marginality enabled a handful of Dutch, German, and Swiss thinkers to take the initial lead in arguing that rights were universal. As early as 1625, a Dutch Calvinist jurist, Hugo Grotius, put forward a notion of rights that was applicable to all of mankind, not just one country or legal tradition. He defined "natural rights" as something self-possessed and conceivable separately from God's will. He also suggested that people could use their rights—unaided by religion—to establish the contractual foundations for social life. His German follower Samuel Pufendorf, the first professor of natural law at Heidelberg, featured Grotius's achievements in his general history of natural law teachings published in 1678. Although Pufendorf criticized Grotius on certain points, he helped solidify Grotius's reputation as a prime source of the universalist stream of rights thinking.[3]

The Swiss natural law theorists built upon these ideas in the early eighteenth century. The most influential of them, Jean-Jacques Burlamaqui, taught law in Geneva. He synthesized the various seventeenth-century natural law writings in *The Principles of Natural Law* (1747). Like his predecessors, Burlamaqui provided little specific legal or political content to the notion of universal natural rights; his main purpose was to prove their existence and their derivation from reason and human nature. He updated the concept by linking it to what the contemporary Scottish philosophers called an internal moral sense (thus anticipating the argument of my first chapters). Immediately translated into English and Dutch, Burlamaqui's work was widely used as a kind of textbook of natural law and natural rights in the last half of the eighteenth century. Rousseau, among others, took Burlamaqui as a point of departure.[4]

Burlamaqui's work fed a more general revival of natural law and natural rights theories across Western Europe and the North American colonies. Jean Barbeyrac, another Genevan Protestant, published a new French translation of Grotius's key work in 1746; he had previously issued a French translation of one of Pufendorf's works on natural law. An adulatory biography of Grotius by the Frenchman Jean Lévesque de Burigny appeared in 1752 and was translated into English in 1754. In 1754, Thomas Rutherforth published his lectures given at Cambridge University on Grotius and natural law. Grotius, Pufendorf, and Burlamaqui were all well known to American revolutionaries, such as Jefferson and Madison, who read in the law.[5]

The English had produced two major universalist thinkers in the seventeenth century: Thomas Hobbes and John Locke. Their works were well known in the British North American colonies, and Locke in particular helped shape American political thinking, perhaps even more than he influenced English views. Hobbes had less impact than Locke because he believed that natural rights had to be surrendered to an absolute authority in order to prevent the "war of all against all" that would otherwise ensue. Whereas Grotius had equated natural rights with life, body, freedom, and honor (a list that seemed to call slavery, in particular, into question), Locke defined natural rights as "Life, Liberty and Estate." Since he emphasized property—Estate—Locke did not challenge slavery. He justified slavery for captives taken in a just war. Locke even proposed legislation to ensure that "every freeman of Carolina shall have absolute power and authority over his negro slaves."[6]

Yet, despite the influence of Hobbes and Locke, much if not most English, and therefore American, discussion of natural rights in the first half of the eighteenth century focused on the particular historically based rights of the freeborn English man, not universally applicable rights. Writing in the 1750s, William Blackstone explained why his countrymen would focus on their particular rights rather than on universal ones: "These [natural liberties] were formerly, either by inheritance or purchase, the rights of all mankind; but, in most other countries of the world being now more or less debased and destroyed, they at present may be said to remain, in a peculiar and emphatical manner, the rights of the people of England." Even if rights had once been universal, claimed the prominent jurist, only the superior English had managed to hold on to them.[7]

From the 1760s on, nonetheless, the universalistic strand of rights began to intertwine with the particularistic one in the British North American colonies. In *The Rights of the British Colonies Asserted and Proved* (1764), for example, the Boston lawyer James Otis affirmed both the natural rights of colonists

("Nature has placed all such in a state of equality and perfect freedom") and their political and civil rights as British citizens: "Every British subject born on the continent of America, or in any other of the British dominions, is by the law of God and nature, by the common law, and by act of parliament . . . entitled to all the natural, essential, inherent and inseparable rights of our fellow subjects in Great Britain." Still, from Otis's "rights of our fellow subjects" in 1764 it required another giant step to reach Jefferson's "unalienable rights" of "all men" of 1776.[8]

The universalistic strand of rights thickened in the 1760s and especially the 1770s as the breach widened between the North American colonies and Great Britain. If the colonists wanted to establish a new, separate country, they could hardly rely merely on the rights of freeborn Englishmen. Otherwise, they were looking at reform, not independence. Universal rights provided a better rationale, and accordingly, American election sermons in the 1760s and 1770s began to cite Burlamaqui by name in defense of "the rights of mankind." Grotius, Pufendorf, and especially Locke appeared among the most frequently cited authors in political writings, and Burlamaqui could be found in increasing numbers of private and public libraries. When British authority began to collapse in 1774, the colonists came to consider themselves in something like the state of nature they had read about. Burlamaqui had asserted, "The idea of *Right*, and even more that of *natural law*, are manifestly related to man's nature. It is therefore from this *nature* itself of man, from his *constitution*, and from his *condition* that we must deduce the principles of this science." Burlamaqui talked only of man's nature in general, not about the condition of American colonists or the constitution of Great Britain, but the constitution and condition of universal mankind. Such universalist thinking enabled the colonists to imagine a break with tradition and British sovereignty.[9]

Even before Congress declared independence, the colonists called state conventions to replace British rule, sent instructions with their delegates to demand independence, and began drafting state constitutions that often included bills of rights. The Virginia Declaration of Rights of June 12, 1776, proclaimed that "all men are by nature equally free and independent and have certain inherent rights," which were defined as "the enjoyment of life and liberty, with the means of acquiring and possessing property, and pursuing and obtaining happiness and safety." More important still, the Virginia Declaration went on to offer a list of specific rights such as freedom of the press and freedom of religious opinion; it helped set the template not only for the Declaration of Independence but also for the eventual Bill of Rights of the U.S. Constitution. By the spring of 1776, declaring independence—and declaring universal rather than British rights—had gathered momentum in political circles.[10]

The events of 1774–76 thus temporarily fused particularistic and universalistic thinking about rights in the insurgent colonies. In response to Great Britain, the colonists could cite their already existing rights as British subjects and at the same time claim the universal right to a government that secured their unalienable rights as equal men. Yet, since the latter in effect abrogated the former, as the Americans moved more decisively toward independence they felt the need to declare their rights as part of the transition from a state of nature back into civil government—or from a state of subjection to George III forward into a new republican polity. Universalistic rights would never have been declared in the American colonies without the revolutionary moment created by the resistance to British authority. Although everyone did not agree on the importance of declaring rights or on the content of the rights to be declared, independence opened the door to the declaration of rights.[11]

Even in Great Britain, a more universalistic notion of rights began to creep into discourse in the 1760s. Talk of rights had quieted down with the restoration of stability after the 1688 revolution that had resulted in the Bill of Rights. The number of book titles that included some mention of "rights" steadily declined in Britain from the early 1700s to the 1750s. As international discussion of natural law and natural rights intensified, the numbers then began to rise again in the 1760s and continued to grow thereafter. In a long pamphlet of 1768 denouncing aristocratic patronage of clerical positions in the Church of Scotland, the author called on both "the natural rights of mankind" and "the natural and civil rights of FREE BRITONS." Similarly, the Anglican preacher William Dodd argued that popery was "inconsistent with the Natural Rights of MEN in general and of ENGLISHMEN in particular." Still, the oppositional politician John Wilkes always employed the language of "your birth-right as ENGLISHMEN" when defending his case in the 1760s. *The Letters of Junius*, anonymous letters published against the British government in the late 1760s and early 1770s, also used the language of "the rights of the people" to refer to rights under English tradition and law.[12]

War between the colonists and the British crown brought the universalist strain more fully into the open in Britain itself. A tract of 1776 signed "M.D." cites Blackstone to the effect that the colonists "carry with them only so much of the English laws as is applicable to their own situation"; therefore, if ministerial "innovations" violate "their native rights as [English] freemen," the chain of government is broke," and the colonists can be expected to exert their "natural rights." Richard Price made the appeal to universalism very explicit in his immensely influential pamphlet of 1776, *Observations on the Nature of Civil Liberty, the Principles of Government, and the Justice and Policy of the War with America*. It went through no less than fifteen editions in London in 1776 and was reprinted in the same year in Dublin, Edinburgh, Charleston, New York, and Philadelphia. Price based his support for the colonists on "the general principles of Civil Liberty," that is, "what reason and equity, and the rights of humanity give," not precedent, statute or charters (the practice of English liberty in the past). Price's pamphlet was translated into French, German, and Dutch. His Dutch translator, Joan Derk van der Capellen tot den Poll, wrote to Price in December 1777 and recounted his own support, in a speech subsequently printed and widely circulated, of the American cause: "I consider the Americans to be brave men who defend in a moderate, pious, couragious manner the rights which they hold, as being men, not from the legislative power of England, but from *God* himself."[13]

Price's pamphlet ignited a fierce controversy in Britain. Some thirty pamphlets appeared almost immediately in response, accusing Price of false patriotism, factiousness, parricide, anarchy, sedition, and even treason. Price's pamphlet put "the natural rights of mankind," "the rights of human nature," and especially "the unalienable rights of human nature" on the agenda in Europe. As one author clearly recognized, the crucial question was this: "Whether there are inherent rights in Human Nature, so connected with the will, that such rights cannot be alienated." It was only sophistry, claimed this opponent, to argue that "there are certain rights of Human Nature which are unalienable." These had to be given up—one had "to relinquish the guidance of one's self by one's own will"—in order to enter the civil state. The polemics show that the meaning of natural rights, civil liberty, and democracy now occupied and were debated by many of Britain's best political minds.[14]

The distinction between natural and civil liberty put forward by Price's opponents serves as a reminder that the articulation of natural rights engendered its own countertradition, which continues to the present day. Like natural rights, which grew up in opposition to governments perceived as despotic, the countertradition too was reactive, arguing either that natural rights were a fabrication or that they could never be unalienable (and thus were irrelevant). Hobbes had already argued in the mid-seventeenth century that natural rights had to be given up (and therefore were not unalienable) in order to establish an orderly civil society. Robert Filmer, the English proponent of patriarchal authority, explicitly refuted Grotius in 1679 and pronounced the doctrine of "natural freedom" an "absurdity." In *Patriarcha* (1680), he again contradicted the notion of the natural equality and liberty of mankind, arguing that all people are born subjects of their parents; the only natural right, in Filmer's view, inhered in the regal power that derives from the original model of patriarchal power and is confirmed in the Ten Commandments.[15]

More influential in the long run was the view of Jeremy Bentham, who argued that only positive (actual rather than ideal or natural) law mattered. In 1775, long before he became famous as the father of Utilitarianism, Bentham wrote a critique of Blackstone's *Commentaries on the Laws of England*. In it he laid out his rejection of the concept of natural law: "There are no such things as any '*precepts*,' nothing by which man is '*commanded*' to do any of those acts pretended to be enjoined by the pretended law of Nature. If any man knows of any let him produce them. If they were producible, we should not need to be puzzling out the business of 'discovering' them, as our author [Blackstone] soon after tells us we must, by the help of reason."

Bentham objected to the idea that natural law was innate in the person and discoverable by reason. He therefore basically rejected the entire natural law tradition and with it natural rights. The principle of utility (the greatest happiness of the greatest number, an idea he borrowed from Beccaria), he would later argue, served as the best measure of right and wrong. Only calculations based on fact rather than judgments based on reason could provide the basis for the law. Given this position, his later rejection of the French Declaration of the Rights of Man and Citizen is less surprising. In a pamphlet reviewing the French Declaration article by article he categorically denied the existence of natural rights. "Natural rights is simple nonsense: natural and imprescriptible rights, rhetorical nonsense, nonsense upon stilts."[16]

Despite its critics, rights talk was gathering momentum after the 1760s. "Natural rights," now supplemented by "the rights of mankind," "the rights of humanity," and "the rights of man," became common currency. Its political potential vastly enhanced by the American conflicts of the 1760s and 1770s, talk of universal rights shifted back across the Atlantic to Great Britain, the Dutch Republic, and France. In 1768, for example, the reform-minded French economist Pierre-Samuel du Pont de Nemours offered his own definition of the "rights of each man." His list included freedom to choose an occupation, free trade, public education, and proportional taxation. In 1776, du Pont volunteered to go to the American colonies and report on events to the French government (an offer left on the table). Du Pont later became a close friend of Jefferson's and in 1789 was elected a deputy to the Third Estate.[17]

Although the Declaration of Independence might not have been as "all-but-forgotten" as Pauline Maier recently proclaimed, the universalist idiom of rights essentially returned back home to Europe after 1776. The new state governments of the United States began adopting individual bills of rights as early as 1776, yet the Articles of Confederation of 1777 included no bill of rights, and the Constitution of 1787 was approved without one. The U.S. Bill of Rights only came into being with the ratification of the first ten amendments to the Constitution in 1791, and it was a deeply particularistic document: it protected American citizens against encroachment by their federal government. In comparison, the Declaration of Independence and the Virginia Declaration of Rights of 1776 had made much more universalistic claims. By the 1780s, rights in America had taken a back seat to concerns about building a new national institutional framework. As a consequence, the French Declaration of the Rights of Man and Citizen of 1789 actually preceded the American Bill of Rights, and it immediately attracted international attention.[18]

Declaring Rights in France

Despite the American turn away from universalism in the 1780s, "the rights of man" got a great boost from the American example. Without it, in fact, human rights might have withered on the vine. After sparking widespread interest in the "rights of man" in the early 1760s, Rousseau himself became disenchanted. In a long letter written in January 1769 about his religious convictions, Rousseau railed against the excessive use of "this beautiful word 'humanity.'" Worldly sophisticates, "the least human of people," invoked it so often that it was "becoming insipid, even ridiculous." Humanity had to be impressed on hearts, Rousseau insisted, not just printed on pages in books. The inventor of the phrase "rights of man" did not live to see the full impact of American independence; he died in 1778, the year that France joined the American side against Great Britain. While Rousseau knew of Benjamin Franklin, a veritable celebrity in France since his arrival as minister for the rebellious colonists in 1776, and on one occasion defended the Americans' right to protect their liberties even if they were "obscure or unknown," he expressed little interest in American affairs.[19]

The repeated references to humanity and rights of man continued despite Rousseau's scorn, but they might have been ineffectual if events in America had not given them a sharper edge. Between 1776 and 1783, nine different French translations of the Declaration of Independence and at least five French translations of various state constitutions and bills of rights provided specific applications of rights doctrines and helped crystallize the sense that French government too could be established on new grounds. Although some French reformers favored an English-style constitutional monarchy, and Condorcet for one expressed disappointment with the "aristocratic spirit" of the new U.S. Constitution, many enthused about the American ability to get out from under the dead weight of the past and establish self-government.[20]

The American precedents became all the more compelling as the French entered a state of constitutional emergency. In 1788, facing a bankruptcy caused in large measure by French participation in the American War of Independence, Louis XVI agreed to convoke the Estates-General, which had last met in 1614. As elections of delegates began, declaratory rumbles could already be heard. In January 1789, Jefferson's friend Lafayette prepared a draft declaration and in the weeks that followed Condorcet quietly formulated his own. The king had asked the clergy (the First Estate), the nobles (the Second Estate), and ordinary people (the Third Estate) not only to elect delegates but also to write up lists of their grievances. A number of the lists drawn up in February, March, and April 1789 referred to "the inalienable rights of man," "the imprescriptible rights of free men," "the rights and the dignity of man and the citizen," or "the rights of enlightened and free men," but "rights of man" predominated. The language of rights was now diffusing rapidly in the atmosphere of growing crisis.[21]

A few grievance lists—more often those of the nobles than the clergy or Third Estate—explicitly demanded a declaration of rights (usually those that also asked for a new constitution). The nobility of the Béziers region in the south, for instance, requested that "the general assembly take as its true preliminary task the examination, drafting, and declaration of the rights of man and citizen." The grievance list of the Third Estate of the outer Paris region titled its second section "Declaration of rights" and provided a list of those rights. Virtually all of the lists asked for specific rights in some form or another: liberty of the press, freedom of religion in a few cases, equal taxation, equality of treatment under the law, protection from arbitrary arrest, and the like.[22]

The delegates came with their grievance lists to the official opening of the Estates-General on May 5, 1789. After weeks of futile debate over procedure, the deputies of the Third Estate unilaterally pronounced themselves members of a National Assembly on June 17; they claimed to represent the entire nation, not just their "estate." Many clerical deputies soon joined them and before long the nobles had no choice but to either leave or join too. On June 19, in the very midst of these struggles, a deputy requested that the new Assembly embark immediately on the "great task of a declaration of rights," which he insisted had been mandated by the electors; though far from universally demanded, the idea was most certainly in the air. A Committee on the Constitution was set up on July 6, and on July 9 the committee announced to the National Assembly that it would begin with a "declaration of the natural and impre-scriptible rights of man," labeled in the recapitulation of the session "the declaration of the rights of man."[23]

Thomas Jefferson, then in Paris, wrote to Thomas Paine in England on July 11 with a breathless account of unfolding events. Paine was the author of *Common Sense* (1776), the single most influential pamphlet of the American independence movement. According to Jefferson, the deputies of the National Assembly "have prostrated the old government, and are now beginning to build one from the foundation." He reported that they considered the very first task to be the drafting of "a Declaration of the natural and imprescriptible rights of man"—the very terms of the Committee on the Constitution. Jefferson consulted closely with Lafayette, who read his own draft proposal of a declaration to the Assembly that same day. Several other prominent deputies now rushed to get their proposals into print. Terminology varied: "the rights of man in society," "the rights of a French citizen," or simply "rights," but "the rights of man" predominated in the titles.[24]

On July 14, three days after Jefferson wrote to Paine, crowds in Paris armed themselves and attacked the Bastille prison and other symbols of royal authority. The king had ordered thousands of troops to move into Paris, causing many deputies to fear a counterrevolutionary coup. The king withdrew his soldiers, but the question of a declaration remained unresolved. In late July and early August, the deputies were still debating whether they needed a declaration, whether it should go at the head of the constitution, and whether it should be accompanied by a declaration of a citizen's duties. Division about the necessity of a declaration reflected fundamental disagreements over the course of events. If monarchical authority simply needed a few repairs, then a declaration of the "rights of man" could hardly be necessary. For those, in contrast, who agreed with Jefferson's diagnosis that the government had to be rebuilt from scratch, a declaration of rights was essential.

The Assembly finally voted on August 4 to draw up a declaration of rights without duties. No one then or since has adequately explained how opinion finally shifted in favor of drafting such a declaration, in large part because the deputies were so busy confronting day-to-day issues that they did not grasp the larger import of each of their decisions. As a result, their letters and even later memoirs proved tantalizingly vague about the shifting tides of opinion. We do know that the majority had come to believe that an entirely new groundwork was required. The rights of man provided the principles for an alternative vision of government. As the Americans had before them, the French declared rights as part of a growing rupture with established authority. Deputy Rabaut Saint-Etienne remarked on the parallel on August 18: "like the Americans, we want to regenerate ourselves, and therefore the declaration of rights is essentially necessary."[25]

Debate quickened in mid-August, even as some deputies openly derided the "metaphysical discussion." Faced with a bewildering array of alternatives, the National Assembly chose to consider a compromise document drawn up by a largely anonymous subcommittee of forty members. In the midst of continuing uncertainty and anxiety about the future, the deputies devoted six days to tumultuous debate (August 20–24, August 26). They agreed to seventeen amended articles out of the twenty-four proposed (in the United States the individual states ratified only ten of the first twelve amendments proposed for the Constitution). Exhausted by the discussion of articles and amendments, on August 27 the Assembly voted to postpone any further discussion until after drawing up a new constitution. They never reopened the question. In this somewhat back-handed fashion, the Declaration of the Rights of Man and Citizen took its definitive shape.*

The French deputies declared that all men, and not just French men, were "born and remain free and equal in rights" (Article 1). Among the "natural, inalienable, and sacred rights of man" were liberty, property, security, and resistance to oppression (Article 2). Concretely, this meant that any limits on rights had to be established in law (Article 4). "All citizens" had the right to take part in the formation of the law, which should be the same for everyone (Article 6), and to consent to taxation (Article 14), which should be apportioned equally according to the capacity to pay (Article 13). In addition, the declaration forbade "arbitrary orders" (Article 7), unnecessary punishments (Article 8), any legal presumption of guilt (Article 9), or unnecessary government appropriation of property (Article 17). In somewhat vague terms, it insisted that "no one should be disturbed for his opinions, even in religion" (Article 10) while more vigorously asserting freedom of the press (Article 11).

* See the Appendix for the full text.

In one document, therefore, the French deputies tried to encapsulate both legal protections of individual rights and a new grounds for governmental legitimacy. Sovereignty rested exclusively in the nation (Article 3), and "society" had the right to hold every public agent accountable (Article 15). No mention was made of the king, French tradition, history or custom, or the Catholic Church. Rights were declared "in the presence and under the auspices of the Supreme Being," but however "sacred," they were not traced back to that supernatural origin. Jefferson had felt the need to assert that all men were "endowed by their Creator" with rights; the French deduced rights from the entirely secular sources of nature, reason, and society. During the debates, Mathieu de Montmorency had affirmed that "the rights of man in society are eternal" and "no sanction is needed to recognize them." The challenge to the old order in Europe could not have been more forthright.[26]

None of the articles of the declaration specified the rights of particular groups. "Men," "man," "each man," "all citizens," "every citizen," "society," "any society" were contrasted to "nobody," "no individual," "no man." It was literally all or nothing. Classes, religions, and sexes made no appearance in the declaration. Although the absence of specificity would soon create problems, the generality of the assertions should not be surprising. The Committee on the Constitution had originally undertaken to prepare as many as four different documents about rights: (1) a declaration of the rights of man; (2) of the rights of the nation; (3) of the rights of the king; and (4) of the rights of citizens under the French government. The document adopted combined the first, second, and fourth but without defining the qualifications for citizenship. Before going on to specifics (the rights of the king or the qualifications for citizenship), the deputies first endeavored to set down general principles for all government. In this regard, Article 2 is typical: "The purpose of all political association is the preservation of the natural and imprescriptible rights of man." The deputies wanted to set forth the basis of all political association—not monarchy, not French government, but of all political association. They would have to turn to French government soon enough.[27]

The act of declaring did not resolve all the issues. In fact, it gave greater urgency to some questions—the rights of those without property or of religious minorities, for example—and opened up new ones about groups such as slaves or women who had had no previous political standing (to be examined in the next chapter). Perhaps those opposing a declaration had sensed that the declaring itself would have a galvanizing effect. Declaring did more than clarify articles of doctrine; by declaring, the deputies effectively seized sovereignty. As a result, declaring opened up a previously unimagined space for political debate: If the nation was sovereign, what was the role of the king, and who best represented the nation? If rights served as the foundation of legitimacy, what justified their limitation to people of certain ages, sexes, races, religions, or wealth? The language of human rights had germinated for some time in the new cultural practices of individual autonomy and bodily integrity, but then it burst forth suddenly in times of rebellion and revolution. Who should, would, or could control its effects?

Declaring rights had consequences outside France, too. The Declaration of the Rights of Man and Citizen transformed everyone's language virtually overnight. The change can be traced especially clearly in the writings and speeches of Richard Price, the dissenting British preacher who had sparked controversy with his talk of "the rights of humanity" in support of the American colonists in 1776. His 1784 pamphlet *Observations on the Importance of the American Revolution* continued in the same vein; it compared the American independence movement to the introduction of Christianity and predicted that it would "produce a general diffusion of the principles of humanity" (notwithstanding slavery, which he roundly condemned). In a sermon of November 1789, Price now endorsed the new French terminology: "I have lived to see the rights of men better understood than ever, and nations panting for liberty, which seemed to have lost the idea of it. . . . After sharing in the benefits of one Revolution [1688], I have been spared to be a witness to two other Revolutions [American and French], both glorious."[28]

Edmund Burke's 1790 pamphlet against Price, *Reflections on the Revolution in France*, unleashed in its turn a frenzy of discussion on the rights of man in various languages. Burke argued that the "new conquering empire of light and reason" could not provide an adequate foundation for successful government, which had to be rooted instead in a nation's longstanding traditions. In his indictment of the new French principles, Burke singled out the declaration for especially harsh condemnation. His language infuriated Thomas Paine, who seized on this notorious passage in his riposte of 1791, *Rights of Man: Being an Answer to Mr. Burke's Attack on the French Revolution*.

"Mr. Burke with his usual outrage," Paine wrote, "abused the Declaration of the Rights of Man. . . . This he calls 'paltry and blurred sheets of paper about the rights of man.' Does Mr. Burke mean to deny that man has any rights? If he does, then he must mean that there are no such things as rights anywhere, and that he has none himself; for who is there in the world but man?" Although Mary Wollstonecraft's response, *Vindication of the Rights of Men, in a Letter to the Right Honourable Edmund Burke; occasioned by his Reflections on the*

Revolution in France, had appeared earlier, in 1790, Paine's *Rights of Man* had an even more immediate and stupendous impact, in part because he took the occasion to argue against all forms of hereditary monarchy, including the English one. His work appeared in several English editions in just the first year of its publication.[29]

As a consequence, the use of rights language increased dramatically after 1789. Evidence for this surge can be found readily in the number of titles in English using the word "rights": it quadrupled in the 1790s (418) as compared to the 1780s (95) or any previous decade during the eighteenth century. Something similar happened in Dutch; *rechten van den mensch* appeared for the first time in 1791 with the translation of Paine and then was followed by many uses in the 1790s. *Rechten des menschen* followed soon after in the German-speaking lands. Somewhat ironically, then, the polemics between English-language writers brought the French "rights of man" to an international audience. The impact was greater than it had been after 1776, for the French had a monarchy like those of most other European nations and they never gave up the language of universalism. The writings inspired by the French Revolution also pushed the American discussion of rights into higher gear; Jeffersonians constantly invoked the "rights of man," but the Federalists spurned language associated with "democratic excess" or threats to established authority. Such disputes helped disseminate the language of human rights all over the Western world.[30]

Abolishing Torture and Cruel Punishment

Six weeks after passing the Declaration of the Rights of Man and Citizen, and even before voting qualifications had been determined, the French deputies abolished all uses of judicial torture as part of a stopgap reform of criminal procedure. On September 10, 1789, the Paris city council formally petitioned the National Assembly in the name of "reason and humanity" for immediate judicial reforms that would both "rescue innocence" and "better establish proofs of crime and make condemnation more certain." The city council members made the request because so many people had been arrested by the new National Guard, commanded in Paris by Lafayette, in the weeks of upheaval following July 14. Would the habitual secrecy of judicial proceedings foster manipulation and chicanery by the enemies of the Revolution? In response, the National Assembly named a Committee of Seven to draw up the most pressing reforms, not just for Paris but for the entire country. On October 5, under the pressure of a massive march to Versailles, Louis XVI finally gave his formal approval to the Declaration of the Rights of Man and Citizen. The marchers forced the king and his family to move to Paris from Versailles on October 6. In the midst of this renewed agitation, on October 8–9, the Assembly passed the decree proposed by its committee. At the same time, the deputies voted to join the king in Paris.[31]

The Declaration of the Rights of Man and Citizen had laid out only general principles of justice: the law should be the same for everyone, it should not permit arbitrary imprisonment or punishments other than those "strictly and obviously necessary," and the accused should be considered innocent until judged guilty. The decree of October 8–9, 1789, began with an invocation of the declaration: "The National Assembly, considering that one of the principal rights of man, which it has recognized, is that of enjoying, when accused of a criminal offense, the full extent of liberty and security for the defense that can be reconciled with the interest of society which demands the punishment of crimes. . . ." It then went on to specify procedures, most of them designed to ensure transparency to the public. In a move inspired by distrust of the sitting judiciary, the decree required the election of special commissioners in every district to assist in all criminal cases, including oversight of the collection of evidence and testimony. It guaranteed the access of the defense to all information gathered and the public nature of all criminal proceedings, thus putting into practice one of Beccaria's most cherished principles.

The shortest of the twenty-eight articles in the decree, Article 24, is the most interesting for our purposes here. It abolished all forms of torture and also the use of a low, humiliating stool (the *sellette*) for the final interrogation of the accused before his or her judges. Louis XVI had previously suppressed the "preparatory question," the use of torture to get confessions of guilt, but he had only provisionally forbidden the use of the "preliminary question," torture to get names of accomplices. The king's government had eliminated the *sellette* in May 1788, but because this action was so recent, the deputies felt the need to make their own position clear. The *sellette* was an instrument of humiliation and represented the kind of assault on individual dignity that the deputies now regarded as unacceptable. The deputy presenting the decree for the committee reserved his discussion of these measures for the very end in order to underline their symbolic importance. He had insisted to his colleagues from the beginning that "you cannot leave in the current Code stains that revolt humanity; you want them to disappear straightaway." Then he turned almost lachrymose when he reached the subject of torture:

We believe that we owe it to humanity to offer you a final observation. The king has already . . . banished from France the absurdly cruel practice of tearing from the accused, by means of torture, the confession of crimes . . . but he has left to you the glory of completing this great act of reason and justice. There remains still in our code preliminary torture . . . [the most unspeakable refinements of cruelty] are still used to obtain the revelation of accomplices. Fix your eyes on this remnant of barbarism, will you not, Sirs, and obtain its proscription from your hearts? That would be a beautiful, a touching spectacle for the universe: to see a king and a nation, united by the indissoluble bonds of a reciprocal love, rivaling each other's zeal for the perfection of the laws, and trying to outdo each other in raising monuments to justice, liberty, and humanity.

In the wake of declaring rights, torture was now finally and completely abolished. The abolition of torture had not been on the agenda of the Paris city government on September 10, but the deputies could not resist taking the opportunity presented to make it the capstone of their first revision of the criminal code.[32]

When the time came to complete revision of the penal code more than eighteen months later, the deputy assigned to present the reform invoked all the notions that had become familiar during the campaigns against torture and cruel punishment. Louis-Michel Lepeletier de Saint-Fargeau, once a judge in the Parlement of Paris, climbed up to the rostrum on May 23, 1791, to provide the rationale of the Committee on Criminal Law (a continuation of the Committee of Seven appointed in September 1789). He denounced the "atrocious tortures imagined in barbaric centuries and nonetheless retained in centuries of enlightenment," the lack of proportion between crimes and punishments (one of Beccaria's prime complaints), and the generally "absurd ferocity" of the previous laws. "The principles of humanity" would now shape the penal code, which would in the future rest on rehabilitation through work rather than sacrificial retribution through pain.[33]

So successful had been the campaigns against torture and cruel punishment that the committee put the section on punishments before the section defining crimes in the new penal code. All societies experience crime, but punishment reflects the very nature of a polity. The committee proposed a complete overhaul of the penal system to embody the new civic values: in the name of equality, everyone would be tried in the same courts under the same law and be susceptible to the same punishments. Deprivation of liberty would be the signal punishment, which meant that being sent to sea on the galleys and banishment would be replaced by imprisonment and forced labor. A criminal's fellow citizens would learn nothing about the significance of punishment if the criminal was simply sent elsewhere, out of public view. The committee even advocated eliminating the death penalty except for rebellion against the state, but knew it would face resistance on this point. The deputies voted to reinstate the death penalty for a few crimes, though they excluded all religious crimes such as heresy, sacrilege, or practice of magic. (Sodomy, previously punishable by death, was no longer listed as a crime.) The death penalty would now be rendered only by decapitation, previously reserved to nobles. The guillotine, invented to make decapitation as painless as possible, went into operation in April 1792. Breaking on the wheel, burning at the stake, "those tortures that accompanied the death penalty," were to disappear; "all these legal horrors are detested by humanity and by public opinion," insisted Lepeletier. "These cruel spectacles degrade public morals and are unworthy of a humane and enlightened century."[34]

Since rehabilitation and the reentry of the criminal into society were the chief aims, bodily mutilation and branding became intolerable. Lepeletier nonetheless lingered some time over the question of branding; how would society protect itself against convicted offenders without some kind of permanent sign of their status? He concluded that under the new order it would be impossible for vagabonds or criminals to go unnoticed because municipalities would keep exact registers with the names of every inhabitant. To mark their bodies permanently would prevent them from reintegrating into society. In this as in the question of pain more generally, the deputies had to walk a fine line; punishment was supposed to be simultaneously a deterrent and yet readaptive in its effects. Punishment could not be so degrading as to prevent those convicted from joining society again. As a consequence, while the penal code prescribed public exposure of those convicted, sometimes in chains, it carefully limited the exposure (at most three days) depending on the severity of the offense.

The deputies also wanted to wipe away the religious coloring of punishment. They eliminated the formal act of penitence (amende honorable) in which the convict, dressed only in a shirt, with a rope around his neck and a torch in hand, went to a church door and begged forgiveness from God, king, and justice. In its place the committee proposed a rights-based punishment called "civic degradation," which might be the sole punishment or might be added on to a term of imprisonment. Its procedures were laid out in detail by Lepeletier. The convict would be conducted to a specified public place, where the clerk of the criminal court would read these words aloud: "Your country has convicted you of a dishonorable action. The law and the court take away your standing as a French citizen." The convict would then be put in an iron collar where he would remain exposed to the public for two hours. His name, his crime, and his judgement would be written on a placard placed below his head. Women, foreigners, and recidivists posed a problem, however; how could they lose their voting rights or right to hold office when they had no such rights? Article 32 specifically addressed this point: in the case of a sentence of "civic degradation" against women, foreigners, or recidivists, they would be condemned to the iron collar for two hours and would wear a placard similar to the one prescribed for men, but the clerk would not read the phrase regarding the loss of civic standing.[35]

"Civic degradation" might sound formulaic, but it pointed to the reorientation not only of the penal code but of the political system more generally. The convict was now a citizen, not a subject; therefore, he or she (women were "passive" citizens) could not be made to endure torture, unnecessarily cruel punishments, or excessively dishonoring penalties. When Lepeletier presented the reform of the penal code, he distinguished between two kinds of punishments: corporal punishments (prison, death) and dishonoring punishments. Though all punishment had a shaming or dishonoring dimension, as Lepeletier himself asserted, the deputies wanted to circumscribe the use of dishonoring punishments. They kept public exposure and the iron collar but suppressed the act of penitence, use of stocks and pillory, dragging of the body on a hurdle after death, judicial reprimand, and declaring a case against the accused open indefinitely (implying therefore guilt). "We propose," said Lepeletier, "that you adopt the principle [of dishonoring punishment] but multiply less the variations, which by dividing it up weaken this salutary and terrible thought: society and the laws pronounce an anathema against someone who has defiled himself by crime." Shaming a criminal could be carried out in the name of society and the laws, but not in the name of religion or the king.[36]

In another move that signified a fundamental realignment, the deputies decided that the new dishonoring punishments applied only to the individual criminal, not to his or her family. With traditional types of dishonoring punishment, family members of convicts suffered the consequences directly. None of them could buy offices or hold public positions, their property was subject to confiscation in some cases, and they were considered equally dishonored by the community. In 1784, the young lawyer Pierre-Louis Lacretelle won a prize from the Metz Academy for an essay arguing that the shame of dishonoring punishments should not be extended to family members. The second prize went to a young lawyer from Arras with a remarkable future, Maximilien Robespierre, who took the same position.

This attention to dishonoring punishment reflects a subtle but momentous shift in the concept of honor: with the rise of a notion of human rights, the traditional understanding of honor was coming under attack. Honor had been the most important personal quality under the monarchy; indeed, Montesquieu argued in his *Spirit of Laws* (1748) that honor was the animating principle of monarchy as a form of government. Many considered honor the special province of the aristocracy. In his essay on dishonoring punishments, Robespierre had traced the practice of shaming entire families back to the defects of the notion of honor itself:

If one considers the nature of this honor, fertile in caprices, always inclined to an excessive delicacy, often appreciating things for their glamour rather than for their intrinsic value, and men for their accessories, titles that are foreign to them, rather than for their personal qualities, one could easily understand how it [honor] could deliver up to contempt those who hold dear a villain punished by society.

Yet Robespierre also denounced the reserving of decapitation (thought more honorable) to nobles alone. Did he want all people to be equally honorable or to give up on honor itself?[37]

Even before the 1780s, however, honor was undergoing changes. "Honor," according to the 1762 edition of the dictionary of the Académie Française, signifies "virtue, probity." "In speaking of women," however, "honor signifies chastity, modesty." Increasingly in the second half of the eighteenth century, the distinctions in honor divided men from women more than aristocrats from commoners. For men, honor was becoming linked to virtue, the quality Montesquieu associated with republics; all citizens were honorable if they were virtuous. Under the new dispensation, honor had to do with actions, not birth. The distinction between men and women carried over from honor into questions of citizenship as well as forms of punishment. Women's honor (and virtue) was private and domestic; men's was public. Men and women alike could be shamed in punishment, but only men had political rights to lose. In punishment as in rights, aristocrats and commoners were now equal; men and women were not.[38]

The dilution of honor did not escape notice. In 1794, the

writer Sébastien-Roch Nicolas Chamfort, one of the members of the elite Académie Française, satirized the change:

> It is a recognized truth that our century has put words in their place; by banishing scholastic, dialectical, and metaphysical subtleties, it has returned to the simple and true in physics, morals, and politics. Speaking only of morals, one senses how much this word, honor, incorporates complex and metaphysical ideas. Our century felt the drawbacks of these and to bring everything back to the simple, to prevent every abuse of words, it has established that honor remains integral to any man who has never been an ex-convict. In the past this word was a source of equivocations and contestations; at present, nothing could be clearer. Has a man been put in the iron collar or not? This is the state of the question. It is a simple question of fact which can be easily answered by the court clerk's registers. A man who has not been put in the iron collar is a man of honor who may lay claim to anything, places in the ministry, etc. He gains entrance to professional bodies, to the academies, to sovereign courts. One senses how much clarity and precision save us from quarrels and discussions, and how much the commerce of life becomes convenient and easy.

Chamfort had his own reasons for taking honor seriously. An abandoned child of unknown parents, Chamfort made a literary reputation and became the personal secretary of Louis XVI's sister. He killed himself at the height of the Terror not long after writing these words. During the Revolution, he first attacked the prestigious Académie Française, which had elected him in 1781, and then repented of his actions and defended it. Elevation to the Académie was the greatest honor that could be bestowed on a writer under the monarchy. The Académie was abolished in 1793 and revived under Napoleon. Chamfort grasped not only the magnitude of the change in honor—the difficulty of maintaining social distinctions in an impatiently equalizing world—but also the connection of the new penal code to it. The iron collar had become the lowest common denominator of loss of honor.[39]

The new penal code was only one of the many consequences that followed from the Declaration of the Rights of Man and Citizen. The deputies had responded to the urging of duc de Montmorency to "set a great example" by drawing up a declaration of rights, and within weeks of doing so, they began to discover how unpredictable the effects of such example setting could be. "The action of stating, telling, setting forth, or announcing openly, explicitly or formally" that was implied in declaring had a logic all its own. Rights once announced openly raised new questions—questions previously unasked and previously unaskable. Declaring turned out to be only the first step in a highly charged process, one that continues to our day.

4

"THERE WILL BE NO END OF IT"

The Consequences of Declaring

JUST BEFORE CHRISTMAS 1789, the deputies of the French National Assembly found themselves in the midst of a peculiar debate. It began on December 21, when a deputy raised the issue of the voting rights of non-Catholics. "You have declared that all men are born and remain free and equal in rights," he reminded his fellow deputies. "You have declared that no one can be disturbed for his religious opinions." Many Protestants sit as deputies among us, he observed, and so the Assembly should immediately decree that non-Catholics be eligible to vote, hold office, and aspire to any civil or military post, "like other citizens."

"Non-Catholics" comprised an odd category. When Pierre Brunet de Latuque used it in his proposed decree, he clearly meant Protestants. But did it not include Jews as well? France

was home to some 40,000 Jews in 1789 in addition to its
100,000–200,000 Protestants (Catholics made up the other 99
percent of the population). Two days after Brunet de Latuque's
initial intervention, Comte Stanislas de Clermont-Tonnerre
decided to push right into the thicket. "There is no middle way
possible," he insisted. Either you establish an official religion of
the state, or you admit to voting and public office members of
any religion. Clermont-Tonnerre insisted that religious belief
should not be a cause for exclusion from political rights and that
therefore Jews too should have equal rights. But that was not all.
Profession should not be a cause for exclusion either, he argued.
Executioners and actors, denied political rights in the past,
should now gain entry too. (Executioners had been considered
dishonorable because they killed people for a living, and actors
because they pretended to be someone else.) Clermont-Tonnerre
believed in consistency: "we should either forbid plays altogether or remove the dishonor associated with acting."[1]

Rights questions thus revealed a tendency to cascade. Once
the deputies considered the status of Protestants as a disenfranchised religious minority, Jews were bound to come up; as soon
as religious exclusions made it to the agenda, professional ones
were not long in following. Already in 1776 John Adams had
feared an even more radical progression in Massachusetts. To
James Sullivan he wrote,

Depend upon it, Sir, it is dangerous to open so fruitfull a
Source of Controversy and altercation; as would be
opened by attempting to alter the Qualifications of Vot-
ers. There will be no End of it. New Claims will arise.
Women will demand a Vote. Lads from 12 to 21 will
think their Rights not enough attended to, and every

Man, who has not a Farthing, will demand an equal
Voice with any other in all Acts of State.

Adams did not really think that women or children would ask
for the right to vote, but he did dread the consequences of
extending suffrage to men without property. It was easiest to
argue against "every Man, who has not a Farthing" by pointing
to even more preposterous requests that might come from those
on rungs further down the social ladder.[2]

In both the new United States and France, declarations of
rights referred to "men," "citizens," "people," and "society"
without addressing differences in political standing. Even before
the French Declaration was drafted, an astute constitutional the-
orist, abbé Sieyès, had argued for a distinction between the natural and civil rights of citizens on the one hand and political
rights on the other. Women, children, foreigners, and those who
paid no taxes should be "passive" citizens only. "Those alone
who contribute to the public establishment are like the true
shareholders in the great social enterprise. They alone are the
true active citizens."[3]

The same principles had long been in force on the other side
of the Atlantic. The thirteen colonies denied the vote to women,
African-Americans, Native Americans, and the propertyless. In
Delaware, for example, the suffrage was limited to adult white
males who owned fifty acres of land, had resided in Delaware for
two years, were native-born or naturalized, denied the authority
of the Roman Catholic Church, and acknowledged that the Old
and New Testaments were divinely inspired. After independence, some states enacted more liberal provisions. Pennsylvania,
for example, extended voting rights to all free adult men who
paid taxes of any amount, and New Jersey briefly allowed prop-

ertied women to vote; but most states retained their property qualifications and many kept religious tests, at least for a time. John Adams captured the dominant view: "[s]uch is the Frailty of the human Heart, that very few Men, who have no Property, have any judgment of their own."[4]

The basic chronology of the extension of rights is easier to follow in France because political rights were defined by the national legislature, whereas in the new United States such rights were regulated by the individual states. In the week of October 20–27, 1789, the deputies passed a series of decrees setting the conditions for eligibility for voting: (1) to be French or to have become French through naturalization; (2) to have reached one's majority, set then at twenty-five years of age; (3) to have resided in the precinct for at least one year; (4) to pay direct taxes at a rate equal to the local value of three days of work (a higher rate was required for eligibility for office); and (5) not to be a domestic servant. The deputies said nothing about religion, race, or sex in setting these requirements, though it was clearly assumed that women and slaves were excluded.

Over the next months and years, group after group came up for specific discussion and eventually most of them got equal political rights. Protestant men gained their rights on December 24, 1789, as did all professions. Jewish men finally obtained the same access on September 27, 1791. Some, but not all, free black men won political rights on May 15, 1791, only to lose them on September 24 and then have them reinstated and applied more generally on April 4, 1792. On August 10, 1792, voting rights were extended to all men (in metropolitan France) except servants and the unemployed. On February 4, 1794, slavery was abolished and equal rights granted at least in principle to slaves. Despite this almost unimaginable extension of political rights to groups previously disenfranchised, the line was drawn at women: women never gained equal political rights during the Revolution. They did, however, gain equal inheritance rights and the right to divorce.

The Logic of Rights: Religious Minorities

The French Revolution, more than any other event, revealed that human rights have an inner logic. As the deputies faced the need to turn their lofty ideals into specific laws, they inadvertently developed a kind of conceivability or thinkability scale. No one knew in advance which groups were going to come up for discussion, when they would come up, or what the resolution of their status would be. But sooner or later, it became clear that granting rights to some groups (Protestants, for example) was more easily imagined than granting them to others (women). The logic of the process determined that as soon as a highly conceivable group came up for discussion (propertied males, Protestants), those in the same kind of category but located lower on the conceivability scale (propertyless males, Jews) would inevitably appear on the agenda. The logic of the process did not necessarily move events in a straight line forward, but in the long run it tended to do so. Thus, for example, the opponents of Jewish rights used the case of the Protestants (unlike Jews, they were Christians at least) to convince the deputies to table the question of Jewish rights. Yet in less than two years, Jews nevertheless got equal rights, in part because the explicit discussion of their rights had made granting equal rights to Jews more imaginable.

In the workings of this logic, the supposedly metaphysical nature of the Declaration of the Rights of Man and Citizen proved to be a very positive asset. Precisely because it left aside any question of specifics, the July–August 1789 discussion of general principles helped set in motion ways of thinking that eventually fostered more radical interpretations of the specifics required. The declaration was designed to articulate the universal rights of humanity and the general political rights of the French nation and its citizens. It offered no specific qualifications for active participation. The institution of a government required movement from the general to the specific; as soon as elections were set up, the definition of qualifications for voting and holding office became urgent. The virtue of beginning with the general became apparent once the specific came into question.

Protestants were the first identity group to come up for consideration, and the discussion of them established an enduring characteristic of the subsequent disputes: a group could not be considered in isolation. Protestants could not come up without raising the question of Jews. Similarly, the rights of actors could not be questioned without raising the specter of executioners, or the rights of free blacks without drawing attention to the slaves. When pamphleteers wrote about women's rights, they inevitably compared them to those of propertyless men and slaves. Even discussions about the age of adulthood (it was lowered from twenty-five to twenty-one in 1792) depended on its comparison to childhood. The status and rights of Protestants, Jews, free blacks, or women were determined in large measure by their place in the larger network of groups constituting the polity.

Protestants and Jews had already come up together in the debates about drafting a declaration. The young noble deputy comte de Castellane had argued that Protestants and Jews should enjoy the "most sacred of all rights, that of freedom of religion." Yet even he insisted that no specific religion should be cited in the declaration. Rabaut Saint-Etienne, himself a Calvinist pastor from Languedoc where many Calvinists lived, referred to the demand of his local grievance list for freedom of religion for non-Catholics. Rabaut explicitly included Jews among non-Catholics, but his argument, like those of everyone else in the debate, concerned freedom of religion, not the political rights of minorities. After hours of tumultuous debate, the deputies adopted a compromise article in August which made no mention of political rights (Article 10 of the declaration): "No one should be disturbed for his opinions, even in religion, provided that their manifestation does not trouble the public order as established by law." The formulation was deliberately ambiguous and was even interpreted by some as a victory for the conservatives, who vociferously opposed freedom of religion. Would not public worship by Protestants "trouble the public order"?[5]

By December, less than six months later, most of the deputies nevertheless took freedom of religion for granted. But did freedom of religion then imply equal political rights for religious minorities as well? Brunet de Latuque raised the issue of Protestants' political rights just a week after regulations were drawn up for municipal elections on December 14, 1789. He reported to his colleagues that non-Catholics were being excluded from voting lists on the pretext that they had not been included by name in the regulations. "You have certainly not wished, Sirs," he said hopefully, "to let religious opinions be an official reason for excluding some citizens and admitting others." Brunet's language was telling: the deputies were now having to interpret their previous actions in the light of the present. Opponents of the Protestants wanted to claim that Protestants could not participate because the Assembly had not voted a decree to that effect; after all, Protestants had been excluded from political office by law since the 1685 Revocation of the Edict of Nantes, and no subsequent law had formally revised their political status. Brunet and his supporters argued that the general principles proclaimed in the Declaration of the Rights of Man and Citizen admitted no exceptions, that all those who fulfilled the age and economic conditions of eligibility had to be automatically eligible, and that therefore the previous strictures against Protestants were no longer valid.[6]

In other words, the abstract universalism of the declaration was now coming home to roost. Neither Brunet nor anyone else brought up the question of women's rights at this point; automatic eligibility apparently did not encompass sexual difference. But the minute the status of Protestants was raised in this fashion, the floodgates opened. Some deputies reacted with alarm. Clermont-Tonnerre's proposed extension outward from Protestants to all religions and professions ignited an intense debate. Although the question of Protestants' rights had started the discussion, almost everyone now granted that they should enjoy the same rights as Catholics. Extending rights to executioners and actors aroused only isolated, largely frivolous objections, but the suggestion of granting political rights to Jews provoked furious resistance. Even a deputy open to an eventual emancipation of the Jews argued that "Their idleness, their lack of tact, a necessary result of the laws and humiliating conditions to which they are subjected in many places, all work towards rendering them odious." Giving them rights, in his view, would only unleash a popular backlash against them (and in fact anti-Jewish riots had already taken place in eastern France). On December 24, 1789—Christmas Eve—the Assembly voted to extend equal political rights to "non-Catholics" and all professions, even while tabling the question of the political rights of Jews. The vote in favor of Protestant political rights was evidently massive, according to participants, and one deputy wrote in his journal of "the joyfulness that manifested itself at the moment the decree passed."[7]

The turnaround in opinion about Protestants was astounding. Before the Edict of Toleration of 1787, Protestants had not been able to legally practice their religion, marry, or pass on their property. After 1787, they could practice their religion, marry before local officials, and register the births of their children. They gained only civil rights, however, not equal rights to political participation, and they still did not enjoy the right of practicing their religion publicly. That was reserved solely to Catholics. Some of the high courts had continued to resist application of the edict right into 1788 and 1789. In August 1789, therefore, it was far from evident that most deputies supported true freedom of religion. Yet by the end of December they had granted equal political rights to Protestants.

What explained the change of mind? Rabaut Saint-Etienne attributed the transformation in attitudes to the display of civic responsibility by Protestant deputies. Twenty-four Protestants, including himself, had been elected deputies in 1789. Even before then Protestants had held local offices despite official proscriptions, and in the uncertainty of the early months of 1789, many Protestants had participated in the elections for the Estates-General. The leading historian of the National Assembly, Timothy Tackett, traces the change in opinion about Protestants to internal political struggles within the Assembly; moderates found the obstructionism of the right increasingly distasteful and so aligned themselves with the left, which supported extension of rights. Yet even Tackett's prime example of obstructionism, the obstreperous clerical deputy abbé Jean

Maury, argued in favor of the rights of Protestants. Maury's posi-tion provides a clue to the process, for he linked support of the political rights of Protestants to denial of those of Jews: "The Protestants have the same religion and the same laws as us . . . they already enjoy the same rights." Maury sought to distinguish in this fashion between Protestants and Jews. However, the Spanish and Portuguese Jews of southern France immediately began preparing to petition the National Assembly with the claim that they too were already exercising their political rights on the local level. The attempt to play one religious minority off another only widened the crack in the door.[8]

The status of Protestants was transformed by both theory and practice, that is, by the discussion of general principles of freedom of religion and by the actual participation of Protestants in local and national affairs. Brunet de Latuque had invoked the general principle when he claimed that the deputies cannot have wanted "religious opinions be an official reason for excluding some citizens and admitting others." Not wanting to concede the general point, Maury had to grant the practical one; Protes-tants already exercised the same rights as Catholics. The general discussion in August had purposely left these matters unre-solved, opening the door to later reinterpretations and even more important, not closing the door to participation in local affairs. Protestants and even some Jews had rushed to make the most of the new opportunities presented.

Unlike Protestants before the 1787 Edict of Toleration, French Jews suffered no penalties for publicly professing their religion, but they enjoyed few civil and no political rights. In fact, the Frenchness of the Jews was to some extent in question. The Calvinists were French people who had gone astray by embracing heresy, whereas the Jews were originally foreigners who constituted a separate nation within France. Thus, the Alsatian Jews were known officially as "the Jewish nation of Alsace." But "nation" had a less nationalistic meaning at this time than it would have later in the nineteenth and twentieth centuries. Like most Jews in France, the Alsatian Jews constituted a nation insofar as they lived within a Jewish community whose rights and obligations had been set forth in special letters patent by the king. They had the right to govern some of their own affairs and even decide cases in their own courts, but they also suffered from a host of restrictions on the kinds of trades they could practice, the places where they could live, and the professions to which they might aspire.[9]

Enlightenment writers had written frequently about the Jews, though not always positively, and after the granting of civil rights to Protestants in 1787 attention shifted to improving the situation of the Jews. Louis XVI set up a commission to study the question in 1788, too late for action to be taken before the Revolution. Although Jewish political rights ranked lower than Protestant ones in conceivability, the Jews ultimately benefited from the attention drawn toward them. Explicit discussion did not immediately translate into rights, however. Three hundred and seven of the grievance lists drawn up in spring 1789 explicitly mentioned Jews, but opinion in them was sharply divided. Seventeen percent urged limitation on the number of Jews allowed in France and 9 percent advocated their expulsion, whereas only 9–10 percent urged improvement in their conditions. Amid the thousands of grievance lists, a mere eight advocated granting equal rights to Jews. Still, that was more than made the same claim for women.[10]

Jewish rights seem to fit the general rule that first efforts to raise the issue of rights often backfire. The largely negative position of the grievance lists foreshadowed the refusal of the deputies to grant political rights to Jews in December 1789. Over the next twenty months, however, the logic of rights drove the discussion forward. Only a month after the discussion of Jewish rights was tabled, the Spanish and Portuguese Jews of southern France presented their petition to the Assembly claiming that, like Protestants, they were already participating in politics in some southern French cities such as Bordeaux. Speaking for the Committee on the Constitution, the liberal Catholic bishop Charles-Maurice de Talleyrand-Périgord essentially endorsed their position. The Jews were not asking for new rights of citizenship, he insisted; they were just asking "to continue to enjoy those rights" since they, like Protestants, were already exercising them. The Assembly could thus grant rights to some Jews without changing the status of Jews in general. In this way, the argument from practice could be turned against those who wanted categorical distinctions.[11]

Talleyrand's speech provoked an uproar, especially among the deputies from Alsace-Lorraine, which was home to the largest Jewish population. The Jews of eastern France were Ashkenazim, who spoke Yiddish. The men wore beards, unlike the Sephardim of Bordeaux, and French regulations restricted them largely to moneylending and peddling as occupations. There was little love lost between them and their peasant debtors. The deputies from the region wasted no time in pointing out the inevitable consequence of following Talleyrand's lead: "the exception for the Jews of Bordeaux [largely Sephardim] will soon result in the same exception for the other Jews of the kingdom." Over vociferous objections, the deputies nonetheless voted 374 to 224 that "all Jews known as Portuguese, Spanish, and Avignonese Jews will continue to exercise the rights which they have exercised up to the present" and will therefore "exercise the rights of active citizens as long as they meet the requirements set by the decrees of the National Assembly [for active citizenship]."[12]

The vote in favor of rights for some Jews did make refusing it for others more difficult in the long run. On September 27, 1791, the Assembly revoked all its previous reservations and exceptions in regard to Jews, thus granting all of them equal rights. It also required that Jews swear a civic oath renouncing the special privileges and exemptions negotiated by the monarchy. In the words of Clermont-Tonnerre: "We must refuse everything to the Jews as a nation and accord everything to Jews as individuals." In exchange for giving up their own courts and laws, they would become individual French citizens like all others. Once again, practice and theory worked in dynamic relation to each other. Without the theory, that is the principles enunciated in the declaration, the reference to some Jews already practicing these rights would have had little impact. Without the reference to practice, the theory might have remained a dead letter (as it apparently continued to be for women).[13]

Rights were not just granted by the legislative body, however. The debates over rights galvanized the minority communities to speak for themselves and to demand equal recognition. Protestants had greater access since they could speak through their deputies already elected to the National Assembly. Yet Parisian Jews, who had no corporate status and numbered only a few hundred in total, presented their first petition to the National Assembly as early as August 1789. They were already asking the deputies "to consecrate our title and rights of Citizens." A week later, representatives of the much larger community of Jews in Alsace and Lorraine published an open letter asking for citizenship, too. When the deputies recognized the rights of southern Jews in January 1790, the Jews of Paris, Alsace, and Lorraine banded together to present a joint petition. Since some deputies had questioned whether Jews really wanted French citizenship, the petitioners made their position crystal clear: "They ask that the degrading distinctions that they have suffered to this day be abolished and that they be declared CITI- ZENS." The petitioners knew exactly which buttons to push. After a long review of all the longstanding prejudices against the Jews, they concluded with an invocation of historical inevitabil- ity: "Everything is changing; the lot of the Jews must change at the same time; and the people will not be more surprised by this particular change than by all those which they see around them everyday. . . . [A]ttach the improvement of the lot of the Jews to the revolution; amalgamate, so to speak, this partial revolution to the general revolution." They dated their pamphlet with the very date the Assembly voted to make an exception for the southern Jews.[14]

Within two years, then, religious minorities had gained equal rights in France. Prejudice had certainly not disappeared, especially with regard to the Jews. Still, some sense of the enor- mity of such a change in such a short time can be established by simple comparisons. In Great Britain, Catholics first gained access to the armed forces, the universities, and the judiciary in 1793. British Jews had to wait until 1845 to achieve the same concessions. Catholics could be elected to the British Parliament only after 1829, Jews after 1858. The record in the new United States was a bit better. The small Jewish population in the British North American colonies, numbering only about 2,500, did not have political equality. After independence, most of the new United States continued to restrict officeholding (and in some states, voting) to Protestants. The first amendment to the Constitution, drawn up in September 1789 and ratified in 1791, guaranteed freedom of religion, and gradually thereafter the states removed their religious tests. The process usually proceeded in the same two stages seen in Britain: first Catholics, then Jews, gained full political rights. Massachusetts, in 1780, for example, opened officeholding to anyone "of the Christian religion," though it waited until 1833 to do so for all religions. Following Jefferson's lead, Virginia moved more quickly, granting equal rights in 1785, with South Carolina and Pennsylvania following in 1790. Rhode Island only acted in 1842.[15]

Free Blacks, Slavery, and Race

The bulldozer force of the revolutionary logic of rights can be seen even more clearly in the French decisions about free blacks and slaves. Again, comparison is telling; France granted equal political rights to free blacks (1792) and emancipated the slaves (1794) long before any other slaveholding nation. Even though the new United States granted rights to religious minorities much earlier than did its British cousins, it lagged far behind when it came to the question of slavery. After years of petition campaigns spearheaded by the Quaker-inspired Society for the Abolition of the Slave Trade, the British Parliament voted to end participation in the slave trade in 1807 and decided in 1833 to abolish slavery in the British colonies. The record in the United States was more dismal because the Constitutional Convention of 1787 did not grant the federal government control over slavery. Even though Congress also voted to forbid the import of slaves in 1807, the United States did not officially abolish slavery until 1865, when the Thirteenth Amendment to the Constitution was ratified. Moreover, the status of free blacks actually declined in many states after 1776, reaching its nadir in the notorious *Dred Scott* case of 1857, when the U.S. Supreme Court declared that neither slaves nor free blacks were citizens. *Dred Scott* was only overturned in 1868 when the Fourteenth Amendment to the U.S. Constitution was ratified, guaranteeing that "All persons born or naturalized in the United States and subject to the jurisdiction thereof, are citizens of the United States and of the State wherein they reside."[16]

Abolitionists in France followed the English lead by setting up a sister society in 1788 modeled on the British Society for the Abolition of the Slave Trade. Lacking broad backing, the French Society of the Friends of Blacks might have foundered had it not been for the events of 1789 that put them in the spotlight. The opinions of the Friends of Blacks could not be ignored because among their prominent members were Brissot, Condorcet, Lafayette, and abbé Baptiste-Henri Grégoire, all well-known campaigners for human rights in other arenas. Grégoire, a Catholic clergyman from Lorraine, had argued even before 1789 for relaxation of restrictions against the Jews in eastern France, and in 1789 he published a pamphlet advocating equal rights for free men of color. He drew attention to the burgeoning racism of the white colonists. "The whites," he maintained, "having might on their side, have pronounced unjustly that a darkened skin excludes one from the advantages of society."[17]

Still, the granting of rights to free blacks and mulattoes and the abolition of slavery hardly proceeded by acclamation. The abolitionists were vastly outnumbered in the new National Assembly by those who feared tampering with the slave system and the immense riches it brought to France. The white planters and merchants of the Atlantic port cities generally succeeded in portraying the Friends of Blacks as zealots intent on fomenting slave insurrection. On March 8, 1790, the deputies voted to exclude the colonies from the constitution and therefore from the Declaration of the Rights of Man and Citizen. The spokesman for the colonial committee, Antoine Barnave, explained that "the rigorous and universal application of general principles cannot be suitable for [the colonies] . . . the difference in places, mores, climate, and products seemed to us to require a difference in laws." The decree also made it a crime to incite unrest in the colonies.[18]

Despite this refusal, talk of rights made its way ineluctably down the social scale in the colonies. It began at the top with the white planters of the biggest and richest colony, Saint Domingue (now Haiti). In mid-1788, they demanded reforms in colonial trade and representation at the upcoming Estates-General. Before long, they threatened to demand independence, like the North Americans, if the national government tried to interfere with the slave system. Lower-class whites, on the other hand, expected the Revolution in France to bring them redress against the wealthier whites who had no desire to share political power with mere artisans and shopkeepers.

Far more dangerous to the continuation of the status quo were the rising demands of free blacks and mulattoes. Excluded by royal decree from practicing most professions or even from taking the names of white relatives, free people of color nonetheless owned considerable property: one third of the plantations and one fourth of the slaves in Saint Domingue, for example. They wanted to be treated equally with whites even while maintaining the slave system. One of their delegates to Paris in 1789, Vincent Ogé, tried to win over the white planters by emphasizing their common interests as plantation owners: "We will see blood flowing, our lands invaded, the objects of our industry ravaged, our homes burnt . . . the slave will raise the standard of revolt." His solution was to grant equal rights to free men of color like himself, who would then help contain the slaves, at least for the time being. When his appeal to the white planters failed and the support of the Friends of Blacks proved equally unavailing, Ogé went back to Saint Domingue and in the fall of 1790 raised a revolt of the free men of color. It failed, and he was broken on the wheel.[19]

Support for the rights of free men of color did not stop there, however. Back in Paris, continuing agitation by the Friends of Blacks won a decree in May 1791 granting political rights to all free men of color born of free mothers and fathers. After the slaves of Saint Domingue rebelled in August 1791, the deputies rescinded even this highly restrictive decree, only to pass a more generous one in April 1792. It is not surprising that the deputies would act in a confused fashion, for the situation on the ground in the colonies was bewildering. The slave revolt that began in mid-August 1791 had drawn as many as 10,000 insurgents by the end of the month, a number that continued to grow by leaps and bounds. Armed bands of slaves massacred whites and burned down the sugar cane fields and the plantation houses. Planters immediately blamed the Friends of Blacks and the spread of "commonplaces about the Rights of Man."[20]

Where would the free coloreds position themselves in this struggle? They had served in the militias charged with capturing runaway slaves and sometimes owned slaves themselves. In 1789, the Friends of Blacks had portrayed them both as a bulwark against potential slave uprising and as mediators in any coming abolition of slavery. Now the slaves had risen. Having initially rejected the view of the Friends of Blacks, increasing numbers of deputies in Paris desperately began to endorse it in early 1792. They hoped that the free men of color might ally with French forces and lower-class whites against both the planters and the slaves. A former noble naval officer and plantation owner among the deputies laid out the argument: "This class [poor whites] is reinforced by that of the property-owning free men of color; this is the party of the National Assembly in this island. . . . The fears of our colonists [white planters] are therefore well-founded in that they have everything to fear from the influence of our Revolution on their slaves. The rights of man overturn the system on which rests their fortunes. . . . Only by changing their principles will [the colonists] save their lives and their fortunes." Deputy Armand-Guy Kersaint went on to argue for the gradual abolition of slavery itself. In fact, free blacks and mulattoes played an ambiguous role throughout the slave uprising, sometimes allying with whites against the slaves, sometimes allying with the slaves against the whites.[21]

Once again, the potent combination of theory (declaring rights) and practice (in this case outright revolt and rebellion) forced the hand of the legislators. As Kersaint's argument showed, the rights of man were unavoidably part of the discussion, even in the Assembly that had declared them inapplicable to the colonies. Events pushed the deputies to recognize their applicability in places and in regard to groups they had originally hoped to exclude from them. Those who opposed granting rights to free men of color agreed on one central point with those who supported according those rights: the rights of free men of color could not be separated from consideration of the slave system itself. Once those rights had been acknowledged, the next step became that much more inevitable.

By the summer of 1793, the French colonies were in total upheaval. A republic had been declared in France and war now pitted the new republic against Britain and Spain in the Caribbean. White planters sought alliances with the British. Some of the rebellious slaves of Saint Domingue joined with the Spanish, who controlled the eastern half of the island, Santo Domingo, in exchange for promises of freedom for themselves. But Spain had no intention of abolishing slavery. In August 1793, facing a total breakdown of French authority, two commissioners sent from France began offering emancipation to slaves who fought for the French Republic and then to their families as well. In addition, they promised concessions of land. By the end of the month they were offering freedom to entire provinces. The decree emancipating the slaves of the north opened with Article 1 of the Declaration of the Rights of Man and Citizen, "Men are born and live free and equal in rights." Although initially fearful of a British plot to undermine French power by freeing the slaves, the deputies back in Paris voted to abolish slavery in all the colonies in February 1794. They acted as soon as they heard firsthand reports from three men—a white, a mulatto, and a freed slave—sent from Saint Domingue to explain the necessity of emancipation. In addition to "the abolition of Negro slavery in all the colonies," the deputies decreed "that all men, without distinction of color, residing in the colonies, are French citizens and will enjoy all the rights assured by the constitution."[22]

Was the abolition of slavery an act of pure enlightened altruism? Hardly. The continuing revolt of the slaves in Saint Domingue and its conjunction with war on many fronts left the commissioners, and therefore the deputies back in Paris, little choice, if they wanted to hold on to any portion of their island colony. Yet, as the actions of the British and Spanish revealed, much room remained for maneuvering to keep slavery in place; they could promise piecemeal emancipation to those who came over to their side without offering the general abolition of slavery. But the propagation of "the rights of man" made maintaining slavery much more difficult for the French. As the discussion of rights spread in France, it undercut the legislature's attempt to keep the colonies outside the constitution, even as it ineluctably galvanized the free men of color and slaves themselves to make new demands and fight fiercely for them. From the very beginning, the planters and their allies perceived the threat. The colonial deputies in Paris wrote home secretly to instruct their friends to "keep a watch on persons and things; arrest suspects; seize any writings where even the word 'liberty' is pronounced." While the slaves might not have understood all the fine points of the doctrine of the rights of man, the words themselves came to have an undeniably talismanic effect. The ex-slave Toussaint-Louverture, soon to be leader of the revolt, proclaimed in August 1793 that "I want Liberty and Equality to reign in Saint Domingue. I work to bring them into existence. Unite yourselves to us, brothers [fellow insurgents], and fight with us for the same cause." Without the initial declaration, the abolition of slavery in 1794 would have remained inconceivable.[23]

In 1802, Napoleon sent a huge expeditionary force from France to capture Toussaint-Louverture and reestablish slavery in the French colonies. Transported back to France, Toussaint died in a cold prison, eulogized by William Wordsworth and celebrated by abolitionists everywhere. Wordsworth embraced Toussaint's zeal for freedom:

Though fallen thyself, never to rise again,
Live, and take comfort. Thou hast left behind
Powers that will work for thee; air, earth, and skies;

There's not a breathing of the common wind
That will forget thee; thou hast great allies;
Thy friends are exultations, agonies,
And love, and man's unconquerable mind.

Napoleon's action retarded the definitive abolition of slavery in the French colonies until 1848, when a second republic came to power. Yet he did not succeed in turning back the clock all the way. The slaves of Saint Domingue refused to accept their lot and successfully held out against Napoleon's armies until the French withdrew, leaving behind the first nation led by freed slaves, the independent state of Haiti. Of the 60,000 French, Swiss, German, and Polish soldiers sent to the island, only a few thousand returned back across the ocean. The others had fallen in ferocious combat or to yellow fever, which carried away thousands, including the commander in chief of the expeditionary forces. Even in the colonies where slavery was successfully restored, however, the taste of freedom was not forgotten. After the revolution of 1830 in France replaced the ultra-conservative monarchy, an abolitionist visited Guadeloupe and reported the reaction of the slaves to his tricolor flag, adopted by the republic in 1794. "Glorious sign of our emancipation, we salute you!" shouted fifteen or twenty slaves. "Hello, benevolent flag, which comes to announce from across the seas the triumph of our friends and the hours of our deliverance."[24]

Declaring the Rights of Women

Although the deputies could agree—under pressure—that the declaration of rights applied to "all men, without distinction of color," only a handful could bring themselves to say that it applied to women, too. Nevertheless, women's rights did come up for discussion and the deputies extended women's civil rights in important new directions. Girls gained the right to equal inheritance with their brothers, and wives won the right to divorce on the same grounds as their husbands. Divorce had not been allowed under French law before its enactment in 1792. The restored monarchy abrogated divorce in 1816, and divorce was not reinstituted until 1884, and even then it came with more restrictions than had applied in 1792. Given women's universal exclusion from political rights in the eighteenth century and for most of human history—women did not gain the right to vote in national elections anywhere in the world before the end of the nineteenth century—it is more surprising that women's rights were even discussed in the public arena than that women ultimately did not gain them.

The rights of women clearly ranked lower on the "conceivability" scale than those of other groups. The "woman question" came up periodically in Europe during the seventeenth and eighteenth centuries, especially in regard to women's education, or lack thereof, but the rights of women had not been the focus of sustained discussion in the years leading to either the American or French Revolution. In contrast to French Protestants, Jews, or even slaves, women's status had not been the subject of pamphlet wars, public essay contests, government commissions, or specially organized advocacy organizations, such as the Friends of Blacks. This neglect may have been due to the fact that women were not a persecuted minority. They were oppressed by our standards, and oppressed because of their sex, but they were not a minority and certainly no one was trying to get them to change their identity, as with Protestants or Jews. If some likened their lot to slavery, few pushed the analogy beyond the realm of metaphor. Laws limited women's rights, to be sure, but women did have some rights, unlike slaves. Women were thought to be morally, if not intellectually, dependent on their fathers and husbands, but they were not imagined as devoid of autonomy; indeed, their penchant for autonomy required constant vigilance by supposed authorities of all sorts. Nor were they voiceless, even in political affairs; demonstrations and riots over the price of bread repeatedly demonstrated that truth before and during the French Revolution.[25]

Women simply did not constitute a clearly separate and distinguishable *political* category before the Revolution. The example of Condorcet, the most outspoken male defender of the political rights of women during the Revolution, is telling. As early as 1781, he published a pamphlet calling for the abolition of slavery. In a list that included proposed reforms for peasants, Protestants, and the criminal justice system, as well as establishing free trade and inoculating for smallpox, women were not mentioned. They only became an issue for this human rights pioneer a full year after the Revolution began.[26]

Although a few women voted by proxy in the elections for the Estates-General and a small number of deputies thought that women, or at least property owning widows, might gain the vote in the future, women as such, that is as a potential rights category, appeared not at all in the discussions of the National Assembly between 1789 and 1791. The alphabetical table of the massive *Archives parlementaires* cites "women" only twice, in one case a group of Breton women requesting to take a civic oath and in the other a group of Parisian women sending an address. In contrast, the Jews came up for direct discussion by the deputies on at least seventeen different occasions. By the end of 1789, actors, executioners, Protestants, Jews, free blacks, and even poor men could be imagined as citizens by at least some substantial number of deputies. Despite this continual recalibration of the conceivability scale, equal rights for women remained unimaginable to almost everyone, men and women alike.[27]

Yet even here the logic of rights worked its way, however spasmodically. In July 1790, Condorcet shocked his readership with a startling newspaper editorial, "On the Admission of Women to the Rights of Citizenship." In it he made explicit the rationale for human rights that had been steadily developing in the second half of the eighteenth century: "the rights of men follow only from the fact that they are feeling beings, capable of acquiring moral ideas and of reasoning about these ideas." Did women not have the same characteristics? "Since women have the same qualities," he insisted, "they necessarily have equal rights." Condorcet drew the logical conclusion that his fellow revolutionaries had so much trouble deriving for themselves: "Either no individual in mankind has true rights, or all have the same ones; and whoever votes against the right of another, whatever be his religion, his color, or his sex, has from that moment abjured his own rights."

Here was the modern philosophy of human rights in its pure form, clearly articulated. The particularities of humans (other perhaps than age, children not yet being able to reason on their own) should not weigh in the balance, even of political rights. Condorcet also explained why so many women, as well as men, had accepted in unquestioning fashion the unjustifiable subordination of women. "Habit can familiarize men with the violation of their natural rights to the point that among those who have lost them no one dreams of reclaiming them or believes that he has suffered an injustice." He dared his readers to acknowledge that women had always had rights and that social custom had blinded them to this fundamental truth.[28]

In September 1791, the antislavery playwright Olympe de Gouges turned the Declaration of the Rights of Man and Citizen inside out. Her Declaration of the Rights of Woman insisted that "Woman is born free and remains equal to man in rights" (Article 1). "All citizenesses and citizens, being equal in its [the law's] eyes, should be equally admissible to all public dignities, offices, and employments, according to their ability, and with no other distinction than that of their virtues and talents" (Article 6). The inversion of the language of the official 1789 declaration hardly seems shocking to us now, but it surely did then. In England, Mary Wollstonecraft did not go as far as her French counterparts in demanding absolutely equal political rights for women, but she wrote at much greater length and with searing passion about the ways education and tradition had stunted women's minds. In *Vindication of the Rights of Woman*, published in 1792, she linked the emancipation of women to the explosion of all forms of hierarchy in society. Like de Gouges, Wollstonecraft suffered public vilification for her boldness. De Gouges's fate was even worse, for she went to the guillotine, condemned as an "impudent" counterrevolutionary and unnatural being (a "woman-man").[29]

Once the momentum got going, women's rights were not limited to the publications of a few pathbreaking individuals. Between 1791 and 1793, women set up political clubs in at least fifty provincial towns and cities as well as in Paris. Women's rights came up for debate in the clubs, in newspapers, and in pamphlets. In April 1793, during the consideration of citizenship under a proposed new constitution for the republic, one deputy argued at length in favor of equal political rights for women. His intervention showed that the idea had gained some adherents. "There is no doubt a difference," he granted, "that of the sexes . . . but I do not conceive how a sexual difference makes for one in the equality of rights. . . . Let us liberate ourselves rather from the prejudice of sex, just as we have freed ourselves from the prejudice against the color of Negroes." The deputies did not follow his lead.[30]

Instead, in October 1793, the deputies moved against women's clubs. Reacting to street fights among women over the wearing of revolutionary insignia, the Convention voted to suppress all political clubs for women on the grounds that such clubs only diverted them from their appropriate domestic duties. According to the deputy who presented the decree, women did not have the knowledge, application, devotion, or self-abnegation required for governing. They should stick with "the private functions to which women are destined by nature itself." The rationale hardly sounded new notes; what was new was the need to come out and forbid women from forming and attending political clubs. Women may have come up least and last, but their rights did eventually make the agenda, and what was said about them in the 1790s—especially in favor of rights—had an impact that has lasted down to the present.[31]

The logic of rights had pushed even women's rights out from the obscuring fog of habit, at least in France and England. In the United States, the neglect of women's rights attracted relatively little public discussion before 1792, and no American writings appeared in the revolutionary era that can be compared to those of Condorcet, Olympe de Gouges, or Mary Wollstonecraft. Before the publication of Wollstonecraft's *Vindication of the Rights of Woman* in 1792, in fact, the concept of women's rights got virtually no hearing in either England or America. Wollstonecraft herself had developed her influential notions on the subject in direct response to the French Revolution. In her first work on rights in 1790, *Vindication of the Rights of Men*, she replied to Burke's denunciations of the French rights of man. That led her to consider, in turn, the rights of woman.[32]

If we look beyond the official proclamations and decrees of male politicians, the change in expectations about women's rights is more striking. Surprisingly, for example, Wollstonecraft's *Vindication of the Rights of Woman* could be found in more private American libraries of the early republic than Paine's *Rights of Man*. Though Paine himself paid no attention to women's rights, others did. Early in the nineteenth century, debating societies, graduation addresses, and popular magazines in the United States regularly addressed the gender assumptions behind male suffrage. In France, women seized upon the new openings in publishing created by freedom of the press to write more books and pamphlets than ever before. Women's right to equal inheritance prompted countless lawsuits, as women determined to hold on to what was now rightfully theirs. Rights were not an all-or-nothing proposition, after all. New rights, even if they were not political rights, opened the way to new opportunities for women, and women took them up immediately. As the previous actions of Protestants, Jews, and free men of color had already shown, citizenship is not just something to be granted by the authorities; it is something to be grasped for oneself. One measure of moral autonomy is that capacity to argue, to insist, and, for some, to fight.[33]

After 1793, women found themselves more constrained in the official world of French politics. Yet the promise of rights had not been completely forgotten. In a long review published in 1800 of Charles Théremin's *On the Condition of Women in Republics*, the poet and playwright Constance Pipelet (later known as Constance de Salm) showed that women had not lost sight of the goals first enunciated in the early years of the Revolution:

> One can understand that [under the Ancien Régime] one did not believe it necessary to assure one half of humankind one half of the rights attached to humanity; but it would be more difficult to understand that one could have entirely neglected to recognize [the rights] of women during the last ten years, in those moments when the words equality and liberty have resounded everywhere, in those moments when philosophy, aided by experience, ceaselessly enlightens man about his true rights.

She attributed this neglect of the rights of women to the fact that the male masses easily believed that limiting or even annihilating the power of women would increase the power of men. In her review, Pipelet cited the work of Wollstonecraft on the rights of women, but she did not claim for women the right to vote or hold office.[34]

Pipelet demonstrated a subtle understanding of the tension between the revolutionary logic of rights and the continuing constraints of custom. "It is especially during the revolution . . . that women, following the example of men, have most reasoned about their true essence and have acted in consequence." If obscurity or ambiguity remained on the subject of women's rights (and Pipelet struck a very tentative tone in many of her passages), then it was because the Enlightenment had not progressed far enough; the common people and especially ordinary women remained uneducated. As women gained education, they would inevitably demonstrate their talents, for merit has no sex, Pipelet asserted. She agreed with Théremin that women should be employed as schoolteachers and be allowed to defend their "natural and inalienable rights" in the courts.

If Pipelet herself stopped short of advocating full political rights for women, she was only responding to what she saw as possible—imaginable, arguable—in her own day. But like many others, she saw that the philosophy of natural rights had an implacable logic, even if it had not yet worked itself out in the case of women, that other half of humanity. The notion of "the rights of man," like revolution itself, opened up an unpredictable space for discussion, conflict, and change. The promise of those rights can be denied, suppressed, or just remain unfulfilled, but it does not die.

5

"THE SOFT POWER OF HUMANITY"

Why Human Rights Failed,
Only to Succeed in the Long Run

WERE HUMAN RIGHTS SIMPLY "rhetorical nonsense, nonsense upon stilts," as the philosopher Jeremy Bentham claimed? The long gap in the history of human rights, from their initial formulation in the American and French Revolutions to the United Nations' Universal Declaration in 1948, has to give anyone pause. Rights did not disappear in either thought or action, but the discussions and decrees now transpired almost exclusively within specific national frameworks. The notion of constitutionally guaranteed rights of various sorts—the political rights of workers, religious minorities, and women, for example—continued to gain ground in the nineteenth and twentieth centuries, but talk of universally applicable natural rights subsided.

Workers, for instance, won rights as British, French, German, or American workers. The nineteenth-century Italian nationalist Giuseppe Mazzini captured the new focus on nation when he asked the rhetorical question: "What is a Country . . . but the place in which our individual rights are most secure?" It took two devastating world wars to shatter this confidence in the nation.[1]

Defects of the Rights of Man

Nationalism only gradually took over as the dominant framework for rights after 1815, with the fall of Napoleon and the final end of the Revolutionary era. Between 1789 and 1815, two different conceptions of authority warred with each other: the rights of man on one side and traditional hierarchical society on the other. Each side invoked the nation, though neither side made claims about ethnicity determining identity. By definition, the rights of "man" repudiated any idea that rights depended on nationality. Edmund Burke, on the other side, had tried to link hierarchical society to a certain conception of the nation, by arguing that liberty could only be guaranteed by a government rooted in a nation's history, with the emphasis on history. Rights only worked, he insisted, when they grew out of longstanding traditions and practices.

Supporters of the rights of man had denied the importance of tradition and history. Precisely because it relied on "metaphysical abstractions," the French Declaration, Burke maintained, did not have enough emotional force to compel obedience. How could those "paltry blurred shreds of paper" compare to love of God, awe of kings, duty toward magistrates, reverence of priests, and deference toward one's betters? The revolutionaries would have to use violence to stay in power, he had already concluded in 1790. When the French republicans executed the king and moved toward Terror as an acknowledged system of government, as they did in 1793 and 1794, Burke's forecast seemed to come true. The Declaration of the Rights of Man and Citizen, shelved along with the Constitution of 1791, had not prevented the suppression of dissent and wholesale execution of those perceived as enemies.

Despite Burke's strictures, many writers and politicians in Europe and the United States had enthusiastically greeted the declaration of rights in 1789. As the French Revolution turned more radical, however, public opinion began to divide. Monarchical governments, in particular, reacted strongly against the proclamation of a republic and the execution of the king. In December 1792, Thomas Paine was forced to flee to France when a British court found him guilty of sedition for attacking hereditary monarchy in the second part of his *Rights of Man*. The British government followed up with a systematic campaign of harassment and persecution of the supporters of French ideas. In 1798, only twenty-two years after the declaration of the equal rights of all men, the U.S. Congress passed the Alien and Sedition Acts to limit criticism of the American government. The new spirit of the times can be seen in the remarks made in 1797 by John Robison, a professor of natural philosophy at the University of Edinburgh. He inveighed against "that accursed maxim, which now fills every mind, of thinking continually of our rights, and anxiously demanding them from every quarter." This obsession with rights was "the greatest bane of life," according to Robison, who saw it as a prime cause of the ongoing political upheaval, even in Scotland, and of the war between France and its neighbors that now threatened to engulf all of Europe.[2]

Robison's wariness about rights paled in comparison to the attack missiles launched by counterrevolutionary royalists on the Continent. According to Louis de Bonald, an outspoken conservative, "the revolution began with the declaration of the rights of man and will only finish when the rights of God are declared." The declaration of rights, he asserted, represented the evil influence of Enlightenment philosophy and with it atheism, Protestantism, and Freemasonry, which he lumped together. The declaration encouraged people to neglect their duties and think only of their own individual desires. Since it could not serve as a break on those passions, it therefore led France straight to anarchy, terror, and social disintegration. Only a revived Catholic Church protected by a restored, legitimate monarchy could inculcate true moral principles. Under the Bourbon king reinstalled in 1815, Bonald took the lead in abrogating the revolutionary laws on divorce and reestablishing rigorous censorship before publication.[3]

Before the return of the Bourbon kings, when French republicans and later Napoleon spread the message of the French Revolution through military conquest, the rights of man became entangled with imperialist aggression. To its credit, France's influence induced the Swiss and the Dutch to abolish torture in 1798; Spain followed in 1808 when Napoleon's brother ruled as king. After Napoleon fell, however, the Swiss reintroduced torture, and the Spanish king reestablished the Inquisition, which used torture to get confessions. The French also encouraged the emancipation of the Jews wherever their armies held sway. Although returning rulers took away some of these newly gained rights in the Italian and German states, Jewish emancipation proved permanent in the Netherlands. Because Jewish emancipation was seen as French, bandits who harassed French forces in some newly conquered territories often also targeted Jews.[4]

Napoleon's contradictory interventions showed that rights need not be seen as forming a single package. He introduced religious toleration and equal civil and political rights for religious minorities wherever he ruled. Yet at home in France, he severely limited everyone's freedom of speech and basically eliminated freedom of the press. The French emperor believed that "men are not born to be free. . . . Liberty is a need felt by a small class of people whom nature has endowed with nobler minds than the mass of men. Consequently, it may be repressed with impunity. Equality, on the other hand, pleases the masses." The French did not desire true liberty, in his view; they simply aspired to rise to the top of society. They would sacrifice their political rights in order to ensure their legal equality.[5]

On the question of slavery, Napoleon proved entirely consistent. During a brief lull in the fighting in Europe in 1802, he sent military expeditions to the Caribbean colonies. Although he deliberately left his intentions vague in the beginning, so as not to provoke a general uprising by the freed slaves, the instructions given to his brother-in-law, one of the commanding generals, made his goals clear. Upon arrival the soldiers should occupy key spots and get the lay of the land. Then they should "pursue the rebels without mercy," disarm all blacks, and arrest their leaders and transport them back to France, opening the way to the restoration of slavery. Napoleon felt certain that "the prospect of a black republic is equally disturbing to the Spanish, the English, and the Americans." His plan failed in Saint Domingue, which gained its independence as Haiti, but succeeded elsewhere in the French colonies. As many as 150,000 people died in the fighting on Saint Domingue; one tenth of the population of Guadeloupe was killed or deported.[6]

Napoleon tried to create a hybrid between the rights of man and traditional hierarchical society, but in the end, both sides rejected the bastard offspring. Napoleon put too much emphasis on religious toleration, the abolition of feudalism, and equality before the law to satisfy the traditionalists and curtailed too many political freedoms to appeal to the other side. He could make peace with the Catholic Church, but he never became a legitimate ruler in the eyes of the traditionalists. For the defenders of rights, his insistence on equality before the law failed to counterbalance his revival of nobility and the creation of a hereditary empire. By the time the French emperor fell from power, he was denounced by both traditionalists and defenders of rights as a tyrant, despot, and usurper. One of Napoleon's most persistent critics, the writer Germaine de Staël, proclaimed in 1817 that his only legacy was "a few more secrets in the art of tyranny." De Staël, like all other commentators on both left and right, referred to the deposed leader only by his surname, Bonaparte, and never by his imperial first name, Napoleon.[7]

Nationalism Rushes In

The victory of the forces of order proved ephemeral in the long run, in large part thanks to developments set in motion by their nemesis, Napoleon. Over the course of the nineteenth century, nationalism overtook both sides of the revolutionary debates, transforming the discussion of rights and creating new kinds of hierarchy that ultimately threatened the traditional order. The Corsican upstart's imperialist adventures inadvertently catalyzed the forces of nationalism from Warsaw to Lima. Everywhere he went, he created new entities (the Duchy of Warsaw, the Kingdom of Italy, the Confederation of the Rhine), produced new opportunities, or provoked new animosities that would feed into national aspirations. His Duchy of Warsaw reminded Poles that there had once been a Poland, before it was gobbled up by Prussia, Austria, and Russia. Even though the new Italian and German administrations disappeared after Napoleon's fall, they had shown that national unification was thinkable. By deposing the king of Spain, the French emperor opened the door to South American independence movements in the 1810s and 1820s. Simón Bolívar, liberator of Bolivia, Panama, Colombia, Ecuador, Peru, and Venezuela, spoke the same nascent language of nationalism as his counterparts in Europe. "Our native soil," he enthused, "arouses tender feelings and delightful memories. . . . What claims on love and dedication could be greater?" National feeling offered the emotional power missing in those "paltry blurred shreds of paper" derided by Burke.[8]

In reaction to French imperialism, some German writers rejected all things French—including the rights of man—and developed a new sense of nation, one based explicitly on ethnicity. Lacking a single nation-state structure, German nationalists emphasized instead the mystique of the *Volk* or "folk," a German inner character that distinguished it from other peoples. In the views expressed at the beginning of the nineteenth century by the German nationalist Friedrich Jahn, the first signs of future troubles could already be seen. "The purer a people, the better," he wrote. The laws of nature, he maintained, worked against the mixing of races and peoples. "Sacred rights" for Jahn were those of the German people, and so exasperated was he by French influence that he exhorted his fellow Germans to stop speaking French altogether. Like all succeeding nationalists, Jahn urged the writing and study of patriotic history. Monuments, public funerals, and popular festivals should all focus on things German, not universal ideals. At the very moment when Europeans were fighting their climactic battles against Napoleon's imperial ambitions, Jahn proposed surprisingly wide boundaries for this new Germany. It should include, he asserted, Switzerland, the Low Countries, Denmark, Prussia, and Austria, and a new capital should be built for it called Teutona.[9]

Like Jahn, most early nationalists preferred a democratic form of government because it would maximize the sense of national belonging. As a consequence, traditionalists initially opposed nationalism and German or Italian unification just as much as they had opposed the rights of man. The early nationalists spoke the revolutionary language of messianic universalism, but for them the nation, rather than rights, acted as the springboard for universalism. Bolívar believed that Colombia would light the path to universal liberty and justice; Mazzini, founder of the nationalist Society of Young Italy, proclaimed that the Italians would lead a universal crusade of oppressed peoples for freedom; the poet Adam Mickiewicz thought that the Poles would show the way to universal liberation. Human rights now depended on national self-determination, and the priority necessarily went to the latter.

After 1848, the traditionalists began to accommodate nationalist demands, and nationalism moved from the left to the right of the political spectrum. The failure in 1848 of nationalist and constitutionalist revolutions in Germany, Italy, and Hungary opened the way to these changes. Nationalists interested in guaranteeing rights within the newly proposed nations showed themselves to be all too ready to reject the rights of other ethnic groups. The Germans meeting in Frankfurt drew up a new national constitution for Germany but denied any self-determination to Danes, Poles, or Czechs within their proposed borders. The Hungarians who demanded independence from Austria ignored the interests of Romanians, Slovaks, Croats, and Slovenes who made up more than half the population of Hungary. Interethnic competition doomed the 1848 revolutions and with them the link between rights and national self-determination. The national unification of Germany and Italy was accomplished in the 1850s and 1860s by means of warfare and diplomacy, and the guarantee of individual rights played hardly any role.

Once bursting with enthusiasm for securing rights through the spread of national self-determination, nationalism turned increasingly closed and defensive. The shift reflected the enormity of the task of creating nations. The idea that Europe could be neatly divided into nation-states of relatively homogeneous ethnicity and culture was belied by the linguistic map itself. Every nation state harbored linguistic and cultural minorities in the nineteenth century, even the long-established ones like Great Britain and France. When a republic was declared in France in 1870, half of the citizens could not speak French; the others spoke dialects or regional languages such as Breton, Franco-Provençal, Basque, Alsatian, Catalan, Corsican, Occitan, or in the colonies, Creole. A massive campaign of education had to be undertaken to integrate everyone into the nation. The aspiring nations faced even greater pressures because of greater ethnic heterogeneity; Count Camillo di Cavour, the prime minister of the new Kingdom of Italy, spoke Piedmontese dialect as his first language and less than 3 percent of his fellow citizens spoke standard Italian. The situation was even more chaotic in Eastern

Europe, where many different ethnic groups lived cheek by jowl. A revived Poland, for example, would include not only a substantial community of Jews but also Lithuanians, Ukrainians, Germans, and Belarusians, each with their language and traditions.

The difficulty of creating or maintaining ethnic homogeneity contributed to the growing concern with immigration worldwide. Few objected to immigration before the 1860s, but it came under fire in the receiving countries by the 1880s and 1890s. Australia tried to prevent the influx of Asians so that it might retain its English and Irish character. The United States banned immigration from China in 1882 and from all of Asia in 1917 and then set up quotas in 1924 for everyone else based on the current ethnic composition of the U.S. population. The British government passed an Aliens Act in 1905 to prevent the immigration of "undesirables," which many interpreted to mean East European Jews. Even as workers and servants began to gain equal political rights in these countries, barriers blocked those who did not share the same ethnic origins.

In this new protective atmosphere, nationalism took on a more xenophobic and racist character. Although xenophobia might target any foreign group (Chinese in the United States, Italians in France, or Poles in Germany), the last decades of the nineteenth century saw an alarming rise in anti-Semitism. Right-wing politicians in Germany, Austria, and France used newspapers, political clubs, and, in some cases, new political parties to fan hatred of Jews as enemies of the true nation. After two decades of anti-Semitic propaganda in right-wing newspapers, the German Conservative Party made anti-Semitism an official plank in its platform in 1892. At about the same time, the Dreyfus Affair wreaked havoc in French politics, creating lasting divisions between supporters and opponents of Dreyfus. The affair began in 1894 when a Jewish army officer named Alfred Dreyfus was wrongly accused of spying for Germany. When he was convicted despite mounting evidence of his innocence, the famous novelist Emile Zola published a daring front-page article accusing the French army and government of covering up the attempts to frame Dreyfus. In response to the growing tide of opinion in favor of Dreyfus, a newly formed French Anti-Semitic League fomented riots in many towns and cities that sometimes included attacks by thousands of demonstrators on Jewish properties. The League could mobilize so many people because several cities had newspapers that routinely churned out anti-Semitic diatribes. The government offered Dreyfus a pardon in 1899 and finally exonerated him in 1906. Yet anti-Semitism grew more venomous everywhere. In 1895, Karl Lueger got himself elected mayor of Vienna on an anti-Semitic program. He would become one of Hitler's heroes.

Biological Explanations for Exclusion

As nationalism became more closely entwined with ethnicity, it fed into an increasing emphasis on biological explanations for difference. Arguments for the rights of man had relied on the assumption of sameness of human nature across cultures and classes. After the French Revolution, it became increasingly difficult to simply reassert differences on the basis of tradition, custom, or history. Differences had to have a more solid foundation if men were to maintain their superiority to women, whites to blacks, or Christians to Jews. In short, if rights were to be less than universal, equal, and natural, then reasons had to be given. As a consequence, the nineteenth century witnessed an explosion in biological explanations of difference.

Ironically, then, the very notion of human rights inadvertently opened the door to more virulent forms of sexism, racism, and anti-Semitism. In effect, the sweeping claims about the natural equality of all mankind called forth equally global assertions about natural difference, producing a new kind of opponent to human rights, more powerful and sinister even than the traditionalist ones. The new forms of racism, anti-Semitism, and sexism offered biological explanations for the naturalness of human difference. In the new racism, Jews were not just Christ-killers; their inherent racial inferiority threatened to stain the purity of whites through intermarriage. Blacks were no longer inferior because they were slaves; even as the abolition of slavery progressed around the globe, racism became more, not less, poisonous. Women were not simply less reasonable than men because they were less educated; their biology destined them to the private, domestic life and made them entirely unsuitable for politics, business, or the professions. In these new biological doctrines, education or changes in environment could never change the inherent hierarchical structures in human nature.

Sexism was the least politically organized, least intellectually systematic, and least emotionally negative of the new biological doctrines. After all, no nation could reproduce itself without mothers, so while it might be conceivable to argue that African-American slaves should be sent back to Africa or that Jews should be forbidden to reside in a particular locale, it was not possible to exclude women altogether. Therefore, they could be allowed positive qualities that might be important in the private sphere. Moreover, since women clearly differed from men biologically (though just how much still remains a subject of debate), few dismissed out of hand the biological arguments about the difference between the sexes, which had a much longer history than the biological arguments about race. Yet the French Revolution had shown that even sexual difference, or at least its political relevance, could be questioned. With the emergence of explicit arguments for the political equality of women, the biological argument for women's inferiority shifted. Females no longer occupied a lower rung on the same biological ladder as males, making them biologically similar to males, even if inferior. Females were now increasingly cast as altogether different biologically; they became the "opposite sex."[10]

The precise timing and even nature of this shift in thinking about women is not easy to pin down, but the period of the French Revolution seems to be critical. The French revolutionaries had called upon largely traditional arguments for women's difference when they forbade women to meet in political clubs in 1793. "In general, women are not capable of elevated thoughts and serious meditations," proclaimed the government spokesman. In the following years, however, medical men in France worked hard to give these vague ideas a more biological basis. The leading French physiologist of the 1790s and early 1800s, Pierre Cabanis, argued that women had weaker muscular fibers and more delicate cerebral matter, thus making them unfit for public careers, but their consequent volatile sensibility suited them for the roles of wife, mother, and nurse. Such thinking helped establish a new tradition in which women seemed preordained to fulfill themselves within the confines of domesticity or a separate female sphere.[11]

In his influential tract *The Subjection of Women* (1869), the English philosopher John Stuart Mill questioned the very existence of these biological differences. He insisted that we cannot know how men and women differ in nature because we only see them in their current social roles. "What is now called the nature of women," he argued, "is an eminently artificial thing." Mill linked the reform of women's status to overall social and economic progress. The legal subordination of women, he asserted, "is wrong itself" and "ought to be replaced by a principle of perfect equality, admitting no power or privilege on the one side, nor disability on the other." No equivalent of anti-Semitic leagues or parties was needed, however, to keep the biological argument going strong. In a landmark legal case before the U.S. Supreme Court in 1908, Justice Louis Brandeis trotted out the same old horses when explaining why sex could be a legal basis for classification. The "physical organization of woman," her maternal functions, the rearing of children, and the maintenance of the home put women into a separate and different category. "Feminism" had come into common usage as a term in the 1890s, and resistance to its demands was fierce. Women only got the right to vote in Australia in 1902, in the United States in 1920, in Great Britain in 1928, and in France in 1944.[12]

Like sexism, racism and anti-Semitism took on new forms after the French Revolution. Proponents of the rights of man, though still harboring many negative stereotypes about Jews and blacks themselves, no longer accepted the existence of prejudice as sufficient grounds for an argument. That the rights of Jews in France had always been restricted proved only that habit and custom exercised great power, not that such restrictions were warranted by reason. Similarly, for abolitionists slavery did not demonstrate the inferiority of black Africans; it merely revealed the rapacity of white slavers and planters. Those who rejected the idea of equal rights for Jews or blacks therefore needed a doctrine—a cogently reasoned case—to buttress their position, especially after Jews had gained rights and slavery had been abolished in the British and French colonies, in 1833 and 1848, respectively. Over the course of the nineteenth century, opponents of rights for Jews and blacks increasingly turned to science, or what passed as science, to find that doctrine.

The science of race can be traced back to the end of the eighteenth century and the efforts to classify the peoples of the world. Two strands woven in the eighteenth century twined together in the nineteenth: first, the argument that history had seen the successive development of peoples toward civilization and that whites were the most advanced of the lot; and second, the idea that permanent inherited characteristics divided people by race. Racism, as a systematic doctrine, depended on the conjunction of the two. Eighteenth-century thinkers assumed that all peoples would eventually achieve civilization, whereas nineteenth-century racial theorists believed that only certain races could do so because of their inherent biological qualities. Elements of this conjunction can be found in scientists of the early nineteenth century, such as the French naturalist Georges Cuvier, who wrote in 1817 that "certain intrinsic causes" arrested the development of the Mongolian and Negro races. Only after midcentury, however, did these ideas appear in their fully articulated form.[13]

The epitome of the genre can be found in Arthur de Gobineau's *Essay on the Inequality of the Human Races* (1853–55). Using a hodgepodge of arguments derived from archeology, ethnology, linguistics, and history, the French diplomat and man of letters argued that a biologically based hierarchy of races determined the history of mankind. At the bottom sat the animalistic, unintellectual, and intensely sensual dark-skinned races; next up on the ladder came the apathetic, mediocre, but practical yellow ones; and at the top stood the persevering, intellectually energetic and adventurous white peoples, who balanced "an extraordinary instinct for order" with "a pronounced taste for liberty." Within the white race, the Aryan branch reigned supreme. "Everything great, noble, and fruitful in the works of man on this earth, in science, art and civilization" derives from the Aryans, concluded Gobineau. Migrating from their initial home in Central Asia, the Aryans had provided the original stock for the Indian, Egyptian, Chinese, Roman, European, and even, through colonization, the Aztec and Incan civilizations.[14]

Racial miscegenation explained both the rise and fall of civilizations, according to Gobineau. "The ethnic question dominates all the other problems of history and holds its key," he wrote. Unlike some of his later followers, however, Gobineau thought that the Aryans had already lost their edge through intermarriage and that, though it sickened him, egalitarianism and democracy would eventually triumph, signaling the end of civilization itself. Although Gobineau's fanciful notions got little traction in France, Emperor Wilhelm I of Germany (who ruled from 1861 to 1888) found them so congenial that he conferred honorary citizenship on the Frenchman. They were also taken up by the German composer Richard Wagner and then by Wagner's son-in-law, the English writer and Germanophile Houston Stewart Chamberlain. Through Chamberlain's influence, Gobineau's Aryans became a central element of Hitler's racial ideology.[15]

Gobineau gave a secular and seemingly systematic cast to ideas already in circulation in much of the Western world. In 1850, for example, the Scottish anatomist Robert Knox published *The Races of Men*, in which he argued that "race, or hereditary descent, is everything; it stamps the man." The next year, the head of the Philadelphia typesetters union, John Campbell, offered his *Negro Mania, Being an Examination of the*

Falsely Assumed Equality of the Races of Mankind. Racism was not confined to the southern United States. Campbell cited Cuvier and Knox among others to insist on the savagery and barbarism of Negroes and to argue against any possibility of equality between whites and blacks. Since Gobineau himself had criticized the treatment of African slaves in the United States, his American translators had to excise those sections in order to make the work more palatable to pro-slavery southerners when it was published in English in 1856. The prospect of the abolition of slavery (which only became official in the United States in 1865) thus only heightened the interest in racial science.[16]

As the titles of Gobineau's and Campbell's works demonstrate, the common feature in most racialist thinking was a visceral reaction against the notion of equality. Gobineau confessed to Tocqueville the disgust provoked in him by the "dirty overalls [workers]" who had participated in the revolution of 1848 in France. For his part, Campbell felt revulsion about sharing a political platform with men of color. What had once defined an aristocratic rejection of modern society—having to mix with the inferior orders—now took on a racial meaning. The advent of mass politics in the last half of the nineteenth century may have gradually eroded the sense of class difference (or given the semblance of doing so), but it did not eliminate difference altogether. Difference shifted from the register of class to that of race and sex. The establishment of universal male suffrage combined with the abolition of slavery and the beginning of mass immigration to make equality much more concrete and threatening.[17]

Imperialism further aggravated these developments. Even as the European powers abolished slavery in their plantation colonies, they extended their dominion in Africa and Asia. The French invaded Algeria in 1830 and ultimately incorporated it into France. The British annexed Singapore in 1819 and New Zealand in 1840 and relentlessly increased their control over India. By 1914, Africa had been split up between France, Great Britain, Germany, Italy, Portugal, Belgium, and Spain. Hardly any African states emerged unscathed. Although in some cases foreign rule actually made countries more "backward," by destroying local industries in favor of importations from the imperial center, Europeans generally drew only one lesson from their conquests: they had the right—and the duty—to "civilize" the more backward, barbarian places they governed.

Not all supporters of these imperial ventures promoted explicit racism. John Stuart Mill, who worked for many years for the British East India Company, the effective administrator of British rule in India until 1858, rejected biological explanations of difference. Still, even he believed that the native states of India were "savage," with "little or no law," and living in a condition "very little above the highest of the beasts." Mill notwithstanding, European imperialism and racial science developed a symbiotic relationship: the imperialism of the "conquering races" made racial claims more credible, and racial science helped justify imperialism. In 1861, the British explorer Richard Burton took the soon to be standard line. The African, he said, "partakes largely of the worst characteristics of the lower Oriental types—stagnation of mind, indolence of body, moral deficiency, superstition, and childish passion." After the 1870s, these attitudes found a mass audience in new cheaply produced newspapers, illustrated weeklies, and ethnographic exhibitions. Even in Algeria, considered part and parcel of France after 1848, natives only gained rights over the very long term. In 1865 a government decree declared them subjects, not citizens, whereas in 1870 the French state made Algerian Jews naturalized citizens.

Muslim males only gained equal political rights in 1947. The "civilizing mission" was not a short-term project.[18]

Gobineau had not considered the Jews a special case in his elaboration of racial science, but his followers did. In his *Foundations of the Nineteenth Century*, published in German in 1899, Houston Stewart Chamberlain combined Gobineau's ideas about race and German mysticism about the *Volk* with a vitriolic attack on the Jews, "this alien people" that has enslaved "our governments, our law, our science, our commerce, our literature, our art." Chamberlain offered only one new argument, but it had a direct influence on Hitler: the Aryans and the Jews alone of all peoples had maintained their racial purity, which meant that now they must struggle to the death with each other. In other respects, Chamberlain packaged together a variety of increasingly common ideas.[19]

Although modern anti-Semitism built on the negative Christian stereotypes about Jews that had been circulating for centuries, the doctrine took on new qualities after the 1870s. Unlike blacks, Jews no longer represented an inferior stage of historical development, as they had, for instance, in the eighteenth century. Instead, they stood for the threats of modernity itself: excessive materialism, emancipation of minority groups and their participation in politics, and the "degenerate," "rootless" cosmopolitanism of urban life. Newspaper cartoons depicted Jews as greedy, duplicitous, and lecherous; journalists and pamphleteers wrote of Jewish control of world capital and conspiratorial manipulation of parliamentary parties. (Figure 11) One American cartoon from 1894, less malevolent than many of its European counterparts, shows the continents of the world encircled by the tentacles of an octopus sitting at the site of the British Isles. The octopus is labeled ROTHSCHILD, after the rich

FIGURE 11. *"The French Revolution: Before and Today"* Caran d'Ache in *Psst . . . !,* 1898.

Caran d'Ache was the pseudonym of Emmanuel Poiré, a French political cartoonist who published anti-Semitic caricatures during the Dreyfus Affair in France. This one plays on a common image from the French Revolution of 1789, showing the peasant weighed down by a noble (because nobles were exempt from some taxes). In modern times, the peasant has to carry even more burdens; on his shoulders are a republican politician, a Freemason, and on top, a Jewish financier. Caran d'Ache also published several images ridiculing Zola. From *Psst . . . !,* no. 37, October 15, 1898.

and powerful Jewish family. These modern efforts at defamation got added fuel from *The Protocols of the Elders of Zion*, a fraudulent document purporting to reveal a Jewish conspiracy to set up a supergovernment that would control the whole world. First published in Russia in 1903, exposed as a forgery in 1921, the *Protocols* were nonetheless repeatedly reprinted by the Nazis in Germany and are to this day taught as fact in the schools in some Arab countries. The new anti-Semitism thus combined traditional and modern elements: the Jews should be excluded from rights and even expelled from the nation because they were both too different and too powerful.

Socialism and Communism

Nationalism was not the only new mass movement in the nineteenth century. Like nationalism, socialism and communism took shape in explicit reaction to the perceived limitations of constitutionally framed individual rights. Whereas early nationalists wanted rights for all peoples, rather than just for those with already established states, Socialists and Communists wanted to ensure that the lower classes would enjoy social and economic equality rather than just equal political rights. Yet even as they drew attention to rights that had been shortchanged by the proponents of the rights of man, Socialist and Communist organizations inevitably downgraded the importance of rights as a goal. Marx's own view was clear-cut: political emancipation could be achieved through legal equality within bourgeois society, but true human emancipation required the destruction of bourgeois society and its constitutional protections of private property. Socialists and Communists nonetheless raised two enduring questions about rights: were political rights enough, and could the individual's right to the protection of private property co-exist with society's need to foster the well-being of its less fortunate members?

Just as nationalism had gone through two phases in the nineteenth century, moving from early enthusiasm about self-determination to a more defensive protectionism about ethnic identity, so too socialism evolved over time. It moved from an early emphasis on rebuilding society with peaceful but non-political means to a sharp division between those favoring parliamentary politics and those advocating the violent overthrow of governments. During the first half of the nineteenth century, when trade unions were illegal in most countries and workers did not have the right to vote, Socialists concentrated on revolutionizing the new social relations created by industrialization. They could hardly hope to win elections when workers could not vote, which remained true until at least the 1870s. Instead, Socialist pioneers set up model factories, producers' and consumers' cooperatives, and experimental communities to overcome conflict and alienation between social groups. They wanted to enable the workers and the poor to benefit from the new industrial order, to "socialize" industry and replace competition with cooperation.

Many of these early Socialists shared a distrust of the "rights of man." The leading French Socialist of the 1820s and 1830s, Charles Fourier, argued that constitutions and talk of inalienable rights were a sham. What can the "imprescriptible rights of the citizen" possibly mean, when the indigent man "has neither the liberty to work" nor the authority to demand employment? The right to work trumped all other rights, in his view. Like Fourier, many of the early Socialists cited the failure to grant rights to women as a sign of the bankruptcy of the previous rights doctrines. Could women ever achieve liberation without the abolition of private property and of legal codes upholding patriarchy?[20]

Two factors altered the trajectory of socialism in the second half of the nineteenth century: the advent of universal male suffrage and the rise of communism ("Communist" first appeared as a term in 1840). Socialists and Communists then split between those who aimed to establish a parliamentary political movement with parties and campaigns for office and those, like the Bolsheviks in Russia, who insisted that only a dictatorship of the proletariat and total revolution would transform social conditions. The former believed that the gradual establishment of voting for all men opened the prospect that workers might achieve their goals within parliamentary politics. The British Labour Party, for example, was formed in 1900 out of a variety of preexisting unions, parties, and clubs to promote the interests and election of workers. On the other hand, the Russian Revolution of 1917 encouraged Communists everywhere to believe that total social and economic transformation lay just over the horizon and that participation in parliamentary politics only siphoned off energies needed for other kinds of struggle.

As might be expected, the two branches also differed in their view of rights. Socialists and Communists who embraced the political process also espoused the cause of rights. One of the founders of the French Socialist Party, Jean Jaurès, argued that a Socialist state "only retains its legitimacy to the extent that it secures individual rights." He supported Dreyfus, universal male suffrage, and the separation of church and state, in short, equal political rights for all men as well as improvement in the lives of workers. Jaurès considered the Declaration of the

Rights of Man and Citizen a document of universal significance. Those on the other side followed Marx more closely in arguing, as did one French Socialist opponent of Jaurès, that the bourgeois state could only be "an instrument of conservatism and social oppression."[21]

Karl Marx himself had only discussed the rights of man at any length in his youth. In his essay "On the Jewish Question," published in 1843, five years before *The Communist Manifesto*, Marx condemned the very foundations of the Declaration of the Rights of Man and Citizen. "None of the supposed rights of man," he complained, "go beyond the egoistic man." So-called liberty only regarded man as an isolated being, not as a part of a class or community. The right of property only guaranteed the right to pursue one's own self-interest with no regard for others. The rights of man guaranteed religious freedom when what men needed was freedom from religion; they confirmed the right to own property when what was needed was freedom from property; they included the right to engage in business when what was needed was liberation from business. Marx particularly disliked the political emphasis in the rights of man. Political rights were all about means, he thought, not ends. "Political man" was "abstract, artificial," not "authentic." Man could only recover his authenticity by recognizing that human emancipation could not be achieved through politics; it required a revolution that focused on social relations and the abolition of private property.[22]

These views and later variations on them exercised influence in the Socialist and Communist movement for generations. The Bolsheviks proclaimed a Declaration of Rights of the Working and Exploited People in 1918, but it included not one political or legal right. Its aim was to "abolish all exploitation of man by man, to completely eliminate the division of society into classes, to mercilessly crush the resistance of the exploiters, [and] to establish a socialist organization of society." Lenin himself quoted Marx in arguing against any emphasis on individual rights. The notion of an equal right, Lenin affirmed, is in itself a violation of equality and an injustice because it is based on "bourgeois law." So-called equal rights protect private property and therefore perpetuate exploitation of the workers. Joseph Stalin issued a new constitution in 1936 that claimed to guarantee freedom of speech, of the press, and of religion, but his government did not hesitate to dispatch hundreds of thousands of class enemies, dissidents, and even fellow party members to prison camps or immediate execution.[23]

The World Wars and the Search for New Solutions

Even as the Bolsheviks began establishing their dictatorship of the proletariat in Russia, the astronomical death counts of World War I were prompting the leaders of the soon to be victorious Allies to find a new mechanism for ensuring peace. When the Bolsheviks signed a peace treaty with the Germans in March 1918, Russia had lost nearly 2 million men. By the time the war ended on the western front in November 1918, as many as 14 million people had died, most of them soldiers. Three quarters of the men mobilized to fight in Russia and France ended up either wounded or dead. In 1919, the diplomats who drew up the peace accords set up a League of Nations to maintain peace, oversee disarmament, arbitrate disputes between nations, and guarantee rights for national minorities, women, and children. The League failed despite some noble efforts. The U.S. Senate refused to ratify American participation; Germany and Russia were initially denied membership; and while promoting national self-determination in Europe, the League administered the former German colonies and territories of the now defunct Ottoman Empire through a system of "mandates" justified once again by European advancement over other peoples. Moreover, the League proved powerless to stop the rise of fascism in Italy and Nazism in Germany and therefore could not prevent the outbreak of World War II.

World War II set a new benchmark of barbarity with its almost incomprehensible 60 million deaths. Moreover, the majority of those killed this time were civilians, and 6 million of them were Jews killed only because they were Jews. The mayhem left millions of refugees at the war's end, many of them barely able to imagine a future and living in Displaced Persons camps. Yet others were forced to resettle for ethnic reasons (2.5 million Germans, for example, were expelled from Czechoslovakia in 1946). All of the powers involved in the war targeted civilians at one time or another; but as the war ended, revelations about the scale of the horrors deliberately perpetrated by the Germans shocked the public. Photographs taken at the liberation of the Nazi death camps showed the appalling consequences of anti-Semitism that had been justified by talk of Aryan racial supremacy and nationalist purification. The Nuremberg Trials of 1945–46 not only brought such atrocities to wide public attention but also established the precedent that rulers, officials, and military personnel could be punished for crimes "against humanity."

Even before the war ended, the Allies—in particular the United States, the Soviet Union, and Great Britain—determined to improve on the League of Nations. A conference held at San

Francisco in the spring of 1945 set up the basic structure for a new international body, the United Nations. It would have a Security Council dominated by the great powers, a General Assembly with delegates from all member countries, and a Secretariat headed by a secretary-general to act as an executive. The meeting also provided for an International Court of Justice at The Hague in the Netherlands to replace a similar court established by the League of Nations in 1921. Fifty-one countries signed the United Nations Charter as founding members on June 26, 1945.

Despite the emerging evidence of Nazi crimes against Jews, Gypsies, Slavs, and others, the diplomats meeting in San Francisco had to be prodded and pushed to put human rights on the agenda. In 1944, Great Britain and the Soviet Union had both rejected proposals to include human rights in the charter of the United Nations. Britain feared the encouragement such an action might afford to independence movements in its colonies, and the Soviet Union wanted no interference in its now expanding sphere of influence. In addition, the United States had initially opposed China's suggestion that the charter include a statement on the equality of all races.

Pressure came from two different directions. Many small and medium-size states in Latin America and Asia urged more attention to human rights, in part because they resented the high-handed domination of the great powers over the proceedings. In addition, a multitude of religious, labor, women's, and civic organizations, most of them based in the United States, directly lobbied the conference delegates. Urgent face-to-face pleas from representatives of the American Jewish Committee, the Joint Committee for Religious Liberty, the Congress of Industrial Organizations (CIO), and the National Association for the Advancement of Colored People (NAACP) helped change the minds of officials in the U.S. State Department, who agreed to put human rights in the United Nations Charter. The Soviet Union and Great Britain gave their consent because the charter also guaranteed that the United Nations would never intervene in a country's domestic affairs.[24]

The commitment to human rights was still far from assured. The United Nations Charter of 1945 emphasized international security issues and devoted only a few lines to "universal respect for, and observance of, human rights and fundamental freedoms for all without distinction as to race, sex, language, or religion." But it did set up a Human Rights Commission, which decided that its first task must be the drafting of a bill of human rights. As head of the commission, Eleanor Roosevelt played a central role in getting a declaration drafted and then shepherding it through the complex approval process. A forty-year-old law professor at McGill University in Canada, John Humphrey, prepared a preliminary draft. It then had to be revised by the full commission, circulated to all member states, then reviewed by the Economic and Social Council, and, if approved, sent on to the General Assembly, where it had first to be considered by the Third Committee on Social, Humanitarian, and Cultural Affairs. The Third Committee had delegates from every member state, and as the draft was discussed, the Soviet Union proposed amendments to nearly every article. Eighty-three meetings (of just the Third Committee) and nearly 170 amendments later, a draft was sanctioned for a vote. Finally, on December 10, 1948, the General Assembly approved the Universal Declaration of Human Rights. Forty-eight countries voted in favor, eight abstained, including six Soviet bloc countries, and none opposed.[25]

Like its eighteenth-century predecessors, the Universal Declaration explained in a preamble why such a formal statement had become necessary. "Disregard and contempt for human rights have resulted in barbarous acts which have outraged the conscience of mankind," it asserted. The variation on the language of the original French Declaration of 1789 is telling. In 1789, the French had insisted that "ignorance, neglect or contempt of the rights of man are the sole causes of public misfortunes and governmental corruption." "Ignorance" and even simple "neglect" were no longer possible. By 1948 everyone knew, presumably, what human rights meant. Moreover, the 1789 expression "public misfortunes" hardly captured the magnitude of the events recently experienced. Willful disregard and contempt for human rights had produced acts of almost unimaginable brutality.

The Universal Declaration did not simply reaffirm the eighteenth-century notions of individual rights such as equality before the law, freedom of speech, freedom of religion, the right to participate in government, protection of private property, and the rejection of torture and cruel punishment (see Appendix). It also expressly prohibited slavery and provided for universal and equal suffrage by secret ballot. In addition, it called for freedom of movement, the right to a nationality, the right to marry, and more controversially, the right to social security; the right to work, with equal pay for equal work at a life-sustaining wage; the right to rest and leisure; and the right to education, which should be free at the elementary levels. At a time of hardening lines of conflict in the Cold War, the Universal Declaration expressed a set of aspirations rather than a readily attainable reality. It outlined a set of moral obligations for the world community, but it had no mechanism for enforcement. If it had included a mechanism for enforcement, it would never have passed. Yet, for all its shortcomings, the document would have effects not unlike those of its eighteenth-century predecessors. For more than fifty years, it has set the standard for international discussion and action on human rights.

The Universal Declaration crystallized 150 years of struggle for rights. Throughout the nineteenth and early twentieth centuries, benevolent societies had kept the flame of universal human rights burning as nations turned in upon themselves. Prime among these organizations were the Quaker-inspired societies founded to combat the slave trade and slavery. The British Society for the Abolition of the Slave Trade, set up in 1787, distributed abolitionist literature and images and organized mass petition campaigns directed at Parliament. Its leaders developed close ties with abolitionists in the United States, France, and the Caribbean. When in 1807 Parliament passed a bill to end British participation in the slave trade, the abolitionists renamed their group the Anti-Slavery Society and turned to organizing mass petition campaigns to get Parliament to abolish slavery itself, which it finally did in 1833. The British and Foreign Anti-Slavery Society then took up the baton and agitated for the end of slavery elsewhere, especially in the United States.

On the suggestion of American abolitionists, the British society organized a world antislavery convention in London in 1840 to coordinate the international fight against slavery. Although the delegates refused to allow female abolitionists to participate in any formal way, and thus helped precipitate the women's suffrage movement, they did boost the international anti-slavery cause with the development of new international contacts, information about slave conditions, and resolutions that denounced slavery "as a sin against God" and condemned those churches that supported it, especially in the southern United

States. Even though the "world" convention was dominated by the British and Americans, it set the mold for future international campaigns for women's suffrage, protection of child labor, workers' rights, and a host of other issues, some rights related, and others, such as temperance, not.[26]

During the 1950s and 1960s, the cause of international human rights took a back seat to anticolonial and independence struggles. At the conclusion of World War I, President Woodrow Wilson had famously insisted that a lasting peace must rest on the principle of national self-determination. "Every people," he insisted, "has a right to choose the sovereignty under which they shall live." He had in mind the Poles, Czechs, and Serbs—not the Africans—and he and his Allies granted independence to Poland, Czechoslovakia, and Yugoslavia because they saw themselves as having the right to dispose of the territories previously controlled by the defeated powers. Great Britain agreed to include national self-determination in the Atlantic Charter of 1941 laying out the joint British-U.S. principles for fighting the war, but Winston Churchill insisted that this applied only to Europe and not to Britain's own colonies. African intellectuals disagreed and made it part of their growing campaign for independence. Although the United Nations failed to take a strong stand on decolonization in its first years, by 1952 it had agreed to make self-determination an official part of its program. Most African states regained their independence, either peacefully or by force, in the 1960s. Although they sometimes incorporated into their constitutions the rights enumerated, for example, in the European Convention for the Protection of Human Rights and Fundamental Freedoms of 1950, the legal guarantee of rights frequently fell victim to the vagaries of international and intertribal politics.[27]

In the decades after 1948, an international consensus about the importance of defending human rights took shape by fits and starts. The Universal Declaration initiated the process rather than representing its culmination. Nowhere was the progress of human rights more apparent than among Communists, who had long resisted this call. Beginning in the 1970s, West European Communist parties returned to a position much like that laid out by Jaurès in France at the turn of the century. They replaced "the dictatorship of the proletariat" in their official platforms with the advancement of democracy and explicitly endorsed human rights. At the end of the 1980s, the Soviet bloc began moving in the same direction. Communist Party general secretary Mikhail Gorbachev proposed to the 1988 Communist Party Congress in Moscow that the Soviet Union should henceforth be a state under the rule of law with "maximum protection for the rights and freedom of the Soviet individual." In that same year, a human rights department was established for the first time in a Soviet law school. A certain convergence had taken place. The Universal Declaration of 1948 included social and economic rights—the right to social security, the right to work, the right of education, for instance—and by the 1980s most Socialist and Communist parties had given up their previous hostility to political and civil rights.[28]

Non-governmental organizations (now called NGOs) never disappeared, but they gained more international influence beginning in the 1980s, in large part due to the spread of globalization itself. NGOs such as Amnesty International (founded 1961), Anti-Slavery International (a continuation of the Anti-Slavery Society), Human Rights Watch (founded 1978), and Doctors without Borders (founded 1971), not to mention countless local groups whose activities are unknown outside of their locales, have provided critical support for human rights in the last several decades. These NGOs frequently brought more pressure to bear on offending governments and did more to ameliorate famine, disease, and brutal treatment of dissidents and minorities than the United Nations itself, but almost all of them based their programs on the rights articulated in one or another part of the Universal Declaration.[29]

Needless to say, human rights are still easier to endorse than to enforce. The steady stream of international conferences and conventions against genocide, slavery, the use of torture, and racism, and for the protection of women, children, and minorities shows that human rights remain in need of rescue. The United Nations adopted a Supplementary Convention on the Abolition of Slavery, the Slave Trade, and Institutions and Practices Similar to Slavery in 1956, and yet it is estimated that there are 27 million slaves in the world today. It approved the Convention Against Torture and Other Cruel, Inhuman or Degrading Treatment or Punishment in 1984 because torture had not disappeared when its judicial forms were abolished in the eighteenth century. Rather than being employed in a legally sanctioned setting, torture moved to the backrooms of the secret and not so secret police and military forces of modern states. The Nazis explicitly authorized the use of "the third degree" against Communists, Jehovah's Witnesses, saboteurs, terrorists, dissidents, "antisocial elements," and "Polish or Soviet vagabonds." The categories are no longer exactly the same, but the practice endures. South Africa, the French in Algeria, Chile, Greece, Argentina, Iraq, the Americans at Abu Ghraib—the list never ends. The hope of stopping "barbarous acts" has not yet been fulfilled.[30]

The Limits of Empathy

What are we to conclude from the resurgence of torture and ethnic cleansing, the continuing use of rape as a weapon of war and
enduring oppression of women, the growing sexual traffic in
children and women, and the remaining practices of slavery?
Have human rights failed us by proving inadequate to the task?
A paradox of distance and closeness is at work in modern times.
On the one hand, the spread of literacy and the development of
novels, newspapers, radio, films, television, and the Internet
have made it possible for more and more people to empathize
with those who live far away and in very different circumstances. Pictures of starving children in Bangladesh or accounts
of thousands of murdered men and boys in Srebrenica, Bosnia,
can mobilize millions of people to send money, goods, and sometimes themselves to help people in other places or to urge their
governments or international organizations to intervene. On the
other hand, firsthand accounts tell how neighbors in Rwanda
killed each other over ethnicity and did so with furious brutality. This close-up violence is far from exceptional or recent;
Jews, Christians, and Muslims have long tried to explain why
the biblical Cain, son of Adam and Eve, killed his brother Abel.
As the years have passed since the Nazi atrocities, careful
research has shown that ordinary human beings, without psychological abnormalities or passionate political or religious
convictions, could be induced in the "right" circumstances to
undertake what they knew to be mass murder at close quarters.
The torturers in Algeria, Argentina, and Abu Ghraib all began as
ordinary soldiers, too. The torturers and murderers are like us,
and they often inflict pain on people right in front of them.[31]

Thus, while modern forms of communication have

expanded the means of empathizing with others, they have not been able to ensure that humans will act on the basis of that fellow feeling. Ambivalence about the power of empathy can be found from the mid-eighteenth century onward, and it was expressed even by those who undertook to explain its operation. In his *Theory of Moral Sentiments*, Adam Smith considers the reaction of "a man of humanity in Europe" who hears of an earthquake in China that kills hundreds of millions of people. He will say all the right things, Smith predicts, and go on with his business as if nothing had happened. If, in contrast, he knew he would lose his little finger the next day, he would toss and turn all night. Would he then be willing to sacrifice the hundreds of millions of Chinese in exchange for his little finger? No, he would not, Smith claims. But what makes a person resist this bargain? "It is not the soft power of humanity," Smith insists, that enables us to counteract self-interest. It has to be a stronger power, that of conscience: "It is reason, principle, conscience, the inhabitant of the breast, the man within, the great judge and arbiter of our conduct."[32]

Smith's own list from 1759—reason, principle, conscience, the man within—captures an important element in the current state of debate on empathy today. What is strong enough to motivate us to act on our fellow feeling? The heterogeneity of Smith's list indicates that he had some trouble answering this question himself; is "reason" synonymous with "the inhabitant of the breast"? Smith seemed to believe, as do many human rights activists today, that a combination of rational invocations of rights principles and emotional appeals to fellow feeling can make empathy morally effective. Critics then and many critics now would respond that some sense of higher religious duty needs to be activated in order to make empathy work. In their view, humans cannot overcome their inner propensity to apathy or evil on their own. A former president of the American Bar Association gave expression to this common view. "When human beings are not visualized in God's image," he said, "then their basic rights may well lose their metaphysical *raison d'être*." The idea of human commonality is not sufficient on its own.[33]

Adam Smith focuses on one question when there are really two. Smith considers empathy for those far away to be in the same class with feelings for those close to us, even though he recognizes that what confronts us directly is far more motivating than the problems faced by those far away. The two questions, then, are: what can motivate us to act on our feelings for those far away, and what makes fellow feeling break down so much that we can torture, maim, or even kill those closest to us? Distance and closeness, positive feelings and negative ones, all have to enter into the equation.

From the middle of the eighteenth century onward, and precisely because of the emergence of a notion of human rights, these tensions became ever more deadly. Late eighteenth-century campaigners against slavery, legal torture, and cruel punishment all highlighted cruelty in their emotionally wrenching narratives. They intended to provoke revulsion, but the arousal of sensations through reading and viewing explicit engravings of suffering could not always be carefully channeled. Similarly, the novel that drew intense attention to the travails of ordinary girls took on other, more sinister forms by the end of the eighteenth century. The Gothic novel, exemplified by Matthew Lewis's *The Monk* (1796), featured scenes of incest, rape, torture, and murder, and those sensationalist scenes increasingly seemed to be the point of the exercise rather than the study of interior feelings or moral outcomes. The marquis de

Sade took the Gothic novel a step further into an explicit pornography of pain, deliberately reducing to their sexual core the long, drawn-out seduction scenes of earlier novels like Richardson's *Clarissa*. Sade aimed to reveal the hidden meanings of previous novels: sex, domination, pain, and power rather than love, empathy, and benevolence. "Natural right" for him meant only the right to grab as much power as you could and enjoy wielding it over others. It is no accident that Sade wrote almost all of his novels in the 1790s during the French Revolution.[34]

The notion of human rights thus brought in its train a whole succession of evil twins. The call for universal, equal, and natural rights stimulated the growth of new and sometimes fanatical ideologies of difference. New modes for gaining empathetic understanding opened the way to a sensationalism of violence. The effort to dislodge cruelty from its legal, judicial, and religious moorings made it more accessible as an everyday tool of domination and dehumanization. The utterly dehumanizing crimes of the twentieth century only became conceivable once everyone could claim to be an equal member of the human family. Recognition of these dualities is essential for the future of human rights. Empathy has not been exhausted, as some have claimed. It has become a more powerful force for good than ever before. But the countervailing effect of violence, pain, and domination is also greater than ever before.[35]

Human rights are our only commonly shared bulwark against those evils. We must still continually improve on the eighteenth-century version of human rights, ensuring that the "Human" in the Universal Declaration of Human Rights leaves none of the ambiguities of "man" in the "rights of man." The cascade of rights continues, though always with great conflict about how it should flow: the right of a woman to choose versus the right of a fetus to live, the right to die with dignity versus the absolute right to life, the rights of the disabled, the rights of homosexuals, the rights of children, the rights of animals—the arguments have not and will not end. The eighteenth-century campaigners for the rights of man could condemn their opponents as unfeeling traditionalists, interested only in maintaining a social order predicated on inequality, particularity, and historical custom rather than equality, universality, and natural rights. But we no longer have the luxury of simple rejection of an older view. At the other end of the struggle for human rights, when belief in them has become more widespread, we have to face the world that has been wrought by that endeavor. We have to figure out what to do with the torturers and the murderers, how to prevent their emergence in the future, all the while recognizing that they are us. We can neither tolerate nor dehumanize them.

The human rights framework, with its international bodies, international courts, and international conventions, might be exasperating in its slowness to respond or repeated inability to achieve its ultimate goals, but there is no better structure available for confronting these issues. Courts and governmental organizations, no matter how international in purview, will always be slowed down by considerations of geopolitics. The history of human rights shows that rights are best defended in the end by the feelings, convictions, and actions of multitudes of individuals, who demand responses that accord with their inner sense of outrage. The Protestant pastor Rabaut Saint-Etienne had already grasped this truth in 1787, when he wrote to the French government to complain about the defects of the new edict offering religious toleration to Protestants. "The time has come," he said, "when it is no longer acceptable for a law to overtly overrule the rights of humanity that are very well known all over the world." Declarations—in 1776, 1789, and 1948—provided a touchstone for those rights of humanity, drawing on the sense of what "is no longer acceptable" and in turn helping to make violations all that more inadmissible. The process had and has an undeniable circularity to it: you know the meaning of human rights because you feel distressed when they are violated. The truths of human rights might be paradoxical in this sense, but they are nonetheless still self-evident.

APPENDIX

Three Declarations:
1776, 1789, 1948

Declaration of Independence, 1776

IN CONGRESS, *July 4, 1776.*
The unanimous Declaration of the thirteen united States of America,

When in the Course of human events, it becomes necessary for one people to dissolve the political bands which have connected them with another, and to assume among the powers of the earth, the separate and equal station to which the Laws of Nature and of Nature's God entitle them, a decent respect to the opinions of mankind requires that they should declare the causes which impel them to the separation.

We hold these truths to be self-evident, that all men are created equal, that they are endowed by their Creator with certain unalienable Rights, that among these are Life, Liberty and the pursuit of Happiness.—That to secure these rights, Governments are instituted among Men, deriving their just powers from the consent of the governed,—That whenever any Form of Government becomes destructive of these ends, it is the Right of the People to alter or to abolish it, and to institute new Government, laying its foundation on such principles and organizing its powers in such form, as to them shall seem most likely to effect their Safety and Happiness. Prudence, indeed, will dictate that Governments long established should not be changed for light and transient causes; and accordingly all experience hath shewn, that mankind are more disposed to suffer, while evils are sufferable, than to right themselves by abolishing the forms to which they are accustomed. But when a long train of abuses and usurpations, pursuing invariably the same Object evinces a design to reduce them under absolute Despotism, it is their right, it is their duty, to throw off such Government, and to provide new Guards for their future security.—Such has been the patient sufferance of these Colonies; and such is now the necessity which constrains them to alter their former Systems of Government. The history of the present King of Great Britain is a history of repeated injuries and usurpations, all having in direct object the establishment of an absolute Tyranny over these States. To prove this, let Facts be submitted to a candid world.

He has refused his Assent to Laws, the most wholesome and necessary for the public good.

He has forbidden his Governors to pass Laws of immediate and pressing importance, unless suspended in their operation till his Assent should be obtained; and when so suspended, he has utterly neglected to attend to them.

He has refused to pass other Laws for the accommodation of large districts of people, unless those people would relinquish the right of Representation in the Legislature, a right inestimable to them and formidable to tyrants only.

He has called together legislative bodies at places unusual, uncomfortable, and distant from the depository of their public Records, for the sole purpose of fatiguing them into compliance with his measures.

He has dissolved Representative Houses repeatedly, for opposing with manly firmness his invasions on the rights of the people.

He has refused for a long time, after such dissolutions, to cause others to be elected; whereby the Legislative powers, incapable of Annihilation, have returned to the People at large for their exercise; the State remaining in the mean time exposed to all the dangers of invasion from without, and convulsions within.

He has endeavoured to prevent the population of these States; for that purpose obstructing the Laws for Naturalization of Foreigners; refusing to pass others to encourage their migrations hither, and raising the conditions of new Appropriations of Lands.

He has obstructed the Administration of Justice, by refusing his Assent to Laws for establishing Judiciary powers.

He has made Judges dependent on his Will alone, for the tenure of their offices, and the amount and payment of their salaries.

He has erected a multitude of New Offices, and sent hither swarms of Officers to harrass our people, and eat out their substance.

He has kept among us, in times of peace, Standing Armies without the Consent of our legislatures.

He has affected to render the Military independent of and superior to the Civil power.

He has combined with others to subject us to a jurisdiction foreign to our constitution, and unacknowledged by our laws; giving his Assent to their Acts of pretended Legislation:

For Quartering large bodies of armed troops among us:

For protecting them, by a mock Trial, from punishment for any Murders which they should commit on the Inhabitants of these States:

For cutting off our Trade with all parts of the world:

For imposing Taxes on us without our Consent:

For depriving us in many cases, of the benefits of Trial by Jury:

For transporting us beyond Seas to be tried for pretended offences:

For abolishing the free System of English Laws in a neighbouring Province, establishing therein an Arbitrary government, and enlarging its Boundaries so as to render it at once an example and fit instrument for introducing the same absolute rule into these Colonies:

For taking away our Charters, abolishing our most valuable Laws, and altering fundamentally the Forms of our Governments:

For suspending our own Legislatures, and declaring themselves invested with power to legislate for us in all cases whatsoever.

He has abdicated Government here, by declaring us out of his Protection and waging War against us.

He has plundered our seas, ravaged our Coasts, burnt our towns, and destroyed the lives of our people.

He is at this time transporting large Armies of foreign Mercenaries to compleat the works of death, desolation and tyranny, already begun with circumstances of Cruelty & perfidy scarcely paralleled in the most barbarous ages, and totally unworthy the Head of a civilized nation.

He has constrained our fellow Citizens taken Captive on the high Seas to bear Arms against their Country, to become the executioners of their friends and Brethren, or to fall themselves by their Hands.

He has excited domestic insurrections amongst us, and has endeavoured to bring on the inhabitants of our frontiers, the merciless Indian Savages, whose known rule of warfare, is an undistinguished destruction of all ages, sexes and conditions.

In every stage of these Oppressions We have Petitioned for Redress in the most humble terms: Our repeated Petitions have been answered only by repeated injury. A Prince whose character is thus marked by every act which may define a Tyrant, is unfit to be the ruler of a free people.

Nor have We been wanting in attentions to our Brittish [sic] brethren. We have warned them from time to time of attempts by their legislature to extend an unwarrantable jurisdiction over us. We have reminded them of the circumstances of our emigration and settlement here. We have appealed to their native justice and magnanimity, and we have conjured them by the ties of our common kindred to disavow these usurpations, which, would inevitably interrupt our connections and correspondence. They too have been deaf to the voice of justice and of consanguinity. We must, therefore, acquiesce in the necessity, which denounces our Separation, and hold them, as we hold the rest of mankind, Enemies in War, in Peace Friends.

We, therefore, the Representatives of the united States of America, in General Congress, Assembled, appealing to the Supreme Judge of the world for the rectitude of our intentions, do, in the Name, and by Authority of the good People of these Colonies, solemnly publish and declare, That these United Colonies are, and of Right ought to be Free and Independent States; that they are Absolved from all Allegiance to the British Crown, and that all political connection between them and the State of Great Britain, is and ought to be totally dissolved; and that as Free and Independent States, they have full Power to levy War, conclude Peace, contract Alliances, establish Commerce, and to do all other Acts and Things which Independent States may of right do. And for the support of this Declaration, with a firm reliance on the protection of divine Providence, we mutually pledge to each other our Lives, our Fortunes and our sacred Honor.

Source: Paul Leicester Ford, ed., *The Writings of Thomas Jefferson*, 10 vols. (New York: G. P. Putnam's Sons, 1892–99), vol. 2, pp. 42–58; www.archives.gov/national-archives-experience/charters/declaration_transcript.html

Declaration of the Rights of Man and Citizen, 1789

The representatives of the French people, constituted as a National Assembly, and considering that ignorance, neglect or contempt of the rights of man are the sole causes of public misfortunes and governmental corruption, have resolved to set forth in a solemn declaration the natural, inalienable and sacred rights of man: so that by being constantly present to all the members of the social body this declaration may always remind them of their rights and duties; so that by being liable at every moment to comparison with the aim of any and all political institutions the acts of the legislative and executive powers may be the more fully respected; and so that by being founded henceforward on simple and incontestable principles the demands of the citizens may always tend toward maintaining the constitution and the general welfare.

In consequence, the National Assembly recognizes and declares, in the presence and under the auspices of the Supreme Being, the following rights of man and the citizen:

1. Men are born and remain free and equal in rights. Social distinctions may be based only on common utility.

2. The purpose of all political association is the preservation of the natural and imprescriptible rights of man. These rights are liberty, property, security and resistance to oppression.

3. The principle of all sovereignty rests essentially in the nation. No body and no individual may exercise authority which does not emanate expressly from the nation.

4. Liberty consists in the ability to do whatever does not harm another; hence the exercise of the natural rights of each man has no other limits than those which assure to other members of society the enjoyment of the same rights. These limits can only be determined by the law.

5. The law only has the right to prohibit those actions which are injurious to society. No hindrance should be put in the way of anything not prohibited by the law, nor may any one be forced to do what the law does not require.

6. The law is the expression of the general will. All citizens have the right to take part, in person or by their representatives, in its formation. It must be the same for everyone whether it protects or penalizes. All citizens being equal in its eyes are equally admissible to all public dignities, offices and employments, according to their ability, and with no other distinction than that of their virtues and talents.

7. No man may be indicted, arrested or detained except in cases determined by the law and according to the forms which it has prescribed. Those who seek, expedite, execute or cause to be executed arbitrary orders should be punished; but citizens summoned or seized by virtue of the law should obey instantly, and render themselves guilty by resistance.

8. Only strictly and obviously necessary punishments may be established by the law, and no one may be punished except by

virtue of a law established and promulgated before the time of the offense, and legally applied.

9. Every man being presumed innocent until judged guilty, if it is deemed indispensable to arrest him, all rigor unnecessary to securing his person should be severely repressed by the law.

10. No one should be disturbed for his opinions, even in religion, provided that their manifestation does not trouble public order as established by law.

11. The free communication of thoughts and opinions is one of the most precious of the rights of man. Every citizen may therefore speak, write and print freely, if he accepts his own responsibility for any abuse of this liberty in the cases set by the law.

12. The safeguard of the rights of man and the citizen requires public powers. These powers are therefore instituted for the advantage of all, and not for the private benefit of those to whom they are entrusted.

13. For maintenance of public authority and for expenses of administration, common taxation is indispensable. It should be apportioned equally among all the citizens according to their capacity to pay.

14. All citizens have the right, by themselves or through their representatives, to have demonstrated to them the necessity of public taxes, to consent to them freely, to follow the use made of the proceeds, and to determine the means of apportionment, assessment, and collection, and the duration of them.

15. Society has the right to hold accountable every public agent of the administration.

16. Any society in which the guarantee of rights is not assured or the separation of powers not settled has no constitution.

17. Property being an inviolable and sacred right, no one may be deprived of it except when public necessity, certified by law, obviously requires it, and on the condition of a just compensation in advance.

Source: *La Constitution française, Présentée au Roi par l'Assemblée Nationale, le 3 septembre 1791* (Paris, 1791), author's translation.

Universal Declaration of Human Rights, 1948

PREAMBLE

Whereas recognition of the inherent dignity and of the equal and inalienable rights of all members of the human family is the foundation of freedom, justice and peace in the world,

Whereas disregard and contempt for human rights have resulted in barbarous acts which have outraged the conscience of mankind, and the advent of a world in which human beings shall enjoy freedom of speech and belief and freedom from fear and want has been proclaimed as the highest aspiration of the common people,

Whereas it is essential, if man is not to be compelled to have recourse, as a last resort, to rebellion against tyranny and oppression, that human rights should be protected by the rule of law,

Whereas it is essential to promote the development of friendly relations between nations,

Whereas the peoples of the United Nations have in the Charter reaffirmed their faith in fundamental human rights, in the dignity and worth of the human person and in the equal rights of men and women and have determined to promote social progress and better standards of life in larger freedom,

Whereas Member States have pledged themselves to achieve, in co-operation with the United Nations, the promotion of universal respect for and observance of human rights and fundamental freedoms,

Whereas a common understanding of these rights and freedoms is of the greatest importance for the full realization of this pledge,

Now, Therefore THE GENERAL ASSEMBLY proclaims THIS UNIVERSAL DECLARATION OF HUMAN RIGHTS as a common standard of achievement for all peoples and all nations, to the end that every individual and every organ of society, keeping this Declaration constantly in mind, shall strive by teaching and education to promote respect for these rights and freedoms and by progressive measures, national and international, to secure their universal and effective recognition and observance, both among the peoples of Member States themselves and among the peoples of territories under their jurisdiction.

Article 1. All human beings are born free and equal in dignity and rights. They are endowed with reason and conscience and should act towards one another in a spirit of brotherhood.

Article 2. Everyone is entitled to all the rights and freedoms set forth in this Declaration, without distinction of any kind, such as race, colour, sex, language, religion, political or other opinion, national or social origin, property, birth or other status. Furthermore, no distinction shall be made on the basis of the political, jurisdictional or international status of the country or territory to which a person belongs, whether it be independent, trust, non-self-governing or under any other limitation of sovereignty.

Article 3. Everyone has the right to life, liberty and security of person.

Article 4. No one shall be held in slavery or servitude; slavery and the slave trade shall be prohibited in all their forms.

Article 5. No one shall be subjected to torture or to cruel, inhuman or degrading treatment or punishment.

Article 6. Everyone has the right to recognition everywhere as a person before the law.

Article 7. All are equal before the law and are entitled without any discrimination to equal protection of the law. All are entitled to equal protection against any discrimination in violation of this Declaration and against any incitement to such discrimination.

Article 8. Everyone has the right to an effective remedy by the competent national tribunals for acts violating the fundamental rights granted him by the constitution or by law.

Article 9. No one shall be subjected to arbitrary arrest, detention or exile.

Article 10. Everyone is entitled in full equality to a fair and public hearing by an independent and impartial tribunal, in the determination of his rights and obligations and of any criminal charge against him.

Article 11. (1) Everyone charged with a penal offence has the right to be presumed innocent until proved guilty according to law in a public trial at which he has had all the guarantees necessary for his defence.

(2) No one shall be held guilty of any penal offence on account of any act or omission which did not constitute a penal offence, under national or international law, at the time when it was committed. Nor shall a heavier penalty be imposed than the one that was applicable at the time the penal offence was committed.

Article 12. No one shall be subjected to arbitrary interference with his privacy, family, home or correspondence, nor to attacks upon his honour and reputation. Everyone has the right to the protection of the law against such interference or attacks.

Article 13. (1) Everyone has the right to freedom of movement and residence within the borders of each state.

(2) Everyone has the right to leave any country, including his own, and to return to his country.

Article 14. (1) Everyone has the right to seek and to enjoy in other countries asylum from persecution.

(2) This right may not be invoked in the case of prosecutions genuinely arising from non-political crimes or from acts contrary to the purposes and principles of the United Nations.

Article 15. (1) Everyone has the right to a nationality.

(2) No one shall be arbitrarily deprived of his nationality nor denied the right to change his nationality.

Article 16. (1) Men and women of full age, without any limitation due to race, nationality or religion, have the right to marry and to found a family. They are entitled to equal rights as to marriage, during marriage and at its dissolution.

(2) Marriage shall be entered into only with the free and full consent of the intending spouses.

(3) The family is the natural and fundamental group unit of society and is entitled to protection by society and the State.

Article 17. (1) Everyone has the right to own property alone as well as in association with others.

(2) No one shall be arbitrarily deprived of his property.

Article 18. Everyone has the right to freedom of thought, conscience and religion; this right includes freedom to change his religion or belief, and freedom, either alone or in community with others and in public or private, to manifest his religion or belief in teaching, practice, worship and observance.

Article 19. Everyone has the right to freedom of opinion and expression; this right includes freedom to hold opinions without interference and to seek, receive and impart information and ideas through any media and regardless of frontiers.

Article 20. (1) Everyone has the right to freedom of peaceful assembly and association.

(2) No one may be compelled to belong to an association.

Article 21. (1) Everyone has the right to take part in the government of his country, directly or through freely chosen representatives.

(2) Everyone has the right of equal access to public service in his country.

(3) The will of the people shall be the basis of the authority of government; this will shall be expressed in periodic and genuine elections which shall be by universal and equal suffrage and shall be held by secret vote or by equivalent free voting procedures.

Article 22. Everyone, as a member of society, has the right to social security and is entitled to realization, through national effort and international co-operation and in accordance with the organization and resources of each State, of the economic, social and cultural rights indispensable for his dignity and the free development of his personality.

Article 23. (1) Everyone has the right to work, to free choice of employment, to just and favourable conditions of work and to protection against unemployment.

(2) Everyone, without any discrimination, has the right to equal pay for equal work.

(3) Everyone who works has the right to just and favourable remuneration ensuring for himself and his family an existence worthy of human dignity, and supplemented, if necessary, by other means of social protection.

(4) Everyone has the right to form and to join trade unions for the protection of his interests.

Article 24. Everyone has the right to rest and leisure, including reasonable limitation of working hours and periodic holidays with pay.

Article 25. (*1*) Everyone has the right to a standard of living adequate for the health and well-being of himself and of his family, including food, clothing, housing and medical care and necessary social services, and the right to security in the event of unemployment, sickness, disability, widowhood, old age or other lack of livelihood in circumstances beyond his control.

(*2*) Motherhood and childhood are entitled to special care and assistance. All children, whether born in or out of wedlock, shall enjoy the same social protection.

Article 26. (*1*) Everyone has the right to education. Education shall be free, at least in the elementary and fundamental stages. Elementary education shall be compulsory. Technical and professional education shall be made generally available and higher education shall be equally accessible to all on the basis of merit.

(*2*) Education shall be directed to the full development of the human personality and to the strengthening of respect for human rights and fundamental freedoms. It shall promote understanding, tolerance and friendship among all nations, racial or religious groups, and shall further the activities of the United Nations for the maintenance of peace.

(*3*) Parents have a prior right to choose the kind of education that shall be given to their children.

Article 27. (*1*) Everyone has the right freely to participate in the cultural life of the community, to enjoy the arts and to share in scientific advancement and its benefits.

(*2*) Everyone has the right to the protection of the moral and material interests resulting from any scientific, literary or artistic production of which he is the author.

Article 28. Everyone is entitled to a social and international order in which the rights and freedoms set forth in this Declaration can be fully realized.

Article 29. (1) Everyone has duties to the community in which alone the free and full development of his personality is possible.

(2) In the exercise of his rights and freedoms, everyone shall be subject only to such limitations as are determined by law solely for the purpose of securing due recognition and respect for the rights and freedoms of others and of meeting the just requirements of morality, public order and the general welfare in a democratic society.

(3) These rights and freedoms may in no case be exercised contrary to the purposes and principles of the United Nations.

Article 30. Nothing in this Declaration may be interpreted as implying for any State, group or person any right to engage in any activity or to perform any act aimed at the destruction of any of the rights and freedoms set forth herein.

Source: Mary Ann Glendon, *A World Made New: Eleanor Roosevelt and the Universal Declaration of Human Rights* (New York: Random House, 2001), pp 310–14; www.un.org/ Overview/rights.html

Notes

Introduction

1. *The Papers of Thomas Jefferson*, ed. Julian P. Boyd, 31 vols. (Princeton: Princeton University Press, 1950–), vol. 1 (1760–1776), esp. p. 423, but see also pp. 309–433.

2. D. O. Thomas, ed., *Political Writings / Richard Price* (Cambridge and New York: Cambridge University Press, 1991), p. 195. Burke quote from paragraph 144, available online at *Reflections on the French Revolution.* vol. XXIV, Part 3. New York: P. F. Collier & Son, 1909–14; Bartleby.com, 2001. www.bartleby.com/24/3/ [January 21, 2005].

3. Jacques Maritain, one of the leaders of the UNESCO Committee on the Theoretical Bases of Human Rights, quoted in Mary Ann Glendon, *A World Made New: Eleanor Roosevelt and the Universal Declaration of Human Rights* (New York: Random House, 2001), p. 77. On the American Declaration, see Pauline Maier, *American Scripture: Making the Declaration of Independence* (New York: Alfred A. Knopf, 1997), pp. 236–41.

4. On the difference between the American Declaration of Independence and the English Declaration of Rights of 1689, see Michael P. Zuckert, *Natural Rights and the New Republicanism* (Princeton: Princeton University Press, 1994), esp. pp. 3–25.

5. The Jefferson quote comes from Andrew A. Lipscomb and Albert E. Bergh, eds., *The Writings of Thomas Jefferson*, 20 vols. (Washington, DC: Thomas Jefferson Memorial Association of the United States, 1903–04), vol. 3, p. 421. I have been able to trace Jefferson's usage of terms on the University of Virginia library Web site of his quotations: http://etext.lib.virginia.edu/jefferson/quotations. There is more to be done on the question of human rights terms, and as online databases expand and are refined, such research will become less cumbersome. "Human rights" is used from the very early years of the eighteenth century in English, but most often occurs in conjunction with religion, as in "divine and human rights" or even "divine divine right" vs. "divine human right." The latter occurs in Matthew Tindal, *The Rights of the Christian Church Asserted, against the Romish, and All Other Priests who Claim an Independent Power over It* (London, 1706), p. liv; the former in, e.g., *A Compleat History of the Whole Proceedings of the Parlia-*

ment of Great Britain against Dr. Henry Sacheverell (London, 1710), pp. 84 and 87.

6. The language of human rights is most easily traced in French thanks to ARTFL, an online database of some 2,000 French texts from the thirteenth to the twentieth century. ARTFL includes only a selection of texts written in French, and it favors literature over other categories. For a description of the resource, see http://humanities.uchicago.edu/orgs/ ARTFL/artfl.flyer.html. Nicolas Lenglet-Dufresnoy, *De l'usage des romans. Où l'on fait voir leur utilité et leurs différents caractères. Avec une bibliothèque des romans, accompagnée de remarques critiques sur leurs choix et leurs éditions* (Amsterdam: Vve de Poilras, 1734; Geneva: Slatkine Reprints, 1970), p. 245. Voltaire, *Essay sur l'histoire générale et sur les moeurs et l'esprit des nations, depuis Charlemagne jusqu'à nos jours* (Geneva: Cramer, 1756), p. 292. Consulting *Voltaire électronique*, a searchable CD-ROM of Voltaire's collected works, I found *droit humain* used seven times (*droits humains* in the plural never), four of them in *Treatise on Tolerance*, and one in each of three other works. In ARTFL, the expression shows up once in Louis-François Ramond, *Lettres de W. Coxe à W. Melmoth* (Paris: Belin, 1781), p. 95; but in the context, it means human law as opposed to divine law. The search function of the electronic Voltaire makes it virtually impossible to quickly determine whether Voltaire used *droits de l'homme* or *droits de l'humanité* in any of his works (it will only give you the thousands of references to *droits* and *homme*, for example, in the same work, not in a consecutive phrase, in contrast to ARTFL).

7. ARTFL gives as the citation Jacques-Bénigne Bossuet, *Méditations sur L'Evangile* (1704; Paris: Vrin, 1966), p. 484.

8. Rousseau may have taken the term "rights of man" from Jean-Jacques Burlamaqui, who used it in the table of contents of *Principes du droit naturel par J. J. Burlamaqui, Conseiller d'Etat, & ci-devant Professeur en droit naturel & civil à Genève* (Geneva: Barrillot et fils, 1747), part one, chap. VII, sect. 4 ("Fondement général des Droits de l'homme"). It appears as "rights of man" in the English translation by Nugent (London, 1748). Rousseau discusses Burlamaqui's ideas of *droit naturel* in his *Discours sur l'origine et les fondements de l'inégalité parmi les hommes*, 1755, *Oeuvres Complètes*, ed. Bernard Gagnebin and Marcel Raymond, 5 vols. (Paris: Gallimard, 1959–95), vol. 3 (1966), p. 124. The report on *Manco* comes from *Mémoires secrets pour servir à l'histoire de la République des lettres en France, depuis MDCCLXII jusqu'à nos jours*, 36 vols. (London: J. Adamson, 1784–89, vol. 1, p. 230. The *Mémoires secrets* covered the years 1762–87. Not the work of a single author (Louis Petit de Bachaumont died in 1771) but probably several hands, the "memoirs" included

reviews of books, pamphlets, plays, musical performances, art exhibitions, and sensational court cases—See Jeremy D. Popkin and Bernadette Fort, *The* Mémoires secrets *and the Culture of Publicity in Eighteenth-Century France* (Oxford: Voltaire Foundation, 1998), and Louis A. Olivier, "Bachaumont the Chronicler: A Questionable Renown," in *Studies on Voltaire and the Eighteenth Century*, vol. 143 (Voltaire Foundation: Banbury, Oxford, 1975), pp. 161–79. Since the volumes were published after the dates they purported to cover, we cannot be entirely certain that usage of "rights of man" was as common as the writer infers by 1763. In Act One, Scene II, Manco recites: "Born, like them, in the forest, but quick to know ourselves/ Demanding both the title and the rights of our being/ We have recalled to their surprised hearts/ Both this title and these rights too long profaned"—Antoine Le Blanc de Guillet, *Manco-Capac, Premier Ynca du Pérou, Tragédie, Représentée pour la premiere fois par les Comédiens François ordinaires du Roi, le 12 Juin 1763* (Paris: Belin, 1782), p. 4.

9. "Rights of man" appears once in William Blackstone, *Commentaries on the Laws of England*, 4 vols. (Oxford, 1765–69), vol. 1 (1765), p. 121. The first use I have found in English is in John Perceval, Earl of Egmont, *A Full and Fair Discussion of the Pretensions of the Dissenters, to the Repeal of the Sacramental Test* (London, 1733), p. 14. It also appears in the 1773 "poetical epistle" *The Dying Negro*, and in an early tract by the abolitionist leader Granville Sharp, *A Declaration of the People's Natural Right to a Share in the Legislature* . . . (London, 1774), p. xxv. I found these using the online service of Thomson Gale, Eighteenth-Century Collections Online, and am grateful to Jenna Gibbs-Boyer for help with this research. Quote from Condorcet in *Oeuvres complètes de Condorcet*, ed. by Maire Louise Sophie de Grouchy, marquise de Condorcet, 21 vols. (Brunswick: Vieweg; Paris: Henrichs, 1804), vol. XI, pp. 240–42, 251, 249. Sieyès used the term *droits de l'homme* only once: "Il ne faut point juger de ses [Third Estate's] demandes par les observations isolées de quelques auteurs plus ou moins instruits des droits de l' homme"—Emmanuel Sieyès, *Le Tiers-Etat* (1789; Paris: E. Champion, 1888), p. 36. In his letter to James Madison from Paris dated January 12, 1789, Thomas Jefferson sent Madison Lafayette's draft declaration. Its second paragraph began, "Les droits de l'homme assurent sa proprieté, sa liberté, son honneur, sa vie"—*Jefferson Papers*, vol. 14, p. 438. Condorcet's draft is dated to some time prior to the opening of the Estates-General on May 5, 1789, in Iain McLean and Fiona Hewitt, *Condorcet: Foundations of Social Choice and Political Theory* (Aldershot, Hants: Edward Elgar, 1994), p. 57, and see pp. 255–70 for the draft declaration "of rights," which uses the expression "rights of man" but not in its title. See the texts of the various projects

for a declaration in Antoine de Baecque, ed., *L'An I des droits de l'homme* (Paris: Presses du CNRS, 1988).

10. Blackstone, *Commentaries on the Laws of England*, vol. 1, p. 121. P. H. d'Holbach, *Système de la Nature* (1770; London, 1771), p. 336. H. Comte de Mirabeau, *Lettres écrites du donjon* (1780; Paris, 1792), p. 41.

11. Quoted in Lynn Hunt, ed., *The French Revolution and Human Rights: A Brief Documentary History* (Boston: Bedford Books/St. Martin's Press, 1996), p. 46.

12. Denis Diderot and Jean Le Rond d'Alembert, eds., *Encyclopédie ou Dictionnaire raisonné des sciences, arts, et des métiers*, 17 vols. (Paris, 1751–80), vol. 5 (1755), pp. 115–16. This volume includes two different articles on "Droit Naturel." The first is titled "Droit Naturel (Morale)," pp. 115–16, and begins with Diderot's characteristic editorial asterisk (signaling his authorship); the second is titled "Droit de la nature, ou Droit naturel," pp. 131–34, and is signed "A" (Antoine-Gaspard Boucher d'Argis). Information on authorship comes from John Lough, "The Contributors to the *Encyclopédie*," in Richard N. Schwab and Walter E. Rex, *Inventory of Diderot's Encyclopédie*, vol. 7: *Inventory of the Plates, with a Study of the Contributors to the Encyclopédie by John Lough* (Oxford: Voltaire Foundation, 1984), pp. 483–564. The second article by Boucher d'Argis consists of a history of the concept and is largely based on Burlamaqui's 1747 treatise, *Principes du droit naturel*.

13. Burlamaqui, *Principes du droit naturel*, p. 29 (his emphasis).

14. J. B. Schneewind, *The Invention of Autonomy: A History of Modern Moral Philosophy* (Cambridge: Cambridge University Press, 1998), p. 4. Autonomy seems to be the crucial element lacking in natural law theories up to the middle of the eighteenth century. As Haakonssen argues, "According to most natural lawyers in the seventeenth and eighteenth centuries, moral agency consisted in being subject to natural law and carrying out the duties imposed by such law, whereas rights were derivative, being mere means to the fulfilment of duties"—Knud Haakonssen, *Natural Law and Moral Philosophy: From Grotius to the Scottish Enlightenment* (Cambridge: Cambridge University Press, 1996), p. 6. In this regard, Burlamaqui, such a great influence on the Americans in the 1760s and 1770s, may well mark an important transition. Burlamaqui insists that men are subject to a superior power, but that that power must accord with man's inner nature: "In order for a law to regulate human actions, it must absolutely accord with the nature and the constitution of man and it must relate in the end to his happiness, which is what reason necessarily makes him seek out"—Burlamaqui, *Principes*, p. 89. On the general importance of autonomy to human rights, see Charles Taylor, *Sources of the Self: The Making of Modern Identity* (Cambridge, MA: Harvard University Press, 1989), esp. p. 12.

15. I traced "torture" in ARTFL. Marivaux's phrase comes from *Le Spectateur français* (1724) in Frédéric Deloffre and Michel Gilet, eds., *Journaux et oeuvres diverses* (Paris: Garnier, 1969), p. 114. Montesquieu, *The Spirit of the Laws*, trans. and ed. Anne M. Cohler, Basia Carolyn Miller, and Harold Samuel Stone (Cambridge: Cambridge University Press, 1989), pp. 92–93.

16. My view is clearly a much rosier one than that elaborated by Michel Foucault, who emphasizes psychological surfaces rather than depth and connects new views of the body to the rise of discipline rather than freedom. See, e.g., Foucault's *Discipline and Punish: The Birth of the Prison*, trans. Alan Sheridan (New York: Vintage, 1979).

17. Benedict Anderson, *Imagined Communities: Reflections on the Origin and Spread of Nationalism* (London: Verso, 1983), esp. pp. 25–36.

18. Leslie Brothers, *Friday's Footprint: How Society Shapes the Human Mind* (New York: Oxford University Press, 1997). Kai Voigeley, Martin Kurthen, Peter Falkai, and Walfgang Maier, "Essential Functions of the Human Self Model Are Implemented in the Prefrontal Cortext," *Consciousness and Cognition*, 8 (1999): 343–63.

Chapter 1

1. François-Marie Arouet de Voltaire to Marie de Vichy de Chamrond, marquise du Deffand, March 6, 1761, in *Correspondance complète de Jean Jacques Rousseau*, ed. R. A. Leigh, 52 vols. (Geneva: Institut et Musée Voltaire, 1965–98), vol. 8 (1969), p. 222. Jean Le Rond d'Alembert to Rousseau, Paris, February 10, 1761, in *Correspondance complète de Jean Jacques Rousseau*, vol. 8, p. 76. For the reader responses cited in this and the following paragraph, see Daniel Mornet, *J.-J. Rousseau: La Nouvelle Héloïse*, 4 vols. (Paris: Hachette, 1925), vol. 1, pp. 246–49.

2. On the English translations, see Jean-Jacques Rousseau, *La Nouvelle Héloïse*, trans. Judith H. McDowell (University Park, PA: Pennsylvania State University Press, 1968), p. 2. On the French editions, see Jo-Ann E. McEachern, *Bibliography of the Writings of Jean Jacques Rousseau to 1800*, vol. 1: *Julie, ou la Nouvelle Héloïse* (Oxford: Voltaire Foundation, Taylor Institution, 1993), pp. 769–75.

3. Alexis de Tocqueville, *L'Ancien Régime*, ed. J. P. Mayer (1856; Paris: Gallimard, 1964), p. 286. Olivier Zunz was kind enough to give me this reference.

4. Jean Decety and Philip L. Jackson, "The Functional Architecture of Human Empathy," *Behavioral and Cognitive Neuroscience Reviews*, 3 (2004): 71–100; see esp. p. 91.

5. On the general evolution of the French novel, see Jacques Rustin, *Le Vice à la mode: Etude sur le roman français du XVIIIe siècle de Manon*

Lescaut à l'apparition de La Nouvelle Héloïse (1731–1761) (Paris: Ophrys, 1979), p. 20. I compiled figures on the publication of new French novels from Angus Martin, Vivienne G. Mylne, and Richard Frautschi, *Bibliographie du genre romanesque français, 1751–1800* (London: Mansell, 1977). On the English novel, see James Raven, *British Fiction 1750–1770* (Newark, DE: University of Delaware Press, 1987), pp. 8–9, and James Raven, "Historical Introduction: The Novel Comes of Age," in Peter Garside, James Raven, and Rainer Schöwerling, eds., *The English Novel, 1770–1829: A Bibliographical Survey of Prose Fiction Published in the British Isles* (London and New York: Oxford University Press, 2000), pp. 15–121, esp. pp. 26–32. Raven shows that the percentage of epistolary novels dropped from 44 percent of all novels in the 1770s to 18 percent in the 1790s.

6. This is not the place for an exhaustive list of works. Most influential for me has been Benedict Anderson, *Imagined Communities: Reflections on the Origin and Spread of Nationalism* (London: Verso, 1983).

7. [abbé Marquet] *Lettre sur Pamela* (London, 1742), pp. 3, 4.

8. I have kept the original punctuation. *Pamela: or, Virtue Rewarded. In a Series of Familiar Letters from a Beautiful Young Damsel to her Parents: In four volumes. The sixth edition; corrected. By the late Mr. Sam. Richardson* (London: William Otridge, 1772), vol. 1, pp. 22–23.

9. Aaron Hill to Samuel Richardson, December 17, 1740. Hill begs Richardson to reveal the author's name, no doubt suspecting it is Richardson himself—Anna Laetitia Barbauld, ed., *The Correspondence of Samuel Richardson, Author of Pamela, Clarissa, and Sir Charles Grandison. Selected from the Original Manuscripts . . .* , 6 vols. (London: Richard Phillips, 1804), vol. I, pp. 54–55.

10. T. C. Duncan Eaves and Ben D. Kimpel, *Samuel Richardson: A Biography* (Oxford: Clarendon Press, 1971), pp. 124–41.

11. Bradshaigh letter dated January 11, 1749, quoted in Eaves and Kimpel, *Samuel Richardson*, p. 224. Edwards letter of January 26, 1749, in Barbauld, ed., *Correspondence of Samuel Richardson*, vol. III, p. 1.

12. On French personal libraries, see François Jost, "Le Roman épistolaire et la technique narrative au XVIIIe siècle," in *Comparative Literature Studies*, 3 (1966): 397–427, esp. pp. 401–02. This is based on a study by Daniel Mornet from 1910. On newsletter reactions (newsletters written by intellectuals in France for foreign rulers who wanted to follow the latest developments in French culture), see *Correspondance littéraire, philosophique et critique par Grimm, Diderot, Raynal, Meister, etc., revue sur les textes originaux, comprenant outre ce qui a été publié à diverses époques les fragments supprimés en 1813 par la censure, les parties inédites conservées à la Bibliothèque ducale de Gotha et à l'Arsenal à Paris,* 16 vols. (Paris: Garnier,

1877–82; Nendeln, Lichtenstein: Kraus, 1968), pp. 25 and 248 (January 25, 1751, and June 15, 1753). Abbé Guillaume Thomas Raynal was the author of the first and Friedrich Melchior Grimm most likely wrote the second.

13. Richardson did not return Rousseau's compliment; he claimed to have found it impossible to read *Julie* (he did, however, die the year of *Julie*'s publication in French). See Eaves and Kimpel, *Samuel Richardson*, p. 605, for Rousseau's quote and Richardson's response to *Julie*. Claude Perroud, ed., *Lettres de Madame Roland*, vol. 2 (1788–1793) (Paris: Imprimerie Nationale, 1902), pp. 43–49, esp. p. 48.

14. Robert Darnton, *The Great Cat Massacre and Other Episodes in French Cultural History* (New York: W. W. Norton, 1984), quote p. 243. Claude Labrosse, *Lire au XVIIIe siècle: la Nouvelle Héloïse et ses lecteurs* (Lyon: Presses Universitaires de Lyon, 1985), quote p. 96.

15. For a recent review of writing on the epistolary novel, see Elizabeth Heck-endorn Cook, *Epistolary Bodies: Gender and Genre in the Eighteenth-Century Republic of Letters* (Stanford: Stanford University Press, 1996). On the origins of the genre, see Jost, "Le Roman épistolaire."

16. W. S. Lewis, ed., *The Yale Edition of Horace Walpole's Correspondence*, vol. 22 (New Haven, 1960), p. 271 (Letter to Sir Horace Mann, December 20, 1764). *Remarks on Clarissa, Addressed to the Author. Occasioned by some critical Conversations on the Characters and Conduct of that Work. With Some Reflections on the Character and Behaviour of Prior's Emma* (London, 1749), pp. 8 and 51.

17. *Gentleman's Magazine*, 19 (June 1749), pp. 245–46, and 19 (August 1749), pp. 345–49, quotes on pp. 245 and 346.

18. N. A. Lenglet-Dufresnoy, *De l'usage des romans, où l'on fait voir leur utilité et leurs différents caractères*, 2 vols. (1734. Geneva: Slatkine Reprints, 1979), quotes, pp. 13 and 92 [vol. 1: 8 and 325 in original]. Twenty years later, Lenglet-Dufresnoy was invited to collaborate with other Enlightenment figures on Diderot's *Encyclopédie*.

19. Armand-Pierre Jacquin, *Entretiens sur les romans* (1755; Geneva: Slatkine Reprints, 1970), quotes pp. 225, 237, 305, 169, and 101. The anti-novel literature is discussed in Daniel Mornet, *J.-J. Rousseau: La Nouvelle Héloïse*, 4 vols. (Paris: Hachette, 1925), vol. 1.

20. Richard C. Taylor, "James Harrison, 'The Novelist's Magazine,' and the Early Canonizing of the English Novel," *Studies in English Literature, 1500–1900*, 33 (1993): 629–43, quote p. 633. John Tinnon Taylor, *Early Opposition to the English Novel: The Popular Reaction from 1760 to 1830* (New York: King's Crown Press, 1943), p. 52.

21. Samuel-Auguste Tissot, *L'Onanisme* (1774; Latin edn. 1758; Paris: Editions de la Différence, 1991), esp. pp. 22 and 166–67. Taylor, *Early Opposition*, p. 61.

22. Gary Kelly, "Unbecoming a Heroine: Novel Reading, Romanticism, and Barrett's *The Heroine*," *Nineteenth-Century Literature*, 45 (1990): 220–41, quote p. 222.

23. (London: Printed for C. Rivington, in St. Paul's Church-Yard; and J. Osborn [etc.], 1741).

24. Jean-Jacques Rousseau, *Julie, or The New Heloise*, trans. Philip Stewart and Jean Vaché, vol. 6 of Roger D. Masters and Christopher Kelly, eds., *The Collected Writings of Rousseau* (Hanover, NH: University Press of New England, 1997), quotes pp. 3 and 15.

25. "Eloge de Richardson," *Journal étranger*, 8 (1762; Geneva: Slatkine Reprints, 1968), 7–16, quotes pp. 8–9. For a more detailed analysis of this text, see Roger Chartier, "Richardson, Diderot et la lectrice impatiente," *MLN*, 114 (1999): 647–66. It is not known when Diderot first read Richardson; references to him in Diderot's correspondence only begin to appear in 1758. Grimm referred to Richardson in his correspondence as early as 1753—June S. Siegel, "Diderot and Richardson: Manuscripts, Missives, and Mysteries," *Diderot Studies*, 18 (1975): 145–67.

26. "Eloge," pp. 8, 9.

27. Ibid., p. 9.

28. Henry Home, Lord Kames, *Elements of Criticism*, 3rd edn., 2 vols. (Edinburgh: A. Kincaid & J. Bell, 1765), vol I, pp. 80, 82, 85, 92. See also Mark Salber Phillips, *Society and Sentiment: Genres of Historical Writing in Britain, 1740-1820* (Princeton: Princeton University Press, 2000), pp. 109–10.

29. Julian P. Boyd, ed., *The Papers of Thomas Jefferson*, 30 vols. (Princeton: Princeton University Press, 1950–), vol. 1, pp. 76–81.

30. Jean Starobinski demonstrates that this debate about the effects of identification applied to the theater as well, but argues that Diderot's analysis of Richardson constitutes an important turning point in developing a new attitude toward identification—"'Se mettre à la place': la mutation de la critique de l'âge classique à Diderot," *Cahiers Vilfredo Pareto*, 14 (1976): 364–78.

31. On this point, see esp. Michael McKeon, *The Origins of the English Novel, 1600–1740* (Baltimore: Johns Hopkins University Press, 1987), p. 128.

32. Andrew Burstein, *The Inner Jefferson: Portrait of a Grieving Optimist* (Charlottesville, VA: University of Virginia Press, 1995), p. 54. J. P. Brissot de Warville, *Mémoires (1754–1793); publiés avec étude critique et notes par Cl. Perroud* (Paris: Picard, n.d.), vol. 1, pp. 354–55.

33. Immanuel Kant, "An Answer to the Question: What is Enlightenment?" in *What Is Enlightenment? Eighteenth-Century Answers and Twentieth-Century Questions*, ed. James Schmidt (Berkeley: University of Califor-

nia Press, 1996), pp. 58–64, quote p. 58. The chronology of autonomy is not easy to pin down. Most historians agree that the scope of individual decision making generally increased between the sixteenth and twentieth centuries in the Western world, even if they disagree about how and why it did so. Countless books and articles have been written about the history of individualism as a philosophical and social doctrine and its associations with Christianity, Protestant conscience, capitalism, modernity, and Western values more generally—See Michael Carrithers, Steven Collins, and Steven Lukes, eds., *The Category of the Person: Anthropology, Philosophy, History* (Cambridge: Cambridge University Press, 1985). A brief review of the literature can be found in Michael Mascuch, *Origins of the Individualist Self: Autobiography and Self-Identity in England, 1591–1791* (Stanford: Stanford University Press, 1996), pp. 13–24. One of the few to relate these developments to human rights is Charles Taylor, *Sources of the Self: The Making of Modern Identity* (Cambridge, MA: Harvard University Press, 1989).

34. Quoted in Jay Fliegelman, *Prodigals and Pilgrims: The American Revolution Against Patriarchal Authority, 1750–1800* (Cambridge: Cambridge University Press, 1982), p. 15.

35. Jean-Jacques Rousseau, *Émile, ou l'Éducation*, 4 vols. (The Hague: Jean Néaume, 1762), vol. I, pp. 2–4. Richard Price, *Observations on The Nature of Civil Liberty, the Principles of Government, and the Justice and Policy of the War with America to which is added, An Appendix and Postscript, containing, A State of the National Debt, An Estimate of the Money drawn from the Public by the Taxes, and An Account of the National Income and Expenditure since the last War*, 9th edn. (London: Edward & Charles Dilly and Thomas Cadell, 1776), pp. 5–6.

36. Lynn Hunt, *The Family Romance of the French Revolution* (Berkeley: University of California Press, 1992), pp. 40–41.

37. Fliegelman, *Prodigals and Pilgrims*, pp. 39, 67.

38. Lawrence Stone, *The Family, Sex and Marriage in England 1500–1800* (London: Weidenfeld & Nicolson, 1977). On swaddling, weaning, and toilet training, see Randolph Trumbach, *The Rise of the Egalitarian Family: Aristocratic Kinship and Domestic Relations in Eighteenth-Century England* (New York: Academic Press, 1978), pp. 197–229.

39. Sybil Wolfram, "Divorce in England 1700–1857," *Oxford Journal of Legal Studies*, 5 (Summer 1985):155–86. Roderick Phillips, *Putting Asunder: A History of Divorce in Western Society* (Cambridge: Cambridge University Press, 1988), p. 257. Nancy F. Cott, "Divorce and the Changing Status of Women in Eighteenth-Century Massachusetts," *William and Mary Quarterly*, 3rd ser., vol. 33, no. 4 (October 1976): 586–614.

40. Frank L. Dewey, "Thomas Jefferson's Notes on Divorce," *William and*

Mary Quarterly, 3rd ser., vol. 39, no. 1, *The Family in Early American History and Culture* (January 1982): 212–23, quotes pp. 219, 217, 216.

41. "Empathy" entered English only in the early twentieth century as a term in aesthetics and psychology. A translation of the German word *Einfühlung*, it was defined as "the power of projecting one's personality into (and so fully comprehending) the object of contemplation"—http://dictionary.oed.com/cgi/entry/00074155?.

42. Francis Hutcheson, *A Short Introduction to Moral Philosophy, in Three Books; Containing the Elements of Ethicks and the Law of Nature*, 1747; 2nd edn. (Glasgow: Robert & Andrew Foulis, 1753), pp. 12–16.

43. Adam Smith, *The Theory of Moral Sentiments*, 3rd edn. (London, 1767), p. 2.

44. Burstein, *The Inner Jefferson*, p. 54; *The Power of Sympathy* was written by William Hill Brown. Anne C. Vila, "Beyond Sympathy: Vapors, Melancholia, and the Pathologies of Sensibility in Tissot and Rousseau," *Yale French Studies*, No. 92, *Exploring the Conversible World: Text and Sociability from the Classical Age to the Enlightenment* (1997): 88–101.

45. There has been much debate about Equiano's background (whether he was born in Africa, as he claimed, or in the United States), but this is not relevant to my point here. For the most recent discussion, see Vincent Carretta, *Equiano, the African: Biography of a Self-Made Man* (Athens, GA: University of Georgia Press, 2005).

46. Abbé Sieyès, *Préliminaire de la constitution française* (Paris: Baudoin, 1789).

47 H. A. Washington, ed., *The Writings of Thomas Jefferson*, 9 vols. (New York: John C. Riker, 1853–57), vol. 7 (1857), pp. 101–03. On Wollstonecraft, see Phillips, *Society and Sentiment*, p. 114, and especially Janet Todd, ed., *The Collected Letters of Mary Wollstonecraft* (London: Allen Lane, 2003), pp. 34, 114, 121, 228, 253, 313, 342, 359, 364, 402, 404.

48. *The Writings of Thomas Jefferson*, ed. Andrew A. Lipscomb and Albert E. Bergh, 20 vols. (Washington, DC: Thomas Jefferson Memorial Association of the United States, 1903–04), vol. 10, p. 324.

Chapter 2

1. The best general account is still David D. Bien, *The Calas Affair: Persecution, Toleration, and Heresy in Eighteenth-Century Toulouse* (Princeton: Princeton University Press, 1960). The tortures of Calas are described in Charles Berriat-Saint-Prix, *Des Tribunaux et de la procédure du grand criminel au XVIIIe siècle jusqu'en 1789 avec des recherches sur la question ou torture* (Paris: Auguste Aubry, 1859), pp. 93–96. I base my description of breaking on the wheel on the report of an eyewitness to breaking on the wheel in Paris—James St. John, Esq., *Letters from France*

to a Gentleman in the South of Ireland: Containing Various Subjects Interesting to both Nations. Written in 1787, 2 vols. (Dublin: P. Byrne, 1788), vol. II: Letter of July 23, 1787, pp. 10–16.

2.   Voltaire published a 21-page pamphlet in August 1762 on Histoire d'Elisabeth Canning et des Calas. He used the case of Elisabeth Canning to show how English justice functioned in a superior manner but most of the pamphlet is devoted to the Calas case. Voltaire's framing of the case in terms of religious intolerance can be seen most clearly in Traité sur la tolérance à l'occasion de la mort de Jean Calas (1763). The quote is taken from Jacques van den Heuvel, ed., Mélanges/Voltaire (Paris: Gallimard, 1961), p. 583.

3.   The connection between torture and Calas can be traced in Voltaire électronique, CD-ROM, ed. Ulla Kölving (Alexandria, VA: Chadwyck-Healey; Oxford: Voltaire Foundation, 1998). The 1766 denunciation of torture can be found in An Essay on Crimes and Punishments, Translated from the Italian, with a Commentary Attributed to Mons. De Voltaire, Translated from the French, 4th edn. (London: F. Newberry, 1775), pp. xli–xlii. For the article on "Torture" in the Philosophical Dictionary, see Theodore Besterman, et al., eds., Les Oeuvres complètes de Voltaire, 135 vols. (1968–2003), vol. 36, ed. Ulla Kölving (Oxford: Voltaire Foundation, 1994), pp. 572–73. Voltaire only argued for the actual abolition of torture in 1778 in his Prix de la justice et de l'humanité.—See Franco Venturi, ed., Cesare Beccaria, Dei Delitti e delle pene, con une raccolta di lettere e documenti relativi alla nascita dell'opera e alla sua fortuna nell'Europa del Settecento (Turin: Giulio Einaudi, 1970), pp. 493–95.

4.   J. D. E. Preuss, Friedrich der Grosse: eine Lebensgeschichte, 9 vols (Osnabrück, West Germany: Biblio Verlag, 1981; reprint of 1832 Berlin edn.), vol. I, pp. 140–41. The French king's decree left open the prospect of reestablishing the question préalable if experience proved it necessary. Moreover, the decree was one of a number related to the crown's effort to diminish the authority of the parlements. After having to register it in a lit de justice, Louis XVI suspended the implementation of all these decrees in September 1788. As a consequence, torture was not definitively abolished until the National Assembly suppressed it on October 8, 1789—Berriat-Saint-Prix, Des Tribunaux, p. 55. See also David Yale Jacobson, "The Politics of Criminal Law Reform in Pre-Revolutionary France," PhD diss., Brown University, 1976, pp. 367–429. For the text of the decrees of abolition, see Athanase Jean Léger et al., eds., Recueil général des anciennes lois françaises depuis l'an 420 jusqu'à la Révolution de 1789, 29 vols. (Paris: Plon, 1824–57), vol. 26 (1824), pp. 373–75, and vol. 28 (1824), pp. 526–32. Benjamin Rush, An Enquiry into the Effects of Public Punishments upon Criminals, and Upon Society. Read

in the Society for Promoting Political Enquiries, Convened at the House of His Excellency Benjamin Franklin, Esquire, in Philadelphia, March 9th, 1787 (Philadelphia: Joseph James, 1787), in Reform of Criminal Law in Pennsylvania: Selected Enquiries, 1787–1810 (New York: Arno Press, 1972), with original page numbering, quote p. 7.

5. On the general establishment and abolition of torture in Europe, see Edward Peters, Torture (Philadelphia: University of Pennsylvania Press, 1985). Although torture was not abolished in some Swiss cantons until the mid-nineteenth century, the practice largely disappeared (at least as legally recognized) in Europe in the course of the Revolutionary and Napoleonic wars. Napoleon abolished it in Spain, for example, in 1808, and it was never reestablished. For the history of the development of juries, see Sir James Fitzjames Stephen, A History of the Criminal Law of England, 3 vols. (1883; Chippenham, Wilts: Routledge, 1996), vol. 1, pp. 250–54. On witchcraft cases and the use of torture, see Alan Macfarlane, Witchcraft in Tudor and Stuart England: A Regional and Comparative Study (London: Routledge & Kegan Paul, 1970), pp. 139–40, and Christina A. Larner, Enemies of God: The Witch-hunt in Scotland (London: Chatto & Windus, 1981), p. 109. As Larner points out, the constant injunctions from Scottish and English judges demanding an end to torture in witchcraft cases show that it remained an issue. James Heath, Torture and English Law: An Administrative and Legal History from the Plantagenets to the Stuarts (Westport, CT: Greenwood Press, 1982), p. 179, details several references to the use of the rack in the sixteenth and seventeenth centuries, but these were not sanctioned by common law. See also Kathryn Preyer, "Penal Measures in the American Colonies: An Overview," American Journal of Legal History, 26 (October 1982): 326–53, esp. p. 333.

6. On the general methods of punishment, see J. A. Sharpe, Judicial Punishment in England (London: Faber & Faber, 1990). Punishment on the pillory could include having one's ears cut off or having one's ear nailed to the pillory (p. 21). Stocks were a wooden device to hold the feet of an offender. The pillory was a device in which offenders stood with their head and hands between two pieces of wood—Leon Radzinowicz, A History of English Criminal Law and Its Administration from 1750, 4 vols. (London: Stevens & Sons, 1948), vol. I, pp. 3–5, and 165–227. For a review of recent research in this now very richly mined vein, see Joanna Innes and John Styles, "The Crime Wave: Recent Writing on Crime and Criminal Justice in Eighteenth-Century England," Journal of British Studies, 25 (October 1986): 380–435.

7. Linda Kealey, "Patterns of Punishment: Massachusetts in the Eighteenth Century," American Journal of Legal History, 30 (April 1986): 163–86,

quote p. 172. William M. Wiecek, "The Statutory Law of Slavery and Race in the Thirteen Mainland Colonies of British America," *William and Mary Quarterly*, 3rd ser., vol. 34, no. 2 (April 1977): 258–80, esp. pp. 274–75.

8. Richard Mowery Andrews, *Law, Magistracy, and Crime in Old Regime Paris, 1735–1789*, vol. 1: *The System of Criminal Justice* (Cambridge: Cambridge University Press, 1994), especially pp. 385, 387–88.

9. Benoît Garnot, *Justice et société en France aux XVIe, XVIIe et XVIIIe siècles* (Paris: Ophrys, 2000), p. 186.

10. Romilly is quoted in Randall McGowen, "The Body and Punishment in Eighteenth-Century England," *Journal of Modern History*, 59 (1987): 651–79, p. 668. Beccaria's famous phrase can be found in *Crimes and Punishments*, p. 2. Jeremy Bentham took Beccaria's motto as the foundation for his doctrine of Utilitarianism. For him, Beccaria was nothing less than "my master, first evangelist of Reason"—Leon Radzinowicz, "Cesare Beccaria and the English System of Criminal Justice: A Reciprocal Relationship," in *Atti del convegno internazionale su Cesare Beccari promosso dall'Accademia delle Scienze di Torino nel secondo centenario dell'opera "Dei delitti e delle pene,"* Turin, October 4–6, 1964 (Turin: Accademia delle Scienze, 1966), pp. 57–66, quote p. 57. On the reception in France and elsewhere in Europe, see the letters reprinted in Venturi, ed., *Cesare Beccaria*, esp. pp. 312–24. Voltaire reported reading Beccaria in a letter of October 16, 1765; in the same letter he refers to the Calas Affair and to the Sirven case (also involving Protestants)—Theodore Besterman, et al., eds., *Les Oeuvres complètes de Voltaire*, 135 vols. (1968–2003), vol. 113, ed. Theodore Besterman, *Correspondence and Related Documents, April–December 1765*, vol. 29 [1973]:346.

11. The Dutch scholar Peter Spierenburg traces moderation of punishment to growing empathy: "The death and suffering of fellow human beings were increasingly experienced as painful, just because other people were increasingly perceived as fellow human beings"—Spierenburg, *The Spectacle of Suffering: Executions and the Evolution of Repression: From a Preindustrial Metropolis to the European Experience* (Cambridge: Cambridge University Press, 1984), p. 185. Beccaria, *Crimes and Punishments*, quotes pp. 43, 107, and 112. Blackstone too argued for punishments proportional to crimes, and he lamented the large number of death penalty offenses in England—William Blackstone, *Commentaries on the Laws of England*, 4 vols., 8th edn. (Oxford: Clarendon Press, 1778), vol. IV, p. 3. Blackstone cites Montesquieu and Beccaria in a note to this page. For the influence of Beccaria on Blackstone, see Coleman Phillipson, *True Criminal Law Reformers: Beccaria, Bentham, Romilly* (Montclair, NJ: Patterson Smith, 1970), esp. p. 90.

12. In recent years scholars have questioned whether Beccaria or the Enlightenment more generally had any role at all in eliminating judicial torture or moderating punishment and even whether the abolition was such a good thing—See John H. Langbein, *Torture and the Law of Proof: Europe and England in the Ancien Régime* (Chicago: University of Chicago Press, 1976); Andrews, *Law, Magistracy, and Crime*, J. S. Cockburn, "Punishment and Brutalization in the English Enlightenment," *Law and History Review*, 12 (1994): 155–79; and esp. Michel Foucault, *Discipline and Punish: The Birth of the Prison*, trans. Alan Sheridan (New York: Vintage, 1979).

13. Norbert Elias, *The Civilizing Process: The Development of Manners*, trans. Edmund Jephcott (German edn., 1939; New York: Urizen Books, 1978), quote pp. 69–70. For a critical view of this narrative, see Barbara H. Rosenwein, "Worrying About Emotions in History," *American Historical Review*, 107 (2002): 821–45.

14. James H. Johnson, *Listening in Paris: A Cultural History* (Berkeley: University of California Press, 1995), quote p. 61.

15. Jeffrey S. Ravel emphasizes the continuing rambunctiousness of the standing pit in *The Contested Parterre: Public Theater and French Political Culture, 1680–1791* (Ithaca, NY: Cornell University Press, 1999).

16. Annik Pardailhé-Galabrun, *The Birth of Intimacy: Privacy and Domestic Life in Early Modern Paris*, trans. Jocelyn Phelps (Philadelphia: University of Pennsylvania Press, 1991). John Archer, "Landscape and Identity: Baby Talk at the Leasowes, 1760," *Cultural Critique*, 51 (2002):143–85.

17. Ellen G. Miles, ed., *The Portrait in Eighteenth Century America* (Newark, DE: University of Delaware Press, 1993), p. 10. George T. M. Shackelford and Mary Tavener Holmes, *A Magic Mirror: The Portrait in France, 1700–1900* (Houston: Museum of the Fine Arts, 1986), p. 9. Walpole quote from Desmond Shawe-Taylor, *The Georgians: Eighteenth-Century Portraiture and Society* (London: Barrie & Jenkins, 1990), p. 27.

18. *Lettres sur les peintures, sculptures et gravures de Mrs. de l'Académie Royale, exposées au Sallon du Louvre, depuis MDCCLXVII jusqu'en MCDDLXXIX* (London: John Adamson, 1780), p. 51 (Salon of 1769). See also Rémy G. Saisselin, *Style, Truth and the Portrait* (Cleveland: Cleveland Museum of Art, 1963), esp. p. 27. The complaints about portraiture and "tableaux du petit genre" continued in the 1770s—*Lettres sur les peintures*, pp. 76, 212, 229. Jaucourt's article can be found in *Encylopédie ou dictionnaire raisonné des sciences, des arts et des métiers*, 17 vols. (Paris, 1751–80), vol. 13 (1765), p. 153. Mercier's comment from the 1780s is quoted in Shawe-Taylor, *The Georgians*, p. 21.

19. On the importance of fabrics and the impact of consumerism on portrait painting in the British North American colonies, see T. H. Breen, "The

Meaning of 'Likeness': Portrait-Painting in an Eighteenth-Century Consumer Society," in Miles, ed., *The Portrait*, pp. 37–60.

20. Angela Rosenthal, "She's Got the Look! Eighteenth-Century Female Portrait Painters and the Psychology of a Potentially 'Dangerous Employment,'" in Joanna Woodall, ed., *Portraiture: Facing the Subject* (Manchester: Manchester University Press, 1997), pp. 147–66 (Boswell quote p. 147). See also Kathleen Nicholson, "The Ideology of Feminine 'Virtue': The Vestal Virgin in French Eighteenth-Century Allegorical Portraiture," in ibid., pp. 52–72. Denis Diderot, *Oeuvres complètes de Diderot, revue sur les éditions originales, comprenant ce qui a été publié à diverses époques et les manuscrits inédits, conservés à la Bibliothèque de l'Ermitage, notices, notes, table analytique. Etude sur Diderot et le mouvement philosophique au XVIIIe siècle, par J. Assézat*, 20 vols. (Paris: Garnier, 1875–77; Nendeln, Lichtenstein: Kraus, 1966), vol. 11: *Beaux-Arts II, arts du dessin (Salons)*, pp. 260–62.

21. Sterne, *A Sentimental Journey*, pp. 158 and 164.

22. Howard C. Rice, Jr., "A 'New' Likeness of Thomas Jefferson," *William and Mary Quarterly*, 3rd ser., vol. 6, no. 1 (January 1949): 84–89. On the process more generally, see Tony Halliday, *Facing the Public: Portraiture in the Aftermath of the French Revolution* (Manchester: Manchester University Press, 1999), pp. 43–47.

23. Muyart did not put his name to the pamphlets defending Christianity: *Motifs de ma foi en Jésus-Christ, par un magistrat* (Paris:Vve Hérissant, 1776) and *Preuves de l'authenticité de nos évangiles, contre les assertions de certains critiques modernes. Lettre à Madame de ***. Par l'auteur de motifs de ma foi en Jésus-Christ* (Paris: Durand et Belin, 1785).

24. Pierre-François Muyart de Vouglans, *Réfutation du Traité des délits et peines, &c.*, printed at the end of his *Les Loix criminelles de France, dans leur ordre naturel* (Paris: Benoît Morin, 1780), pp. 811, 815, and 830.

25. Ibid., p. 830.

26. Spierenburg, *The Spectacle of Suffering*, p. 53.

27. Anon., *Considerations on the Dearness of Corn and Provisions* (London: J. Almon, 1767), p. 31; Anon., *The Accomplished Letter-Writer; or, Universal Correspondent. Containing Familiar Letters on the Most Common Occasions in Life* (London, 1779), pp. 148–50. Donna T. Andrew and Randall McGowen, *The Perreaus and Mrs. Rudd: Forgery and Betrayal in Eighteenth-Century London* (Berkeley: University of California Press, 2001), p. 9.

28. St. John, *Letters from France*, vol. II: Letter of July 23, 1787, p. 13.

29. *Crimes and Punishments*, pp. 2 and 179.

30. For eighteenth-century work on pain, see Margaret C. Jacob and Michael J. Sauter, "Why Did Humphry Davy and Associates Not Pursue the Pain-

Alleviating Effects of Nitrous Oxide?" *Journal of the History of Medicine*, 58 (April 2002): 161–76. Dagge quoted in McGowen, "The Body and Punishment in Eighteenth-Century England," p. 669. For colonial fines, see Preyer, "Penal Measures," pp. 350–51.

31. Eden quoted in McGowen, "The Body and Punishment in Eighteenth-Century England," p. 670. My analysis follows that of McGowen in many respects. Benjamin Rush, *An Enquiry*, see esp. pp. 4, 5, 10, and 15.

32. An essential source not only on the Calas case but the practice of torture more generally is Lisa Silverman, *Tortured Subjects: Pain, Truth, and the Body in Early Modern France* (Chicago: University of Chicago Press, 2001). See also Alexandre-Jérôme Loyseau de Mauléon, *Mémoire pour Donat, Pierre et Louis Calas* (Paris: Le Breton, 1762), pp. 38–39. Elie de Beaumont reports exactly the same words from the mouth of Calas. Voltaire had included them in his account, too. Jean-Baptiste-Jacques Elie de Beaumont, *Mémoire pour Dame Anne-Rose Cabibel, veuve Calas, et pour ses enfans sur le renvoi aux Requêtes de l'Hôtel au Souverain, ordonné par arrêt du Conseil du 4 juin 1764* (Paris: L. Cellot, 1765). Elie de Beaumont represented the Calas family before the Royal Council. On the publication of this kind of legal brief, see Sarah Maza, *Private Lives and Public Affairs: The Causes Célèbres of Prerevolutionary France* (Berkeley: University of California Press, 1993), pp. 19–38.

33. Alain Corbin, Jean-Jacques Courtine, and Georges Vigarello, eds., *Histoire du corps*, 3 vols. (Paris: Editions du Seuil, 2005–06), vol.1: *De la Renaissance aux Lumières* (2005), pp. 306–09. *Crimes and Punishments*, pp. 58 and 60.

34. The Parlement of Burgundy stopped ordering the *question préparatoire* after 1766, and its use of the death penalty declined from 13–14.5 percent of all criminal condemnations in the first half of the eighteenth century to under 5 percent between 1770 and 1789. The use of the *question préalable*, however, apparently continued unabated in France—Jacobson, "The Politics of Criminal Law Reform, pp. 36–47.

35. *Crimes and Punishments*, pp. 60–61 (emphasis in the original). Muyart de Vouglans, *Réfutation du Traité*, pp. 824–26.

36. See Venturi, ed., *Cesare Beccaria*, pp. 30–31, for the definitive 1766 Italian edition (the last one supervised by Beccaria himself). The paragraph appears in the same location in the original English translation, in chap. 11. On the later use of the French order, see for example, *Dei delitti e delle pene. Edizione rivista, coretta, e disposta secondo l'ordine della traduzione francese approvato dall'autore* (London: Presso la Società dei Filosofi, 1774), p. 4. According to Luigi Firpo, this volume was actually printed by Coltellini in Livorno—Luigi Firpo, "Contributo alla bibliografia del Beccaria. (Le edizioni italiane settecentesche del *Dei delitti e*

delle pene)," in *Atti del convegno internazionale su Cesare Beccaria,* pp. 329–453, esp. pp. 378–79.

37. The first French work openly critical of the judicial use of torture appeared in 1682 and was written by a leading magistrate in the Parlement of Dijon, Augustin Nicolas; his argument was against the use of torture in judgments of witchcraft—Silverman, *Tortured Subjects,* p. 161. The most definitive study of the various Italian editions of Beccaria can be found in Firpo, "Contributo alla bibliografia del Beccaria," pp. 329–453. On the English and other translations, see Marcello Maestro, *Cesare Beccaria and the Origins of Penal Reform* (Philadelphia: Temple University Press, 1973), p. 43. I have supplemented his count of the English-language editions with the English Short Title Catalogue. *Crimes and Punishments,* p. iii.

38. Venturi, ed., *Cesare Beccaria,* p. 496. The piece appeared in Linguet's *Annales politiques et littéraires,* 5 (1779).

39. *Encylopédie ou dictionnaire raisonné des sciences, des arts et des métiers,* 17 vols. (Paris, 1751–80), vol. 13 (1765), pp. 702–04. Jacobson, "The Politics of Criminal Law Reform," pp. 295–96.

40. Jacobson, "The Politics of Criminal Law Reform," p. 316. Venturi, ed., *Cesare Beccaria,* p. 517. Joseph-Michel-Antoine Servan, *Discours sur le progrès des connoissances humaines en général, de la morale, et de la législation en particulier* (n.p., 1781), p. 99.

41. I have a more favorable opinion of Brissot's criminal law writings than does Robert Darnton. See, for example, *George Washington's False Teeth: An Unconventional Guide to the Eighteenth Century* (New York: W. W. Norton, 2003), esp. p. 165. Quotes from Brissot come from *Théorie des lois criminelles,* 2 vols. (Paris: J. P. Aillaud, 1836), vol. I, pp. 6–7.

42. The rhetorical strategies are analyzed in depth in Maza, *Private Lives and Public Affairs.* When Brissot published his *Theory of Criminal Laws* (1781), originally written for an essay contest in Bern, Dupaty wrote to him to celebrate their common effort "to make truth triumph and humanity with it." The letter was reprinted in the 1836 edition, *Théorie des lois criminelles,* vol. I, p. vi. [Charles-Marguerite Dupaty], *Mémoire justificatif pour trois hommes condamnés à la roue* (Paris: Philippe-Denys Pierres, 1786), p. 221.

43. Dupaty, *Mémoire justificatif,* pp. 226 and 240. *L'Humanité* appears many times in the brief and in virtually every paragraph in the last pages.

44. Maza, *Private Lives and Public Affairs,* p. 253. Jacobson, "The Politics of Criminal Law Reform," pp. 360–61.

45. Jourdan, ed., *Recueil général des anciennes lois françaises,* vol. 28, p. 528. Muyart de Vouglans, *Les Loix criminelles,* p. 796. In the rank of document-level frequency of subjects (1 being highest, 1125 lowest),

the criminal code ranked 70.5 for the Third Estate, 27.5 for the Nobility, and 337 for the Parishes; legal procedure ranked 34 for the Third Estate, 77.5 for the Nobility, and 15 for the Parishes; criminal prosecution and penalties ranked 60.5 for the Third Estate, 76 for the Nobility, and 171 for the Parishes; and penalties under criminal law ranked 41.5 for the Third Estate, 213.5 for the Nobility, and 340 for the Parishes. The two forms of judicially sanctioned torture did not rank nearly as high because the "preparatory question" had already been definitively eliminated and the "preliminary question" had been provisionally abolished as well. Rank order of subjects comes from Gilbert Shapiro and John Markoff, *Revolutionary Demands: A Content Analysis of the Cahiers de Doléances of 1789* (Stanford: Stanford University Press, 1998), pp. 438–74.

46. Rush, *An Enquiry*, pp. 13 and 6–7.
47. Muyart de Vouglans, *Les Loix criminelles*, esp. pp. 37–38.
48. Antonio Damasio, *The Feeling of What Happens: Body and Emotion in the Making of Consciousness* (San Diego: Harcourt, 1999), and *Looking for Spinoza: Joy, Sorrow, and the Feeling Brain* (San Diego: Harcourt, 2003). Ann Thomson, "Materialistic Theories of Mind and Brain," in Wolfgang Lefèvre, ed., *Between Leibniz, Newton, and Kant: Philosophy and Science in the Eighteenth Century* (Dordrecht: Kluwer Academic Publishers, 2001), pp. 149–73.
49. Jessica Riskin, *Science in the Age of Sensibility: The Sentimental Empiricists of the French Enlightenment* (Chicago: University of Chicago Press, 2002), Bonnet quote p. 51. Sterne, *A Sentimental Journey*, p. 117.
50. Rush, *An Enquiry*, p. 7.

Chapter 3

1. The meaning of "declaration" can be traced in the Dictionnaires d'autrefois function of ARTFL at www.lib.uchicago.edu/etts/ARTFL/projects/dicos/. The official title of the 1689 English Bill of Rights was "An Act Declaring the Rights and Liberties of the Subject and Settling the Succession of the Crown."
2. *Archives parlementaires de 1787 à 1860: Recueil complet des débats legislatifs et politiques des chambres françaises*, series 1, 99 vols. (Paris: Librarie administrative de P. Dupont, 1875–1913), vol. 8, p. 320.
3. On the importance of Grotius and his treatise *On the Law of War and Peace* (1625), see Richard Tuck, *Natural Rights Theories: Their Origin and Development* (Cambridge: Cambridge University Press, 1979). See also Léon Ingber, "La Tradition de Grotius. Les Droits de l'homme et le droit naturel à l'époque contemporaine," *Cahiers de philosophie politique et juridique*, No. 11:"Des Théories du droit naturel" (Caen, 1988): 43–73. On

Pufendorf, see T. J. Hochstrasser, *Natural Law Theories in the Early Enlightenment* (Cambridge: Cambridge University Press, 2000).

4. I have not focused here on the distinction between natural law and natural rights, partly because in French-language works, such as Burlamaqui's, it is often blurred. Moreover, eighteenth-century political figures did not necessarily make clear distinctions themselves. Burlamaqui's 1747 treatise was translated immediately into English as *The Principles of Natural Law* (1748) and then Dutch (1750), Danish (1757), Italian (1780), and eventually Spanish (1825)—Bernard Gagnebin, *Burlamaqui et le droit naturel* (Geneva: Editions de la Fregate, 1944), p. 227. Gagnebin claims that Burlamaqui had less influence in France, but one of the prominent authors writing for the *Encyclopédie* (Boucher d'Argis) used him as his source for one of the articles on natural law. For Burlamaqui's views on reason, human nature, and Scottish philosophy, see J. J. Burlamaqui, *Principes du droit naturel par J.J. Burlamaqui, Conseiller d'Etat, & ci-devant Professeur en droit naturel & civil à Genève* (Geneva: Barrillot et fils, 1747), pp. 1–2 and 165.

5. Jean Lévesque de Burigny, *Vie de Grotius, avec l'histoire de ses ouvrages, et des négociations auxquelles il fut employé,* 2 vols. (Paris: Debure l'aîné, 1752). T. Rutherforth, D.D. F.R.S., *Institutes of Natural Law Being the substance of a Course of Lectures on Grotius de Jure Belli et Paci, read in St. Johns College Cambridge,* 2 vols. (Cambridge: J. Bentham, 1754–56). Rutherford's lectures seem to be a perfect exemplification of Haakonssen's point that the natural law theory emphasis on duties proved to be very difficult to reconcile with the emerging emphasis on personally possessed natural rights (even though Grotius contributed to both). Another Swiss jurist, Emer de Vattel, also wrote extensively about natural law, but he focused more on the relations between nations. Vattel too insisted on the natural liberty and independence of all men. "On prouve en *Droit Naturel,* que tous les hommes tiennent de la Nature une Liberté & une indépendance, qu'ils ne peuvent perdre que par leur consentement"—M. de Vattel, *Le Droit des gens ou principes de la loi naturelle appliqués à la conduite & aux affaires des nations & des souverains,* 2 vols. (Leyden: Aux Dépens de la compagnie, 1758), vol. I, p. 2.

6. John Locke, *Two Treatises of Government* (Cambridge: Cambridge University Press, 1963), pp. 366–67. James Farr, " 'So Vile and Miserable an Estate': The Problem of Slavery in Locke's Political Thought," *Political Theory,* vol. 14, no. 2 (May 1986): 263–89, quote p. 263.

7. William Blackstone, *Commentaries on the Laws of England,* 8th edn., 4 vols. (Oxford: Clarendon Press, 1778), vol. I, p. 129. The influence of natural rights discourse is evident in Blackstone's commentaries for he begins his discussion in Book I with a consideration of "the absolute

rights of individuals," by which he meant "such as would belong to their persons merely in a state of nature, and which every man is entitled to enjoy, whether out of society or in it" (I:123; same wording in 1766 edn., Dublin). There is an immense literature on the relative influence of universalistic and particularistic ideas of rights in the British North American colonies. For an inkling of the debates, see Donald S. Lutz, "The Relative Influence of European Writers on Late Eighteenth-Century American Political Thought," *American Political Science Review*, 78 (1984): 189–97.

8.   James Otis, *The Rights of the British Colonies Asserted and Proved* (Boston: Edes & Gill, 1764), quotes pp. 28 and 35.

9.   On the influence of Burlamaqui in the American conflicts, see Ray Forrest Harvey, *Jean Jacques Bulamaqui: A Liberal Tradition in American Constitutionalism* (Chapel Hill: University of North Carolina Press, 1937), p. 116. On citations of Pufendorf, Grotius, and Locke, see Lutz, "The Relative Influence of European Writers," esp. pp. 193–94, and on Burlamaqui's presence in American libraries, see David Lundberg and Henry F. May, "The Enlightened Reader in America," *American Quarterly*, 28 (1976): 262–93, esp. p. 275. Quote from Burlamaqui, *Principes du droit naturel*, p. 2.

10.   On the increasing desire for declaring independence, see Pauline Maier, *American Scripture: Making the Declaration of Independence* (New York: Alfred A. Knopf, 1997), pp. 47–96. For the Virginia Declaration, see Kate Mason Rowland, *The Life of George Mason, 1725–1792*, 2 vols. (New York: G. P. Putnam's Sons, 1892), vol. I, pp. 438–41.

11.   For a brief but highly pertinent discussion, see Jack N. Rakove, *Declaring Rights: A Brief History with Documents* (Boston: Bedford Books, 1998), esp. pp. 32–38.

12.   I am grateful to Jennifer Popiel for initial research on English titles using the English Short Title Catalogue. I have made no distinction in the use of the term "rights" and have not excluded the considerable number of reprints over the years. The number of uses of rights in titles increased twofold from the 1760s to the 1770s (from 51 in the 1760s to 109 in the 1770s) and then stayed about the same in the 1780s (95). [William Graham of Newcastle], *An Attempt to Prove, That every Species of Patronage is Foreign to the Nature of the Church; and, That any MODIFICATIONS, which either have been, or ever can be proposed, are INSUFFICIENT to regain, and secure her in the Possession of the LIBERTY, where with CHRIST hath made her free....* (Edinburgh: J. Gray & G. Alston, 1768), pp. 163 and 167. Already in 1753, a James Tod had published a pamphlet titled *The Natural Rights of Mankind Asserted: Or a Just and Faithful Narrative of the Illegal Procedure of the Presbytery of*

Edinburgh against Mr. James Tod Preacher of the Gospel. . . . (Edinburgh, 1753). William Dodd, *Popery inconsistent with the Natural Rights of MEN in general, and of ENGLISHMEN in particular: A Sermon preached at Charlotte-Street Chapel* (London: W. Faden, 1768). On Wilkes, see, for example, "To the Electors of Aylesbury (1764)," in *English Liberty: Being a Collection of Interesting Tracts, From the Year 1762 to 1769 containing the Private Correspondence, Public Letters, Speeches, and Addresses, of John Wilkes, Esq.* (London: T. Baldwin, n.d.), p. 125. On Junius, see for example, Letter XII (May 30, 1769) and XIII (June 12, 1769) in *The Letters of Junius*, 2 vols. (Dublin: Thomas Ewing, 1772), pp. 69 and 81.

13. [Manasseh Dawes], *A Letter to Lord Chatham, concerning the present War of Great Britain against America; Reviewing Candidly and Impartially Its unhappy Cause and Consequence; and wherein The Doctrine of Sir William Blackstone as explained in his celebrated Commentaries on the Laws of England, is opposed to Ministerial Tyranny, and held up in favor of America. With some Thoughts on Government by a Gentleman of the Inner Temple* (London: G. Kearsley, n.d.; handwritten 1776), quotes pp. 17 and 25. Richard Price, *Observations on The Nature of Civil Liberty, the Principles of Government, and the Justice and Policy of the War with America to which is added, An Appendix and Postscript, containing, A State of the National Debt, An Estimate of the Money drawn from the Public by the Taxes, and An Account of the National Income and Expenditure since the last War*, 9th edn. (London: Edward & Charles Dilly and Thomas Cadell, 1776), quote p. 7. Price claimed eleven editions of his tract in a letter to John Winthrop—D. O. Thomas, *The Honest Mind: The Thought and Work of Richard Price* (Oxford: Clarendon Press, 1977), pp. 149–50. The success of the pamphlet was instantaneous. Price wrote to William Adams on February 14, 1776, that the pamphlet had appeared three days before and had already almost entirely sold out its edition of 1,000 copies—W. Bernard Peach and D. O. Thomas, eds., *The Correspondence of Richard Price*, 3 vols. (Durham, NC: Duke University Press, and Cardiff: University of Wales Press, 1983–94), vol. I: *July 1748–March 1778* (1983), p. 243. For the complete bibliography, see D. O. Thomas, John Stephens, and P.A.L. Jones, *A Bibliography of the Works of Richard Price* (Aldershot, Hants: Scolar Press, 1993), esp. pp. 54–80. J. D. van der Capellen, letter of December 14, 1777, in Peach and Thomas, eds., *The Correspondence of Richard Price*, vol. I, p. 262.

14. *Civil Liberty Asserted, and the Rights of the Subject Defended, against The Anarchical Principles of the Reverend Dr. Price. In which his Sophistical Reasonings, Dangerous Tenets, and Principles of False Patriotism, contained in his Observations on Civil Liberty, &c. are Exposed and Refuted. In a Letter to a Gentleman in the Country. By a Friend to the*

Rights of the Constitution (London: J. Wilkie, 1776), quotes pp. 38–39. Price's opponents did not necessarily deny the existence of universal rights. Sometimes they simply opposed his specific positions on Parliament or the relation of Great Britain to the colonies. For example, *The Honor of Parliament and the Justice of the Nation Vindicated. In a Reply to Dr. Price's Observations on the Nature of Civil Liberty* (London: W. Davis, 1776) uses the phrase "the natural rights of mankind" throughout in a favorable sense. Similarly, *Experience preferable to Theory. An Answer to Dr. Price's Observations on the Nature of Civil Liberty, and the Justice and Policy of the War with America* (London: T. Payne, 1776) sees no problem with referring to "the rights of human nature" (p. 3) or "the rights of humanity" (p. 5).

15. Filmer's lengthy rebuttal of Grotius can be found in "Observations concerning the Original of Government" in his *The Free-holders Grand Inquest, Touching Our Sovereign Lord the King and his Parliament* (London, 1679). He summarizes his position: "I have briefly presented here the desperate Inconveniences which attend upon the Doctrine of *the natural freedom and community of all things*; these and many more Absurdities are easily removed, if on the contrary we maintain the *natural and private Dominion of Adam*, to be the fountain of all Government and Propriety"—p. 58. *Patriarcha: Or the Natural Power of Kings* (London: R. Chiswel, et al., 1685), esp. pp.1–24.

16. Charles Warren Everett, ed., *A Comment on the Commentaries: A Criticism of William Blackstone's Commentaries on the Laws of England by Jeremy Bentham* (Oxford: Clarendon Press, 1928), quotes pp. 37–38. "Nonsense upon Stilts, or Pandora's Box Opened, or The French Declaration of Rights prefixed to the Constitution of 1791 Laid Open and Exposed," reprinted in Philip Schofield, Catherine Pease-Watkin, and Cyprian Blamires, eds., *The Collected Works of Jeremy Bentham Rights, Representation, and Reform: Nonsense upon Stilts and Other Writings on the French Revolution* (Oxford: Clarendon Press, 2002), pp. 319–75, quote p. 330. The pamphlet, written in 1795, was not published until 1816 (in French) and 1824 (in English).

17. Du Pont also insisted on the reciprocal duties of individuals—Pierre du Pont de Nemours, *De l'Origine et des progrès d'une science nouvelle* (1768), in Eugène Daire, ed., *Physiocrates. Quesnay, Dupont de Nemours, Mercier de la Rivière, l'Abbé Baudeau, Le Trosne* (Paris: Librarie de Guillaumin, 1846), pp. 335–66, quote p. 342.

18. On the "all-but-forgotten" Declaration of Independence, see Maier, *American Scripture*, pp. 160–70.

19. Rousseau's letter criticizing the overuse of "humanity" can be found in R. A. Leigh, ed., *Correspondance complète de Jean Jacques Rousseau*,

vol. 27, *Janvier 1769–Avril 1770* (Oxford: Voltaire Foundation, 1980), p. 15 (Letter from Rousseau to Laurent Aymon de Franquières, January 15, 1769). I am grateful to Melissa Verlet for her research on this point. On Rousseau's knowledge of Franklin and his defense of the Americans, see the account by Thomas Bentley dated August 6, 1776, in Leigh, ed., *Correspondance complète*, vol. 40, *Janvier 1775–Juillet 1778*, pp. 258–63 (". . . the Americans, who he said had not the less right to defend their liberties because they were obscure or unkown," p. 259. Other than this account from a visitor to Rousseau, there is no mention of American affairs in Rousseau's own letters from 1775 to his death.

20. Elise Marienstras and Naomi Wulf, "French Translations and Reception of the Declaration of Independence," *Journal of American History*, 85 (1999):1299–1324. Joyce Appleby, "America as a Model for the Radical French Reformers of 1789," *William and Mary Quarterly*, 3rd ser., vol. 28, no. 2 (April 1971): 267–86.

21. For the uses of these phrases, see *Archives parlementaires*, 1: 711; 2: 57, 139, 348, 383 ; 3: 256, 348, 662, 666, 740; 4: 668; 5: 391, 545. The first six volumes of the *Archives parlementaires* contain only a selection of the thousands of extant grievance lists; the editors included many of the "general" lists (those of the nobles, clergy, and Third Estate of an entire region) and few of those from the preliminary stages. I am grateful to Susan Mokhberi for research on these terms. Most content analysis of the grievance lists was undertaken before scanning and electronic searching became available and therefore reflects the specific interests of the authors and the rather clumsy means of analysis previously available— Gilbert Shapiro and John Markoff, *Revolutionary Demands: A Content Analysis of the Cahiers de Doléances of 1789* (Stanford: Stanford University Press, 1998).

22. *Archives parlementaires*, 2: 348; 5: 238. Beatrice Fry Hyslop, *French Nationalism in 1789 According to the General Cahiers* (New York: Columbia University Press, 1934), pp. 90–97. Stéphane Rials, *La Déclaration des droits de l'homme et du citoyen* (Paris: Hachette, 1989). Rather disappointing is Claude Courvoisier, "Les droits de l'homme dans les cahiers de doléances," in Gérard Chinéa, ed., *Les Droits de l'homme et la conquête des libertés: Des Lumières aux révolutions de 1848* (Grenoble: Presses Universitaires de Grenoble, 1988), pp. 44–49.

23. *Archives parlementaires*, 8: 135, 217.

24. Julian P. Boyd, ed., *The Papers of Thomas Jefferson*, 31 vols. (Princeton: Princeton University Press, 1950–), vol. 15: *March 27, 1789, to November 30, 1789* (1958), pp. 266–69. For the titles of the various projects, see Antoine de Baecque, ed., *L'An I des droits de l'homme* (Paris: Presses du CNRS, 1988). De Baecque provides essential background information on the debates.

25. Rabaut is quoted in de Baecque, *L'An I*, p. 138. On the difficulty of explaining the change in views about the necessity of a declaration, see Timothy Tackett, *Becoming a Revolutionary: The Deputies of the French National Assembly and the Emergence of a Revolutionary Culture (1789-1790)* (Princeton: Princeton University Press, 1996), p. 183.

26. Session of the National Assembly of August 1, 1789, *Archives parlementaires*, 8: 320.

27. The need for four declarations is mentioned in the "recapitulation" given by the Committee on the Constitution on July 9, 1789—*Archives parlementaires*, 8: 217.

28. As quoted in D. O. Thomas, ed., *Richard Price: Political Writings* (Cambridge: Cambridge University Press, 1991), pp. 119 and 195.

29. The passage from *Rights of Man* can be found at " Hypertext on American History from the colonial period until Modern Times," Department of Humanities Computing, University of Groningen, the Netherlands, http://odur.let.rug.nl/~usa/ D/1776-1800/paine/ROM/rofm04.htm (consulted July 13, 2005). Burke's passage can be found at www.bartleby.com/24/3/6.html (April 7, 2006).

30. On English titles, see note 12 above. The number of English titles using rights in the 1770s was 109, much higher than the 1760s but still only one fourth of the number in the 1790s. Dutch titles can be found in the Short Title Catalog of the Netherlands. On German translations of Paine, see Hans Arnold, "Die Aufnahme von Thomas Paines Schriften in Deutschland," *PMLA*, 72 (1959): 365-86. On Jeffersonian Ideas, see Matthew Schoenbachler, "Republicanism in the Age of Democratic Revolution: The Democratic-Republican Societies of the 1790s," *Journal of the Early Republic*, 18 (1998): 237-61. On the impact of Wollstonecraft in the United States, see Rosemarie Zagarri, "The Rights of Man and Woman in Post Revolutionary America," *William and Mary Quarterly*, 3rd ser., vol. 55, no. 2 (April 1998): 203-30.

31. For the September 10, 1789, discussion, see *Archives parlementaires*, 8: 608. On the final discussion and passage, see ibid., 9: 386-87, 392-96. The best account of the politics surrounding the new criminal and penal legislation can be found in Roberto Martucci, *La Costituente ed il problema penale in Francia, 1789-1791* (Milan: Giuffre, 1984). Martucci shows that the Committee of Seven became the Committee on Criminal Law.

32. *Archives parlementaires*, 9: 394-96 (the final decree) and 9: 213-17 (report of the committee given by Bon Albert Briois de Beaumetz). Article 24 in the final decree was a slightly revised version of the original Article 23 submitted by the committee on September 29. See also Edmond Seligman, *La Justice en France pendant la Révolution*, 2 vols. (Paris: Librairie Plon, 1913), vol. 1, pp. 197-204. The language used by the committee bolsters the position taken by Barry M. Shapiro that Enlight-

enment "humanitarianism" did animate the considerations of the deputies—Shapiro, *Revolutionary Justice in Paris, 1789–1790* (Cambridge: Cambridge University Press, 1993).

33. *Archives parlementaires,* 26: 319–32.

34. Ibid., 26: 323. The press focused almost exclusively on the question of the death penalty, though some noted with approval the elimination of branding. The most vociferous opponent of the death penalty was Louis Prudhomme in the *Révolutions de Paris,* 98 (May 21–28, 1791), pp. 321–27, and 99 (May 28–June 4, 1791), pp. 365–470. Prudhomme cited Beccaria in his support.

35. The text of the criminal code can be found in *Archives parlementaires,* 31: 326–39 (session of September 25, 1791).

36. Ibid., 26: 325.

37. Robespierre is quoted with agreement here in the critique that Lacretelle published of the essay: "Sur le discours qui avait obtenu un second prix à l'Académie de Metz, par Maximilien Robespierrre," in Pierre-Louis Lacretelle, *Oeuvres,* 6 vols. (Paris: Bossange, 1823–24), vol. III, pp. 315–34, quote p. 321. For Lacretelle's own essay, see vol. III, pp. 205–314. See also Joseph I. Shulim, "The Youthful Robespierre and His Ambivalence Toward the Ancien Régime," *Eighteenth-Century Studies,* 5 (Spring 1972): 398–420. I was alerted to the importance of honor in the criminal justice system by Gene Ogle, "Policing Saint Domingue: Race, Violence, and Honor in an Old Regime Colony," PhD diss., University of Pennsylvania, 2003.

38. The definition of honor in the dictionary of the Académie Française can be found at ARTFL, http://colet.uchicago.edu/cgi-bin/dico1loo.pl?-strippedhw=honneur.

39. Sébastien-Roch-Nicolas Chamfort, *Maximes et pensées, anecdotes et caractères,* ed. Louis Ducros (1794; Paris: Larousse, 1928), p. 27. Eve Katz, "Chamfort," *Yale French Studies,* No. 40 (1968): 32–46.

Chapter 4

1. *Archives parlementaires,* 10: 693–94, 754–57. On actors, see Paul Friedland, *Political Actors: Representative Bodies and Theatricality in the Age of the French Revolution* (Ithaca, NY: Cornell University Press, 2002), esp. pp. 215–27.

2. Quoted in Joan R. Gundersen, "Independence, Citizenship, and the American Revolution," *Signs: Journal of Women in Culture and Society,* 13 (1987): 63–64.

3. On July 20–21, 1789, Sieyès read his "Reconnaissance et exposition raisonnée des droits de l'homme et du citoyen" to the Committee on the Constitution. It was published as *Préliminaire de la constitution française* (Paris: Baudoin, 1789).

4. On voting qualifications in Delaware and the other thirteen colonies, see Patrick T. Conley and John P. Kaminski, eds., *The Bill of Rights and the States: The Colonial and Revolutionary Origins of American Liberties* (Madison, WI: Madison House, 1992), esp. p. 291. Adams is quoted in Jacob Katz Cogan, "The Look Within: Property, Capacity, and Suffrage in Nineteenth-Century America," *Yale Law Journal*, 107 (1997): 477.

5. Antoine de Baecque, ed., *L'An I des droits de l'homme* (Paris: Presses du CNRS, 1988), p. 165 (August 22), pp. 174–79 (August 23). Timothy Tackett, *Becoming a Revolutionary: The Deputies of the French National Assembly and the Emergence of a Revolutionary Culture (1789–1790)* (Princeton: Princeton University Press, 1996), p. 184.

6. *Archives parlementaires*, 10 (Paris, 1878): 693–95.

7. Ibid.: 780 and 782. The key phrase in the decree reads: "No motive for the exclusion of a citizen from eligibility can be offered other than those which result from constitutional decrees." On the reaction to the decision about Protestants, see *Journal d'Adrien Duquesnoy, Député du tiers état de Bar-le-Duc sur l'Assemblée Constituante*, 2 vols. (Paris, 1894), vol. II, p. 208. See also Raymond Birn, "Religious Toleration and Freedom of Expression," in Dale Van Kley, ed., *The French Idea of Freedom: The Old Regime and the Declaration of the Rights of 1789* (Stanford: Stanford University Press, 1994), pp. 265–99.

8. Tackett, *Becoming a Revolutionary*, pp. 262–63. *Archives parlementaires*, 10 (Paris, 1878): 757.

9. Ronald Schechter, *Obstinate Hebrews: Representations of Jews in France, 1715–1815* (Berkeley: University of California Press, 2003), pp. 18–34.

10. David Feuerwerker, "Anatomie de 307 cahiers de doléances de 1789," *Annales: E.S.C.*, 20 (1965): 45–61.

11. *Archives parlementaires*, 11 (Paris, 1880): 364.

12. Ibid.: 364–65; 31 (Paris, 1888): 372.

13. Clermont-Tonnerre's words come from his December 23, 1789, speech—ibid., 10 (Paris, 1878): 754–57. Some critics take Clermont-Tonnerre's speech to be an example of refusal to countenance ethnic difference within the national community. But a more anodyne interpretation seems warranted. The deputies believed that all citizens should live under the same laws and institutions; therefore, one group of citizens could not be judged in separate courts. I clearly have a more positive view than Schechter, who dismisses the "fabled emancipation of the Jews." The decree of September 27, 1791, he insists, "was merely a revocation of restrictions," and it changed "the status of only a handful of Jews, namely, those who fulfilled the stringent conditions" for active citizenship. That it granted the Jews equal rights with all other French citizens is apparently not all that significant to him, even though Jews did not

gain this equality in the state of Maryland until 1826 or in Great Britain until 1858—Schechter, *Obstinate Hebrews*, p. 151.

14. For a discussion of Jewish petitions, see Schechter, *Obstinate Hebrews*, pp. 165–78, quote p. 166; *Pétition des juifs établis en France, adressée à l'Assemblée Nationale, le 28 janvier 1790, sur l'ajournement du 24 décembre 1789* (Paris: Praul, 1790), quotes pp. 5–6, 96–97.

15. Stanley F. Chyet, "The Political Rights of Jews in the United States: 1776–1840," *American Jewish Archives*, 10 (1958): 14–75. I am grateful to Beth Wenger for her help on this question.

16. A useful overview of the U.S. case can be found in Cogan, "The Look Within." See also David Skillen Bogen, "The Maryland Context of Dred Scott: The Decline in the Legal Status of Maryland Free Blacks, 1776–1810," *American Journal of Legal History*, 34 (1990): 381–411.

17. *Mémoire en faveur des gens de couleur ou sang-mêlés de St.-Domingue, et des autres Iles françoises de l'Amérique, adressé à l'Assemblée Nationale*, par M. Grégoire, curé d'Embermémil, Député de Lorraine (Paris, 1789).

18. *Archives parlementaires*, 12 (Paris, 1881): 71. David Geggus, "Racial Equality, Slavery, and Colonial Secession during the Constituent Assembly," *American Historical Review*, vol. 94, no. 5 (December 1989): 1290–1308.

19. *Motion faite par M. Vincent Ogé, jeune à l'assemblée des colons, habitants de S.-Domingue, à l'hôtel Massiac, Place des Victoires* (probably Paris, 1789).

20. Laurent Dubois, *Avengers of the New World: The Story of the Haitian Revolution* (Cambridge, MA: Belknap Press of Harvard University Press, 2004), p. 102.

21. *Archives parlementaires*, 40 (Paris, 1893): 586 and 590 (Armand-Guy Kersaint, "Moyens proposés à l'Assemblée Nationale pour rétablir la paix et l'ordre dans les colonies").

22. Dubois, *Avengers of the New World*, esp. p. 163. *Décret de la Convention Nationale, du 16 jour de pluviôse, an second de la République françasie, une et indivisible* (Paris: Imprimerie Nationale Exécutive du Louvre, Year II [1794]).

23. Philip D. Curtin, "The Declaration of the Rights of Man in Saint-Domingue, 1788–1791," *Hispanic American Historical Review*, 30 (1950): 157–75, quote p. 162. On Toussaint, see Dubois, *Avengers of the New World*, p. 176. Dubois provides the fullest account of slave interest in the rights of man.

24. On the failure of Napoleon's efforts, see Dubois, *Avengers*. Wordsworth's poem "To Toussaint L'Ouverture" (1803) can be found in E. de Selincourt, ed., *The Poetical Works of William Wordsworth*, 5 vols. (Oxford: Clarendon Press, 1940–49), vol. 3, pp. 112–13. Laurent Dubois, *A Colony of Citizens:*

Revolution and Slave Emancipation in the French Caribbean, 1787–1804 (Chapel Hill: University of North Carolina Press, 2004), quote p. 421.

25. The explanation for the exclusion of women has been much debated of late. See, e.g., the very suggestive intervention by Anne Verjus, *Le Cens de la famille: Les femmes et le vote, 1789–1848* (Paris: Belin, 2002).

26. *Réflexions sur l'esclavage des nègres* (Neufchâtel: Société typographique, 1781), pp. 97–99.

27. For the references to women and Jews, see *Archives parlementaires*, 33 (Paris, 1889): 363, 431–32. On views about widows, see Tackett, *Becoming a Revolutionary*, p. 105.

28. "Sur l'Admission des femmes au droit de cité," *Journal de la Société de 1789*, 5 (July 3, 1790): 1–12.

29. The pieces by Condorcet and Olympe de Gouges can be found in Lynn Hunt, ed., *The French Revolution and Human Rights: A Brief Documentary History* (Boston: Bedford/St. Martin's Press, 1996), pp. 119–21, 124–28. On the reaction to Wollstonecraft and for the best account of her thought, see Barbara Taylor, *Mary Wollstonecraft and the Feminist Imagination* (Cambridge: Cambridge University Press, 2003).

30. The contribution by Pierre Guyomar can be found in *Archives parlementaires*, 63 (Paris, 1903): 591–99. The spokesman for the constitutional committee brought up the question of women's rights on April 29, 1793, and cited two supporters of the idea, one of them Guyomar, only to reject it (pp. 561–64).

31. Lynn Hunt, *The Family Romance of the French Revolution* (Berkeley: University of California Press, 1992), esp. p. 119.

32. Rosemarie Zagarri, "The Rights of Man and Woman in Post-Revolutionary America," *William and Mary Quarterly*, 3rd ser., vol. 55, no. 2 (April 1998): 203–30.

33. Zagarri, "The Rights of Man and Woman"; Carla Hesse, *The Other Enlightenment: How French Women Became Modern* (Princeton: Princeton University Press, 2001); Suzanne Desan, *The Family on Trial in Revolutionary France* (Berkeley: University of California Press, 2004). See also Sarah Knott and Barbara Taylor, eds., *Women, Gender and Enlightenment* (New York: Palgrave/Macmillan, 2005).

34. "Rapport sur un ouvrage du cit. Théremin, intitulé: De la condition des femmes dans une république. Par Constance D. T. Pipelet," *Le Mois*, vol. 5, no. 14, Year VIII (apparently Prairial): 228–43.

Chapter 5

1. Mazzini is quoted in Micheline R. Ishay, *The History of Human Rights: From Ancient Times to the Globalization Era* (Berkeley and London: University of California Press, 2004), p. 137.

2. J. B. Morrell, "Professors Robison and Playfair, and the 'Theophobia Gallica': Natural Philosophy, Religion and Politics in Edinburgh, 1789–1815," *Notes and Records of the Royal Society of London*, vol. 26, no. 1 (June 1971): 43–63, quote pp. 47–48.

3. Louis de Bonald, *Législation primitive* (Paris: Le Clere, Year XI–1802), quote p. 184. See also Jeremy Jennings, "The Declaration des droits de l'homme et du citoyen and Its Critics in France: Reaction and Ideologie," *Historical Journal*, vol. 35, no. 4. (December 1992): 839–59.

4. On the bandit Schinderhannes and his attacks on the French and Jews in the Rhineland in the late 1790s, see T. C. W. Blanning, *The French Revolution in Germany: Occupation and Resistance in the Rhineland, 1792–1802* (Oxford: Clarendon Press, 1983), pp. 292–99.

5. J. Christopher Herold, ed., *The Mind of Napoleon* (New York: Columbia University Press, 1955), p. 73.

6. Laurent Dubois and John D. Garrigus, eds., *Slave Revolution in the Caribbean, 1789–1804: A Brief History with Documents* (Boston: Bedford/St. Martin's Press, 2006), quote p. 176.

7. Germaine de Staël, *Considérations sur la Révolution Française* (1817; Paris: Charpentier, 1862), p. 152.

8. Simon Collier, "Nationality, Nationalism, and Supranationalism in the Writings of Simón Bolívar," *Hispanic American Historical Review*, vol. 63, no. 1 (February 1983): 37–64, quote p. 41.

9. Hans Kohn, "Father Jahn's Nationalism," *Review of Politics*, vol. 11, no. 4 (October 1949): 419–32, quote p. 428.

10. Thomas W. Laqueur, *Making Sex: Body and Gender from the Greeks to Freud* (Cambridge, MA: Harvard University Press, 1990).

11. The French revolutionary views are discussed in Lynn Hunt, *The Family Romance of the French Revolution* (Berkeley: University of California Press, 1992), esp. pp. 119 and 157.

12. The Mill text can be found at www.constitution.org/jsm/women.htm. On Brandeis, see Susan Moller Okin, *Women in Western Political Thought* (Princeton: Princeton University Press, 1979), esp. p. 256.

13. On Cuvier and the question more generally, see George W. Stocking, Jr., "French Anthropology in 1800," *Isis*, vol. 55, no. 2 (June 1964): 134–50.

14. Arthur de Gobineau, *Essai sur l'inégalité des races humaines*, 2nd edn. (Paris: Firmin-Didot, 1884), 2 vols., quote vol. I, p. 216. Michael D. Biddiss, *Father of Racist Ideology: The Social and Political Thought of Count Gobineau* (London: Weidenfeld & Nicolson, 1970), quote p. 113; see also pp. 122–23 for the civilizations based on Aryan stock.

15. Michael D. Biddiss, "Prophecy and Pragmatism: Gobineau's Confrontation with Tocqueville," *The Historical Journal*, vol. 13, no. 4 (December 1970): 611–33, quote p. 626.

16. Herbert H. Odom, "Generalizations on Race in Nineteenth-Century Physical Anthropology," *Isis*, vol. 58, no. 1 (Spring 1967): 4–18, quote p. 8. On the American translation of Gobineau, see Michelle M. Wright, "Nigger Peasants from France: Missing Translations of American Anxieties on Race and the Nation," *Callaloo*, vol. 22, no. 4 (Autumn 1999): 831–52.

17. Biddiss, "Prophecy and Pragmatism," p. 625.

18. Jennifer Pitts, *A Turn to Empire: The Rise of Imperial Liberalism in Britain and France* (Princeton: Princeton University Press, 2005), p. 139. Patrick Brantlinger, "Victorians and Africans: The Genealogy of the Myth of the Dark Continent," *Critical Inquiry*, vol. 12, no. 1 (Autumn 1985): 166–203, quote from Burton, p. 179. See also Nancy Stepan, *The Idea of Race in Science: Great Britain, 1800–1960* (Hamden, CT: Archon Books, 1982), and William H. Schneider, *An Empire for the Masses: The French Popular Image of Africa, 1870–1900* (Westport, CT: Greenwood Press, 1982).

19. Paul A. Fortier, "Gobineau and German Racism," *Comparative Literature*, vol. 19, no. 4 (Autumn 1967): 341–50. For the quote from Chamberlain, see www.hschamberlain.net/grundlagen/division2_chapter5 .html.

20. Robert C. Bowles, "The Reaction of Charles Fourier to the French Revolution," *French Historical Studies*, vol. 1, no. 3 (Spring 1960): 348–56, quote p. 352.

21. Aaron Noland, "Individualism in Jean Jaurès' Socialist Thought," *Journal of the History of Ideas*, vol. 22, no. 1 (January–March 1961): 63–80, quote p. 75. For Jaurès's frequent invocation of rights and his celebration of the declaration, see Jean Jaurès, *Etudes socialistes* (Paris: Ollendorff, 1902), which is available on Frantext at www.lib.uchicago.edu/efts/ARTFL/ databases/TLF/. Jaurès's major opponent, Jules Guesde, is quoted in Ignacio Walker, "Democratic Socialism in Comparative Perspective," *Comparative Politics*, vol. 23, no. 4 (July 1991): 439–58, quote p. 441.

22. Robert C. Tucker, *The Marx-Engels Reader*, 2nd edn. (New York: W. W. Norton, 1978), pp. 43–46.

23. See Vladimir Lenin, *The State and Revolution* (1918) at www.marxists .org/archive/lenin/works/1917/staterev/ch05.htm#s4.

24. Jan Herman Burgers, "The Road to San Francisco: The Revival of the Human Rights Idea in the Twentieth Century," *Human Rights Quarterly*, vol. 14, no. 4 (November 1992): 447–77.

25. The charter's provision is quoted in Ishay, *The History of Human Rights*, p. 216. The essential source on the history of the Universal Declaration is Mary Ann Glendon, *A World Made New: Eleanor Roosevelt and the Universal Declaration of Human Rights* (New York: Random House, 2001).

26. Douglas H. Maynard, "The World's Anti-Slavery Convention of 1840," *Mississippi Valley Historical Review*, vol. 47, no. 3 (December 1960): 452–71.

27. Michla Pomerance, "The United States and Self-Determination: Perspectives on the Wilsonian Conception," *American Journal of International Law*, vol. 70, no. 1 (January 1976): 1–27, quote p. 2. Marika Sherwood, " 'There Is No New Deal for the Blackman in San Francisco': African Attempts to Influence the Founding Conference of the United Nations, April–July, 1945," *International Journal of African Historical Studies*, vol. 29, no. 1 (1996): 71–94. A. W. Brian Simpson, *Human Rights and the End of Empire: Britain and the Genesis of the European Convention* (London: Oxford University Press, 2001), esp. pp. 175–83.

28. Manfred Spieker, "How the Eurocommunists Interpret Democracy," *Review of Politics*, vol. 42, no. 4 (October 1980): 427–64. John Quigley, "Human Rights Study in Soviet Academia," *Human Rights Quarterly*, vol. 11, no. 3 (August 1989): 452–58.

29. Kenneth Cmiel, "The Recent History of Human Rights," *American Historical Review* (February 2004), www.historycooperative.org/journals /ahr/109.1/cmiel.html (April 3, 2006).

30. Edward Peters, *Torture* (Philadelphia: University of Pennsylvania Press, 1985), p. 125.

31. Christopher R. Browning, *Ordinary Men: Reserve Police Battalion 101 and the Final Solution in Poland* (New York: HarperCollins, 1992).

32. The hypothetical case is taken up in Part III, chap. 3 of *The Theory of Moral Sentiments* and can be consulted at www.adamsmith.org/ smith/tms/tms-p3-c3a.htm.

33. Jerome J. Shestack, "The Philosophic Foundations of Human Rights," *Human Rights Quarterly*, vol. 20, no. 2 (May 1998): 201–34, quote p. 206.

34. Karen Halttunen, "Humanitarianism and the Pornography of Pain in Anglo-American Culture," *American Historical Review*, vol. 100, no. 2 (April 1995): 303–34. On Sade, see Hunt, *The Family Romance*, esp. pp. 124–50.

35. Carolyn J. Dean, *The Fragility of Empathy After the Holocaust* (Ithaca, NY: Cornell University Press, 2004).

Permissions

Figure 1

Engraving and etching, 18.3 cm x 13.5 cm. *Collection complète des oeuvres de J. J. Rousseau, Citoyen de Genève*, 25 vols. (Geneva, 1782), III (vol. II of *La Nouvelle Héloïse*): plate placed between pp. 494 and 495 in the UCLA copy. Dept. of Special Collections, Charles E. Young Research Library, UCLA

Figure 2

Engraving, 13.5 cm x 8 cm, signed J. Punt, fecit 1742. Samuel Richardson, *Pamela, ou la vertue recompensée. Traduit de l'Anglois*. Troisième édition, revue, et enrichie de Figures en Tailles-douces, 2 vols. (Amsterdam: Aux Dépens de la compagnie, 1744), vol. I, p. 4. Singer-Mendenhall Collection, Rare Book and Manuscript Library, University of Pennsylvania

Figure 3

Jean Milles de Souvigny, *Praxis criminis persequendi* (Paris: Simon de Colines et Arnold et Charles Les Angeliers, 1541), p. 26 (a misprint for 62). Special Collections, University of Maryland Libraries

Figure 4

de Souvigny, *Praxis criminis persequendi*, p. 61. Special Collections, University of Maryland Libraries

Figure 5

From Pf-6-Fol. Recueil de pièces sur les crimes, délits, jugements criminels, répressions et supplices. Département des Estampes, Bibliothèque Nationale de France

Figure 6

Los Angeles County Museum of Art, M.90.210.1

Figure 7

Mezzotint, 33 cm x 21.7 cm. British Museum, Prints Department, 1902–10–11–3261

Figure 8

Oval in the engraving, 8.7 cm x 7.3 cm. Département des Estampes, Bibliothèque Nationale de France

FIGURE 9

Etching and engraving, 25.75 cm x 40 cm. British Museum, Prints Department, Paulson, 178: 1848–11–25–220

FIGURE 10

Calas Bids Farewell to His Family, Inv. peint et gravé par D. Chodowiecki, à Berlin, 1768. Département des Estampes, Bibliothèque Nationale de France

FIGURE 11

Dept. of Special Collections, Charles E. Young Research Library, UCLA

Index